ADVANCE PRAISE FOR BELFAST DAYS

'The author's honest, humane voice throughout reaches a climax in a passionate, clear-eyed epilogue … Buy it for yourself but, above all, ensure your teenagers read it to appreciate the peace and opportunities they have now which were denied to that earlier generation.'

Anne Cadwallader, author of *Lethal Allies*

'Funny, touching, vivid and real.'

Robin Livingstone, Editor, *Andersonstown News*

'Vivid and disturbing – the terror of war invades the everyday life of a sensitive girl.'

Susan McKay, Derry-born journalist and author of books including
Bear in Mind These Dead and Northern Protestants:
An Unsettled People

'A time machine to the turmoil, trouble and terror of '70s Belfast, *Belfast Days* is a remarkable memoir, bringing heartache and healing in equal measure. A passage into a wretched world of warfare through the unblinking eyes of a teenager whose steady gaze surely shames us into ensuring this path is not walked again.' **Máirtín Ó Muilleoir,**
Former Lord Mayor of Belfast

'*Belfast Days* will be a book you'll want to save for your children and grandchildren to read. Although they might not be growing up in the terror of war and conflict, Eimear's diary will inspire them to use their own unique talents and gifts to bring about a more peaceful world. An object lesson in tolerance and resilience, we can all learn from this book, no matter what our age.'

Laurel Holliday, author of the Children in Conflict series

Eimear O'Callaghan is a former BBC news editor with more than 30 years' experience in print and broadcast journalism. While most of her career was with the BBC, she also worked with the *Irish News* and RTÉ. She left the BBC in 2010 to set up a communications consultancy, Leapfrog Communications, and continues to work as a freelance writer.

Belfast Days
A 1972 Teenage Diary

Eimear O'Callaghan

MERRION

First published in 2014 by Merrion Press
an imprint of Irish Academic Press
8 Chapel Lane
Sallins
Co. Kildare

British Library Cataloguing in Publication Data
An entry can be found on request

978-1-908928-89-4 (paper)
978-1-908928-33-7 (PDF)
978-1-908928-06-0 (epub)
978-1-908928-91-7 (mobi)

Library of Congress Cataloging in Publication Data
An entry can be found on request

Printed by ScandBook AB, Sweden.

Inside design by www.sinedesign.net

For my Father and Mother
Jim and Maura

CONTENTS

ACKNOWLEDGEMENTS

For as long as I remember I have dreamed of writing a book but before 15 June, 2010 I never planned writing *this* one. The seed for *Belfast Days* was planted that day when *The Irish Times* published an article I wrote about the Bloody Sunday Inquiry Report, containing extracts from my teenage diary.

It was the first time that I shared the diary's contents with anyone. I am indebted to *The Irish Times* editor Geraldine Kennedy who made space for the article that would arouse curiosity about my journal at home and further afield. A special mention must also go to BBC producer, J.P. Devlin, who gave me an opportunity to speak about it on Radio 4 and was the first person to suggest I should write a book.

Laurel Holliday, initially a stranger living on the west coast of America, also deserves my thanks. The author of the *Children in Conflict* series tracked me down via the internet after hearing my radio interview and has been unstinting in her advice, support and encouragement ever since.

My heartfelt thanks are owed to the wonderful people at Irish Academic Press/Merrion. I thank Conor Graham in particular for understanding and caring about this book from the moment he received my manuscript. Conor, Lisa Hyde and Maria McGuinness have earned my deepest gratitude for all they have done to make this book the best it can be.

My dear friend and long-suffering colleague Paul McFadden accompanied me on each step of this journey, reading and re-reading every line of each page. He restored my faith in the book when my belief faltered. For his endurance, judgement and candour, I am forever in his debt.

Finally, and most importantly, I have to thank my family. I will always be grateful to my parents, Jim and Maura, for loving and protecting my brothers and me during the darkest days of Northern Ireland's history and for encouraging in me a love of the written word.

This book would not have been possible without the enduring love and support of my husband, Paul McElhone, and our next generation, Maura, Paul and Orla, of whom I am so proud. Thank you all for waiting on me patiently through long days and late nights. A special thanks, too, to our old dog Dustin for keeping me company when the others went to bed.

Thank you all for convincing me I could finish the book and for being a daily reminder of why it matters.

AUTHOR'S NOTE

The events in this book are recorded as the young diarist learned about them, and any inaccuracies are due to the turmoil of the times. In two cases names have been changed.

Map of Greater Belfast

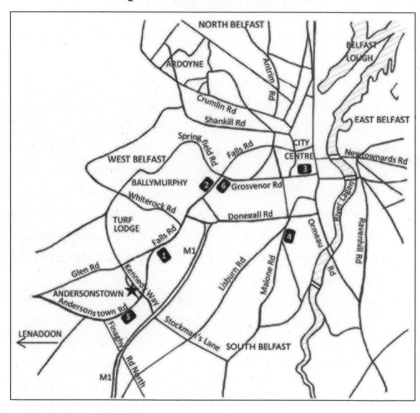

Key:

★ Fruithill Park

1 Milltown Cemetery

2 St. Dominic's Grammar School

3 Belfast City Hall

4 Queen's University

5 Casement Park GAA ground

6 Royal Victoria Hospital

PROLOGUE

'Prayer is our only hope, seeing we haven't got a gun!'

It was in June 2010 – just days before the British Prime Minister delivered the findings of the Bloody Sunday Inquiry – when I stumbled across my old diary, stuffed into a battered briefcase in a spare-room wardrobe. The spine of the journal was faded and frayed, its well-thumbed pages grown dull with the passage of time. The edges of the six glossy, paper butterflies which I pasted on to its cover as a teenager were beginning to curl up and crack, but their colour was as vivid as when they first caught my eye four decades earlier.

I was shocked by the terror which cried out at me from the squiggly handwriting on the page where my record of 1972 happened to fall open: '*May 30 … Came to bed convinced that prayer is our only hope, seeing we haven't got a gun!*'

The spidery, childish handwriting in faded blue ink stopped me in my tracks. What, in God's name, was going on in my 16-year-old mind that made me even think about having a weapon? I couldn't turn a gun on anyone, even if my life depended on it. Yet in West Belfast in 1972 – as a skinny, timid, Catholic teenager, with big, curly, '70s hair – I was confiding to my diary that prayer was the second-best option.

1

If we had been relying on my prayers to save us back then, God help us. I was just a month short of my seventeenth birthday when I penned that desperate entry in my red Collins notebook. I had seldom resorted to prayer except when pleading to St Joseph of Cupertino for help in my O-Level exams the previous summer:

> O Great St Joseph of Cupertino, who while on earth did obtain from God the grace to be asked at your examination only the questions you knew, obtain for me a like favour in the examinations for which I am now preparing ... St Joseph of Cupertino, pray for us. Amen.

I was a sixth year pupil at St Dominic's – Belfast's largest Catholic girls' grammar school – where academic success was all-important. My classmates and I used to pass the grubby, dog-eared prayer to St Joseph between us at exam-times – a picture of 'the flying saint' in religious ecstasy on one side, the miraculous prayer on the other – since part of the deal we agreed with the saint was 'to make you known and cause you to be invoked ...'.

By the late spring of 1972, I would have made any deal God wanted so long as He protected us from the horror which began enveloping Northern Ireland after the Stormont government introduced internment the previous August. I said more prayers and made more promises to 'the Man above' in the first five months of 1972 than in all my previous sixteen and a half years. I kept on praying throughout the summer, into the autumn and all through the winter as violence escalated to a level which would remain unparalleled in the 30 years of 'the Troubles'.

As curiosity subsequently lured me deeper into the diary, I sought out with interest my entry on Bloody Sunday, that awful day in January when members of 1st Battalion, the Parachute Regiment shot dead thirteen civil rights marchers in Derry. I turned back to the first page and embarked on a journey of rediscovery which would gradually explain my teenage desperation in over two hundred scribbled pages.

Notes from 1971: December 25th 1971

On looking back over the past year it is very difficult for anyone not to be filled with a great sense of sorrow, pity and failure. Sorrow, because of the great amount of damage and pain which has been brought to Northern Ireland during 1971 as a result of a long period of injustice and oppression, by a section of our community.

Pity for the families of those people who have lost their lives through shooting and bombing, and pity for the 500 families who spent this Christmas Day without fathers and brothers, because they have been imprisoned without trial in Long Kesh and Crumlin Road internment camps. Internment was introduced into this part of the United Kingdom by Brian Faulkner on August 9, 1971 and its results were tragic ...

By the time my O-Levels came around in the summer of 1971, Northern Ireland's political foundations were shaking.

The mainly nationalist clamour for civil rights, which first manifested itself on the streets in the late 1960s, had unnerved the unionist majority, leaving many of them fearful of being coerced into a United Ireland. Vicious sectarian clashes between Belfast's Protestant and Catholic communities became commonplace. The British Army, which had been welcomed into Catholic areas in 1969, was by then the target of an increasingly ferocious IRA campaign – and met fire with fire.

Declaring in August that Northern Ireland was 'quite simply at war with the terrorist', the Unionist Prime Minister, Brian Faulkner, invoked the Special Powers Act and granted security forces the power to arrest and detain people indefinitely without trial. His decision to introduce internment proved to be disastrous, fanning the flames of republican aggression rather than quelling them. In the two years before detention without trial, fewer than 80 people were killed. By the time I started keeping my diary – just five months later – the death toll had risen to 230.

With growing bewilderment I started to read the pages of my rediscovered journal, some crammed with entries scribbled hastily in biro, others crafted neatly with my treasured Sheaffer fountain pen. I slowly began recalling the solitary hours I would spend filling out line after line in my eight-by-ten foot square bedroom. But the words and sentiments belonged to a person, place and time I no longer recognised.

On the first page, in the top left-hand corner, I had written 'Received from Suzette, Christmas 1971', alongside my name and address. My parents christened me, the eldest of their five children and their only daughter, with the ancient Irish name, Eimear. They loved the sound of it and its origins in the Celtic myths and legends associated with Cooley, my mother's birthplace in the Republic.

The years have given me the confidence to appreciate and even be proud of my name but I can still feel, as though it was yesterday, how the colour would rise in my cheeks, and my mouth would start to dry, as I waited my turn to introduce myself to a group of strangers. Even with new teachers at the start of term in St. Dominic's, the conversation was usually the same:

'And what's *your* name?'
'Eimear.'
'What a lovely name. How do you spell that?'
'E-I-M-E-A-R.'
'Really? I've never heard that one before. Eye-mere.'
'No, Eimear. It rhymes with femur.'
'Oh, sorry. Is it Irish? What does it mean?'
'Yes, it's Irish. But it doesn't mean anything,' I used to reply wearily.

My name did not translate into English but in Belfast in the early 70s, it *did* mean something: it marked me out as a Catholic. In a language and code peculiar to Northern Ireland, we labelled ourselves, and each other, with one tag or the other – Catholic or Protestant. When we met someone new, we circled each other cautiously, looking for 'clues' while trying not to reveal too much about ourselves, trying to work out which 'camp' they belonged to, which 'foot' they 'kicked with'. A name, address or the school attended was enough to tell us whether a new acquaintance was 'from the other side' or was 'one of us'.

Often as a young adult, growing up in such a divided society, I wished I had an 'ordinary' name, one that wasn't so Irish, so Catholic and so difficult to spell. I wanted to be anonymous, like an 'Anne' or 'Claire' or 'Christine'; anything that didn't mean that I might as well have had the word 'Catholic' branded on my forehead.

> ... Ireland once had the reputation of being the 'Land of Saints and Scholars'. This image is certainly far removed from the scene ... when passing through Belfast – a city full of soldiers, here to keep communities apart; bombed buildings; rows of burnt out houses and an air of fear and mistrust in every street.

As I read through my two-page introduction to the diary, its sometimes precocious tone and language embarrassed me. The memories, though, disturbed me. Belfast in 1972 was a dangerous place, where blending into the background and keeping out of harm's way were the order of the day. Sectarian violence meant that no one, from either of our two communities, wanted to run the risk of being singled out for being different. If that meant that 16-year-olds like my friends and me kept to our own tiny patch in predominantly Catholic, nationalist Andersonstown – seldom venturing far beyond school, each other's homes or occasionally the city centre – then so be it. The world we inhabited was, by necessity, small and familiar. But it provided us with relative safety.

The Fruithill Park home that I shared with my parents and four brothers was happy, loving and secure. During weekends and summer evenings, our long back garden, enclosed by hedges and trees, made a perfect playground, football pitch or battleground, depending on which and how many of my brothers and their friends were gathered there.

On Saturday afternoons, the smell of the home baking that my mother and I produced, working side by side, regularly filled our kitchen. The hammering or drilling from my father's enthusiastic DIY efforts often competed with the racket made by the boys and our crazy mongrel dog, Tito. Homework routines were rigorously enforced around the kitchen and living room tables, despite protests from my brothers, and I willingly retreated to my bedroom to escape the happy mayhem.

My parents worked hard and were rightly proud of the comfortable, 1930s, semi-detached house they had saved for and bought when I was finishing primary school and Paul, the youngest, had just turned two. My father, who started his working life as a boy messenger with the Post Office many decades earlier, was well versed in Belfast's unique religious and political geography and knew the areas where his young family was always likely to be safest. Even when the immediate and terrible consequences of internment were first inflicted on nationalist, working-class areas, our lives in quiet, residential Fruithill were initially normal and untroubled.

When I started to record the events of 1972, Paul was just seven and was inseparable from Jim who was three years older. Full of boyish devilment, they operated as a pair –

'partners in crime' – as did the two older boys, Aidan who was twelve and John, fourteen. All of them were still children when the 'excitement' of the Troubles exploded into our lives.

As the eldest of the five and an only girl, I enjoyed the privilege of having one of our four bedrooms to myself. I would spend hours holed up in that small room. My parents, Maura and Jim, would rap on my door to tell me I couldn't possibly be studying properly, as my precious transistor blared out Radio 1 chart hits: Donny Osmond, all hair and American teeth, singing 'Puppy Love'; David Cassidy asking 'Could It Be Forever'; and 'Telegram Sam', 'Jeepster' and 'Metal Guru'. What a great year that was for my favourites – the exotic, glam rockers, T Rex. At night, snuggled up in my narrow single bed, I would try to fall asleep as Radio Luxembourg DJs, with their trans-Atlantic twangs, whispered to me from the radio hidden underneath my blankets.

Outside, on the streets of Belfast, the IRA carried out deadly attacks on British Army patrols with increasing regularity and detonated bombs in the city centre with devastating consequences; soldiers killed members of IRA 'active service units', as well as innocent, unarmed civilians and people allegedly 'acting suspiciously'; sectarian threats and attacks drove families out of their homes, while loyalists abducted and killed random workmen, students and late-night drinkers, just because they were Catholics.

Closeted in my bedroom at the back of the house, I took refuge in music, books and in the pages of the teenage magazine, *Jackie*, with its insights into make-up, fashion, celebrity and, of course, boys. I treasured the pull-out posters of idols like David Cassidy and Marc Bolan, while problem pages opened up a fascinating, new, forbidden world: 'Dear Cathy and Claire, I think my boyfriend ...'; 'Dear Cathy and Claire, what should I do ...'.

A sharp crack of gunfire or the sickening thud of a distant explosion would jolt me back to the reality of West Belfast. And so the depressing, anxious litany of questions and prayers would resume: 'What was that?' – 'Where was it?' – 'Please God, don't let anybody be killed.' – 'Please God don't let it be anybody we know.' The incessant 'chuddering' drone of army helicopters, circling above the rooftops, kept me awake at night. Their powerful, prying searchlights flooded my bedroom with light, casting distorted, ghostly shadows on the walls. Piercing whistles and the racket of metal bin-lids being banged on pavements alerted neighbourhoods to imminent army raids.

Again and again I wondered what it would be like to live in a 'normal' place – going out to discos and shopping with friends, free from the fear of bombs exploding; being able to rely on public transport for going to school – doing the things that ordinary teenagers did. The unexpected discovery of my long-forgotten diary, with its opening grim reminder of the autumn and winter of 1971, prompted me to revisit my ironically named 'Happy Days' scrapbook.

There, in black and white, were appalling images from the streets of Belfast: bare-handed rescuers searching in the dark, through the debris of McGurk's bar after it was bombed by loyalists in December. A schoolgirl, two years younger than me, and a boy – who was even younger – were killed with thirteen other Catholics when the no-warning device exploded. Page after page carried photographs of buildings in flames, army machine-gun posts, bewildered business owners staring in disbelief at the ruins of their livelihoods, and soldiers uncoiling huge rolls of barbed wire to cordon off streets and keep neighbours apart.

I had collected accounts of interrogation and torture written by men interned in Long Kesh since August 1971, as well as a selection of the simple black-and-white Christmas cards they made for their families and friends on 'the outside'. I covered two full pages with a black-and-white photograph that I cut out of the *Belfast Telegraph*, showing 173 tiny white crosses planted in a wintry field, under the grim heading 'And So Ends '71'.

At Midnight Mass in 1971, and for nearly thirty years afterwards, priests asked us to pray for *everyone* who had been killed in the violence of the previous twelve months and for everyone who was separated from their families at Christmas. We all bowed our heads and said our prayers; but secretly, year after year, I prayed selfishly and most fervently that my family and friends would stay safe, and that it would all be over soon. The last lines of my '*Notes from 1971*' entry reminded me of the bleakness of that Christmas:

> *This Christmas Day was celebrated by the internees with a hunger-strike, by people in Andersonstown keeping a 24-hour fast outside the church, by 4,000 people who gave up their homes on Christmas Day to defy the army and to walk 10 miles to Long Kesh – and by 14,000 British soldiers, separated from their families to keep a riot-torn city at peace, for as long as is possible here.*

Not long after my sixteenth birthday, and within weeks of internment being introduced, I made up my mind that I was going to 'break out of it all' and get a taste – if only for a month or so – of the world I glimpsed through the pages of *Jackie*. I wanted to go somewhere bright, sunny and normal; somewhere with no explosions, no bomb scares and no one getting shot. Neither I nor anyone in my family had ever been on a plane or gone to a country where English wasn't the first language but that didn't deter me; if anything, it encouraged and excited me.

When my friend Suzette, who was a student nurse and lived nearby, presented me with a new diary for Christmas, I resolved to be faithful to it. I looked forward to 1972 being *my* year: I would turn 17, get a part-time job, be transformed from an ugly duckling into a beautiful swan and finally find romance, travel and a promising new future.

End-of-year news programmes reminded us sombrely that 150 people had died violently since internment was introduced five months earlier. Naïvely, though, and with the optimism of a schoolgirl who had nobody belonging to her killed or in jail, I was convinced that Northern Ireland would soon settle down and the bloodshed stop.

Even in the bleakest moments of the autumn and winter of 1971, I could not have envisaged the violent depths into which our society was about to plunge headlong. I could not have foreseen the catastrophic repercussions of events like Bloody Sunday. In my political ignorance, I would never have dreamed that within a few months the Unionist-controlled Northern Ireland Government would be replaced with Direct Rule by the British Government at Westminster.

I stayed true to my diary, however, and recorded diligently, with just a few exceptions, my days and nights during what turned out to be the bloodiest year of Northern Ireland's notorious Troubles. The account I unearthed after almost 40 years is not a history: it is the diary of a 16-year-old schoolgirl, woven through with her teenage hopes and fears. The savagery it evokes shocks and appals me, as does its evidence of how speedily and easily a society can violently implode.

It teaches me that the passage of time may soften the stark images and dull the strident sounds of our violent history. It can allow the 'truth' about our past to be distorted. My diary, though, is unsparing. With its brutal candour, it has proved more trustworthy than memory.

CHAPTER 1

'Wish something big would hurry up and happen.'

'Happy New Year, everybody! Happy New Year!' As the clocks struck midnight, my parents and I joined friends in a house not far from our own in West Belfast and celebrated being alive. Two doors away from our own home was about as far as we dared to venture.

As the adults clinked glasses 'To 1972!', the bombers heralded the start of another year in a way with which we were becoming all too familiar. 'Happy New Year, Belfast,' indeed.

Sat, Jan 1 - New Year's Day

Had arranged to go to Dublin for the day with Suzette and got the 8.00 a.m. train. Had a great day there – an atmosphere of freedom and light-heartedness, completely opposite to the atmosphere of death and fear we left behind us.

We welcomed New Year in down in McGlade's and it came in with a bang! Eight explosions rocked the town between midnight and 12.15 …

Aunt Jo telephoned to say she was coming tomorrow – something to brighten up the day. Washed my hair and spent the night playing

Cluedo by the fire.

Only one explosion tonight – reported as a quiet night.

Sun, Jan 2

Auntie Jo, Uncle Jim and family came down from Navan and we persuaded them to stay overnight. Huge Civil Rights Association march planned today to Falls Park. (Ban on marches until February). Daddy and Uncle Jim accompanied it. When it reached the barracks, negotiated with the army – and marchers walked by on the pavement. Estimated crowd of 3,000–5,000.

Murky day and we decided to go to have a look at Long Kesh. About 9 miles outside Belfast.

Very desolate countryside – terrible atmosphere of loneliness and security surrounded the camp. We couldn't see the actual cages – approximately 2 miles inside the main gates.

At the moment, it is 2.00 a.m. Just going to bed – very conscious of military activity up and down Fruithill Park. Puzzled by this because it is unusual in our street.

~~~

We were lucky. A row of sedate, solid houses with mature well-kept gardens lined each side of 'our street' as it climbed up gently from the busy Andersonstown Road, the main thoroughfare through nationalist West Belfast. On the crest of the rise, the street appeared to merge with the grassy, lower slopes of Divis Mountain, one in the chain of hills that border that part of Belfast. Although right in the heart of a nationalist area, which was seldom out of the news, Fruithill was relatively insulated from the turmoil that was steadily encroaching on the sprawling housing estates all around us.

Internment had changed *all* our lives and few nationalist districts escaped the violent reaction to its introduction the previous August. It was impossible for anyone going about their daily business in the west of the city to avoid the strife and unrest that had begun to consume the area: the shooting, rioting, stone-throwing, hijackings and burnings.

Although she had lived in Belfast for nearly 20 years, my mother, Maura, was a relative stranger to such a troubled environment, having been reared in the rural tranquillity of the Cooley Peninsula, across the border in the Republic. She met and fell in love with my Falls Road-born father, Jim, while they were working together in the Civil Service in industrial, post-war Belfast. They spent all their married life in Andersonstown, 50 miles and a cultural world away from her family home on the southern side of the magnificent, fjord-like Carlingford Lough.

Over the space of ten years my parents had five children: me first, followed at regular intervals by my four brothers: John, Aidan, Jim and finally Paul. The rest of my mother's family – her parents, four sisters and one brother, Seamus – all remained in the South. The youngest, Briege, became a nun, joining the Convent of Mercy in Dundalk in the week my mother married. The other sisters left Cooley and reared families in Sligo, Dun Laoghaire and Navan. As the situation in the North deteriorated, they grew understandably more and more reluctant to visit us.

On one of those seemingly interminable days that follow Christmas, we were glad to have her second youngest sister, Jo, and family visiting from across the border in County Meath. I hadn't seen real daylight since I woke, as a sullen, grey sky hung low and heavy over Belfast. The Christmas decorations, already losing their sheen, looked jaded and out of place but Catholic tradition dictated that we should wait until 6 January, the Feast of the Epiphany, before taking them down.

Our aunt, uncle and cousins' arrival was a welcome distraction. It didn't take long though for a dozen adults and children to make our four-bedroomed house feel suffocating. The living room and steamed-up kitchen became uncomfortably warm and crowded.

Even at the best of times, there was little to do in Belfast on a cold, bleak Presbyterian Sunday but there was even less diversion available when that Sunday happened to be the day after New Year's Day. My father, with his mounting concern about the developing political situation, decided that driving out to see the controversial new internment camp, in a disused RAF base near Lisburn, was as interesting a way as any to while away a couple of hours.

As we drove along the M1 motorway in our dark blue Ford Cortina, he slowed the car and pointed out the camp in the distance. Rows of blue-white lights loomed eerily through the mist and drizzle, across acres of flat, forbidding terrain. Huge spotlights burned brightly over the fifteen-foot-high perimeter fences which enclosed the wire cages and Nissen huts where hundreds of men had spent Christmas, interned without trial.

In the weeks before Christmas, I had invariably found myself drawn to detainees' accounts of torture and ill-treatment which were being published regularly in *The Irish News*. But even those compelling descriptions of how the men were 'confined to flooded cages ... with less room than caged animals in the zoo', failed to prepare me for the bleakness of the scene on that first Sunday in January.

Jim and Paul were only 10 and 7 years old but even they knew all about Long Kesh. As soon as they made out the outline of the prison in the grey, cheerless distance, they started to sing:

Armoured cars and tanks and guns
Came to take away our sons,
But every man must stand behind
The men behind the wire

The ballad was already a huge, local hit despite being banned on official radio stations. It blared out day and night on pirate radio, in taxis, pubs and clubs, and at every get-together across West Belfast. With its emotive images of night-time raids, marauding soldiers, crying children and assaults on all things Irish, the song became an anthem and a rallying cry for a generation of young nationalists.

Mon, Jan 3

There was a mini riot around the roundabout at the bottom of the park – only thing of any interest. I felt depressed all day, the atmosphere of tension and fear of what's going to happen got the better of me. Decided I wouldn't go to university in Northern Ireland.

There was one explosion in the afternoon – a lorry with a bomb in it exploded in Calendar Street. As a result, 62 passers-by taken to hospital. Couple of shooting incidents. Daddy apparently just missed the explosion.

Rained tonight, thank goodness – great water shortage.

At about 11.30 p.m. a great flash followed by a huge explosion shook house. Sure Belfast was up in smoke – turned out to be work of God. Thunder!

Tues, Jan 4

Off to a bad start – we didn't surface until twenty to one (disgraceful)! Had a very rushed lunch, Mammy had to be in work at one o'clock.

In the afternoon I had asked Frankie to come down to break the monotony of the holidays. Since the holidays have begun, I haven't seen even one person from school.

Wed, Jan 5

Misty and wet all day. We got up fairly early (for a change!). Mammy and John started the day with a row. Mammy had heard that he and Aidan had thrown paint-bombs yesterday – and I've a queer suspicion that they had! The two boys looked on it as a joke. Soon however all was peaceful again.

I got my hair cut in the afternoon. I was so

embarrassed by it sticking out on end when I came out that I wore a headscarf home and deliberately avoided meeting Michael Ewings, Maurice Murphy etc!

There was 'The Great Debate on Ulster' tonight and inevitably, it was on in our house (as in almost every house in Northern Ireland and Eire). It was unusual for 8 politicians to speak peacefully and with respect to each other. However, nothing came out of it all and was therefore a flop to many people.

Four boys took Jim and Patrick McGlade and beat them up (said it was the treatment given out in Long Kesh!)

Thurs, Jan 6

A Holy Day of Obligation, we went to 11.30 Mass. A cold, dismal day suited the dull atmosphere at home. All the decorations left from Christmas were put away and the last traces of Christmas disappeared.

I wanted to go into town but there seemed to be tension in the air. A lot of military activity and a shop blown up. I decided to go tomorrow instead (hoping I'll get some material to make a pair of trousers). Mammy and Daddy both in good moods.

A huge explosion tonight – have to wait till tomorrow to find out where it was.

Brought the dog out. Very peaceful night, no

*cars on road, no street-lights lit – very normal
here. Another internment camp opens – probably
for women.*

～～～

The 'normal' place where I was reared and was happy to live
was being grotesquely transformed into the most militarised
city in Western Europe. I wanted to go shopping in the
city centre but my parents warned me against it for fear of
IRA bombs. Soldiers – with rifles at the ready – patrolled
our streets in Saracen armoured cars and were bombarded
by bricks, bottles, petrol bombs and nail bombs flung by
Catholic youths. Minor stone-throwing would degenerate
into full-blown rioting, as the security forces responded with
baton charges, rubber bullets and even live ammunition.

Few of our car journeys were completed without us being
stopped and questioned at army checkpoints. Huge coils of
barbed wire denied us access to once familiar streets. I was
terrified that my father, like dozens of other innocent West
Belfast men, could be arrested and interned at any time.

The IRA, the army and loyalist paramilitaries became
more deeply embroiled in their bloody conflicts. In the seven
months before internment was introduced in August 1971,
around thirty people were killed across Northern Ireland. In
the last five months of the year, 150 died.

As 1971 passed into 1972, the life that I longed for as a
16-year-old – the world I read about in *Jackie* every week –
seemed to be slipping further and further beyond my reach.
Our lives had changed.

As the end of the Christmas holidays approached, I was
more preoccupied than ever with the episodes of violence,

upheaval and political bear-baiting being relayed to us night after night on television. My fascination with such matters, though, was nothing new. In the summer of 1969, a month after my fourteenth birthday, I started to compile my first Troubles scrapbook; pasting black-and-white images of civil unrest and Catholic homes ablaze on to its pastel-coloured pages. It was only when Suzette gave me a new diary – its pristine pages begging to be filled – that I felt inspired for the very first time to commit my thoughts to paper.

Once inside my bedroom, tucked away at the end of our narrow, wood-panelled landing, I turned the key in the solid wood door and insulated myself against Tito's noisy yelping and the pestering of my four brothers. I stuck cuttings in my scrapbook and confided in my diary. With the transistor turned up loud, I sat cross-legged on the floor to do homework, my back pressed against the Dimplex radiator for heat. On other nights, I stretched out contentedly on top of my single bed and lost myself in the latest book I was reading: *Once There Was a War*, *Anna Karenina*, *1984* and *Persuasion*, to name but a few. Given any opportunity, I would turn to the Singer sewing machine at the end of my bed, and while away the hours turning out simple garments for my mother or myself.

Suzette, who lived just a couple of doors away, was my most regular visitor. Having already left school, she relished being free from homework and revision and we spent hours in each other's houses – gossiping, listening to music on the radio or playing vinyl records, if I succeeded in commandeering the family record player for my own use. Surrounded by clothes, records, magazines and books strewn untidily about the room, we consumed gallons of tea. Whatever I was doing, I insisted the boys had to knock to get in. When distant plumes of thick smoke signalled a vehicle or building on fire, I would peer out the window guessing at its source, until a news bulletin confirmed a riot or an explosion. Sometimes I sewed; anything to relieve the dreadful boredom of those dismal January days.

Within the first few days of the New Year, it was depressingly clear that the temporary respite provided by the Christmas celebrations had been just that: temporary. As my teenage world continued to contract, the obligation to update my Collins diary became a vital part of my daily routine.

Fri, Jan 7

I wanted to go down town today but not allowed, I go down to Suzette's, she's home for the weekend. Bored in their house – only talk of nursing and holidays.

Went over to the Co-op with Mammy, heard all these stories about men being lifted by army – is very frightening. Daddy could be lifted any time.

Mammy and Daddy went to visit Aunt Alice and Josephine – they weren't in. They had a terrible interrogation at a roadblock by army – names, addresses, occupation, where they were going and why, and then they had to wait to be cleared from army headquarters.

I intended doing some studying for the exams but I just can't be bothered – will do it tomorrow (or some other time).

Sat, Jan 8

Got up to rain and cold and went into town with Mammy. Town was deserted – the same as it was before Christmas – almost as many soldiers as people. I got a letter today from Agnes. She says she's having a great time in the Shetlands – so peaceful and normal.

Last night was a bad night. I was sewing all night. It passes the time instead of sitting watching TV. I can't wait to get back to school on Monday.

Today's exactly one week since New Year's Day. It seems so long since we went to Dublin.

Sun, Jan 9

Dense fog. Went to Mass in St. Michael's new church. Beautiful church, although very plain. We went to an Andersonstown Civil Resistance meeting in the afternoon – a marvellous meeting. John Hume, Paddy Devlin, Jock Stallard (English Labour) and Michael Farrell all there.

Mrs E. came over and we spent the night playing records of the Civil Rights Association.

Shudder at the thought of school tomorrow again. I've a lack of interest in going back for the first time. I can't even find my pencil case. I hope to get half day – if so, I'll be able to get done some of the work that I intended to do over the holidays.

A great escape bid from Crumlin Road jail was foiled last night by the discovery of 3 underground tunnels. S. Kelly, a neighbour and welfare worker, was lifted on Friday and not released after 48 hours. Interned on the Maidstone – shocked to hear this.

~~~

At sixteen and a half, I was midway through my Lower Sixth year at St Dominic's Girls' Grammar School – a diligent student, proud of the exam grades I achieved the previous summer. The start of the autumn term had seen me happy to concentrate single-mindedly on the English, French and Maths I was studying for A-Levels. But, as the world I knew began to disintegrate, I became easily distracted.

With class tests imminent and A-Levels just over a year away, a conscientious voice in my head told me that I should be applying myself seriously to homework and revision. Instead, I was becoming more and more obsessed with what was happening around us.

My father, like many working-class Belfast men of his generation, left school at 14 and was self-educated. My mother, by contrast, had the benefit of a full, convent-school secondary education in Dundalk. What my father lacked, though, in terms of formal education, he more than compensated for through his passion for literature, history and politics, and books were always present in our home. Ensuring that my brothers and I got the best education possible was a priority for both my parents. My father especially urged us to read newspapers, to take an interest in and listen to 'the news' and care about what was happening in our troubled city.

He self-deprecatingly described his job in the Post Office as that of 'a minor civil servant' and claimed the position prevented him from ever becoming *publicly* involved in party politics. I suspect it suited his modest personality to commit himself instead to decades of unpaid, behind-the-scenes involvement in politics, civil rights and social justice issues.

He and my mother were involved with the constitutional, nationalist Social Democratic and Labour Party – the SDLP – since its inception in 1970, and he was a member of the Citizens' Defence Committee – the CDC – for roughly the same time. The latter organisation, which included local business people and members of the Catholic clergy, set itself the tasks of highlighting nationalist grievances, and campaigning peacefully for civil rights and an end to internment.

Night after night – sometimes dodging bullets to get there – he attended meetings of the fledgling SDLP or spent hours with his CDC colleagues in their cold, draughty offices at the bottom of the Falls Road 'trying to keep a lid on things': intervening with the security forces when their behaviour was excessive; recording allegations of army harassment and brutality; detailing sectarian attacks by loyalists; supporting internees' families; and helping to re-house families who'd been intimidated from their homes.

I was proud and excited to accompany him, at the beginning of January, to my first political rally. Both of us were equally curious to hear at first hand, and see in the flesh, some of the public figures who were making the news.

Mon, Jan 10

Back to school but we got half-day. Spent afternoon in the house alone, terrified in case someone should attempt to break in. It was bucketing all day and freezing cold.

There was a big explosion and fire in town – Talbot Street. Building went on fire – just got a slight mention on the news, so commonplace now. Oh! In Derry, 157 pairs of army trousers and 160 flak jackets were stolen from a drycleaners – and then the following day, a riot begins where rioters fired CS gas at the army. Very suspicious!

Denise F. came into school wearing an engagement ring – at least, so we thought. She was only messing by wearing a ring on the wrong hand – gave us all a bit of a jolt.

Tues, Jan 11

The fellow who was shot last week is buried today, so the buses were taken off. It was pouring rain and we had to walk home. We were soaked to the skin, even the lining of my coat got wet.

An explosion shook the school this afternoon but turns out it was only a 2lb bomb at Campbell's shop on the Springfield Road.

Sister Virgilius gave us the cheerful news that our exams start on the 4th. We nearly died of shock but at least we will have half-days off in between

them (something to look forward to).
At the moment, I should be attempting to do
some revision. I'll have to force myself to do it
before it's too late.

～～～

Dragging myself out of bed on those dark, dank mornings, to don my maroon-coloured uniform and go to school, was invariably a chore. The prospect of having to make the two-mile journey to or fro on foot, because the bus service was withdrawn, made it ten times worse. There were many such occasions in 1972.

Our 100-year-old convent school, St Dominic's, graced a sprawling site on the front of the Falls Road, the main thoroughfare from the city centre to West Belfast and the cockpit of much of the unrest. At the first hint of stone-throwing, rioting, hijacking or burning, Belfast Corporation withdrew its buses to protect both passengers and vehicles.

Regardless of the weather, hundreds of students from St Dominic's, St Louise's and St Rose's girls' schools, and St Mary's and the Christian Brothers boys' schools would be left with little choice but to trek up or down the road. We would set out from school in groups of five or six: those of us living in the West, like me and my classmates Eleanor, Oonagh, Maire, Liz and Frankie would head up the Falls Road towards Andersonstown; others, like Agnes and Jackie, who lived in North Belfast would head for the city centre.

Hordes of bedraggled teenagers, in maroon, brown, navy or black uniforms, trudged along wearily, weighed down with books, files, bags and sports-gear. Our outdoor shoes and staid gabardine overcoats would be heavy and sodden from the icy downpours.

On only our second day back at school after the Christmas break, transport was withdrawn because of the disruption likely to be caused by the funeral of a young IRA man, shot dead in a gun battle with the army a few days earlier. We completed our journey on foot, as we would many times that year.

Week in and week out funeral processions passed the front gates of St Dominic's on their way to the vast Milltown Cemetery, halfway along the road between my home and school. There were funerals of IRA men, killed by the police and army or by their own bombs exploding prematurely; of men, women and children shot or blown up by the IRA; of innocent civilians shot dead by the security forces in disputed circumstances, and of victims of loyalist bombers and assassination squads. The coffins might be draped in the Irish Tricolour, buried beneath mounds of plain white flowers, or adorned with colourful family tributes. As the mourners dispersed, it wasn't unusual for a full-scale riot to erupt, especially if the deceased had been killed by the army or the police.

Sometimes we were lucky and succeeded in waving down one of the dilapidated London Hackney cabs which were introduced to the local transport scene around that time by a group of entrepreneurially-minded republicans. Soon there were dozens of these clapped-out vehicles ferrying men, women and children up and down the Falls in droves – to Whiterock, Glen Road and 'Andytown', with drop-offs everywhere in between. As young and old alike embraced this unique, innovative and cheap transport system, 'the black hack' became the most popular and dependable means of transport in and out of West Belfast.

It was not unusual for eight people, laden with bags of shopping, to pile into one vehicle. Friends and relatives sat on each other's knees and toddlers were placed wherever there was room. Three people would squeeze onto the two, fold-down backwards-facing seats, with one of the trio straddling the narrow gap in between. The driver would cram another two people into the single passenger seat beside him. Two or three baby buggies would dangle precariously from the gaping boot, but as long as the doors could be slammed closed nobody complained. The gossip and banter, always witty and often edgy, never ceased.

Unlike the buses, the 'black hacks' had no official 'stops'; passengers simply called out, or used a coin to rap the sliding glass partition separating front and back, when they neared their destination. The most hazardous part of the journey was having to clamber across up to half a dozen people and their bags of shopping, while trying to retain a modicum of decency.

Those journeys were not for the faint-hearted. Winter or summer, the air inside the cabs was thick and stale as odours from sweaty bodies, babies, cigarette smoke, damp clothes, food and alcohol combined in a fetid mix.

The drivers, many of whom had been interned or in jail, knew every twist and turn in the road, every side street and short cut in West Belfast. Regardless of disorder and weather, their battered vehicles trundled through the debris of street battles, negotiating their way around burnt-out vehicles and makeshift barricades. Few incidents, bomb scares or obstacles deterred them from reaching their destinations.

Wed, Jan 12

Oonagh didn't come in today, neither did Eleanor or Jackie. Agnes rang to say she's just back from the Shetlands but will be in school tomorrow. We were trying to arrange our holidays in France – we need something cheap!

Mrs Mc Glade called in tonight and there was one huge explosion – only a mine, although we thought it was in the front garden! I went to bed quite early because I felt miserable and tired – but I read away until one o'clock. I know I'll pay for it in the morning.

Then Daddy told me about man being shot dead on the Falls Road. This morning, a 16-year-old boy shot himself accidentally – and I felt all I wanted was to get out of this place forever.

Thurs, Jan 13

Agnes was back – I was glad to see her, with so many being absent at the moment. She gave me a lovely leather purse from the Shetlands.

Oh, we all had bright ideas about France. Have decided to go to work in the Shetlands for 5 weeks in the summer, can earn £15 a week gutting fish and then we'll go on to France. I suppose it's all very well to dream.

Tonight Mammy made me change from 'Top of the Pops' to the film on the other side. I just left the living-room, came upstairs and sat crying my eyes out – not over TV – just boredom, (fear of exams), and tension.

Another 3 explosions tonight. Another man shot dead.

Fri, Jan 14

Last night, after I wrote my diary, there was a terrible incident outside. Going to bed, 11.30 – heard huge bang and thought it was a nail-bomb in the street. Opened the door and saw and heard the army. A Saracen had crashed into a neighbour's car and wrecked it completely. She was injured and taken to hospital.

Daddy and Mr McGlade began giving off to the soldiers, only to receive ignorance and insolence in return – and were threatened with being 'lifted'. Soldiers drove off, no one bothered about the girl or the car – and that was it!

Had to walk home from school today. IRA funeral, therefore no buses. Suzette is home for the weekend – as usual she was up to see me. Stayed for few hours, then I went down to her house for half an hour or so. I never realised before that I was so nervous till Mrs McGlade told me – every little noise made me jump. Talk about being jittery!

STILL trying to arrange holidays.

~~~

I was delighted to see Agnes back from her short holiday. She was my closest school friend at that particular time and her deceptively 'saintly' demeanour made her a favourite of the nuns. Our friendship, though, extended little beyond class times and phone calls, as she lived in the north of the city on the Cavehill Road. Occasionally, we spent a night in each other's homes but crossing after dark from her part of Belfast to mine, or vice versa, was too fraught with danger for us to do so with any regularity.

By the end of that second week of the new year, when she returned to school with enviable tales of her visit to the Shetland Islands, seven men had been shot dead in separate incidents in Belfast. I realised that despite all my dreams of 1972 being *my* year – when normality would be restored – it was going to be no better than the final months of 1971. The possibility of getting away grew more appealing every day.

I wanted to go to France more than anywhere else and to practise the language I was learning for A-Levels. Regardless though of where I might end up, I needed a part-time job to pay for it. I already knew that the chances of an unqualified 16-year-old like me finding work were slight; my reluctance to work in certain areas reduced them even further.

IRA bomb attacks in the city centre meant that my parents preferred me to look for work locally or in the safer outskirts of the city where we shopped. Working in a staunchly 'Protestant' area was out of the question. I, meanwhile, would happily have settled for a working holiday, if it took me out of Belfast. I was becoming so desperate that even the previously utterly repulsive idea of gutting fish in the Shetland Islands, where Agnes's brother was living, began to look attractive. Some girls at school were considering fruit-picking in

Norfolk as an option but even fish-gutting appealed to me more than such back-breaking work. Besides, I didn't want to go to England.

Sat, Jan 15

Didn't even stir before twenty past eleven. It's a horrible day, raining and foggy and cold. Bought a record this morning by Congregation, 'Softly Whispering I Love You'.

Last night was quiet, only a couple of incidents.

Mon, Jan 17

A boring day. I hate Mondays because we have double classes of everything.

I was speaking to Agnes today. She broke it off with David today because he has been warned what would happen to him if he was seen with her again. (He's not a Catholic).

At about 8 p.m., soldiers arrived outside and searched cars in Kennedy Way. We guessed something was going on – we were right.

On 9 o'clock news, hear that 7 men escaped from the Maidstone and swam to shore, then hijacked a bus (in their underwear) and drove to The Markets. Hope they're not caught.

Mammy rang Auntie Kathleen. She sent us a bouquet of flowers but we never got them.

Tues, Jan 18

Men from the Maidstone still not caught. According to the news, one of the escapees went to a bus driver, told him he had fallen into water and asked for some clothes. Driver brought him in to the fire, gave him his jacket – and then the escapee collected the other 6 and they went off to freedom in the hijacked bus!

Shock announcement today that Faulkner has extended the ban on parades for one year – therefore, no 12th July for the first time ever. Great anger in Orange Order circles.

A man was shot dead tonight. Don't know why yet.

Concert on in school (Thurs) so we have free afternoon. Everybody in school concentrating on our Fancy Fair – no work being done.

Have nearly decided to go on a course to France.

Still trying to get a job somewhere but prospects are rather hopeless. I don't want a job in a shop in town because I wouldn't feel too safe.

Wed, Jan 19

We were making jewellery for Fancy Fair. At lunch-time, we had a 'record session' up in the classroom – charged everyone 1p to get in. Amazing how many people turned up.

I have almost definitely decided now to go on the course to France – at least I hope to go.

I heard someone shouting in language which wasn't actually very refined – and I knew soldiers were in the area. Looked out and they were being stoned out in Fruithill Park. Fired one rubber bullet and went off. I got my new insurance card today although I'm not even working – however, I keep hoping. Big search down the Falls today – found nothing.

Thurs, Jan 20

Slept in this morning. I couldn't be bothered getting up, it was freezing and very icy. We had a Lower Sixth concert today at lunchtime. A few girls performed, and the grand finale was when Mr Garvey, our Science teacher, sang his own composition about the escape of the 7 men from the Maidstone. Many people say that the actual number of escapees was 16. Supposed to have been an attempted break-out from Long Kesh but papers say it was no more than army propaganda stunt.

The soldiers were in the street again tonight. Up and down on foot, and then called in to McGlade's to ask if it would be ok to have a bottle of beer – on duty, too!

Hope for snow, to brighten the place up.

~~~

The dramatic escape from HMS Maidstone – the prison ship moored in Belfast Lough to house internees – was the sort of exploit we only saw on the silver screen. The daring, night-time swim to freedom through the icy waters caused a sensation and was celebrated by nationalists across Belfast and beyond. I cut the escaped prisoners' photographs out of *The Irish News* – along with articles and a cartoon celebrating their breakout – and pasted them into my scrapbook. Nobody I knew wanted the men to be recaptured.

For a brief shining moment, the escapade elevated our messy conflict to the stuff of films and provided some respite from the dreary, grey monotony of that energy-sapping January. Day after day I switched on the lamp on the locker beside my bed and pulled back the curtains on yet another cold, misty morning. It was black dark when I got up at eight o'clock and the nights were already closing in by the time I returned home from school. The hours in between dragged by.

A surprise bouquet of flowers would certainly have brightened my mother's day but it wasn't to be. Her oldest sister Kathleen, who lived in Sligo and whom we seldom saw any more, arranged for some flowers to be sent with love, for no particular reason other than as a surprise, but a riot, hijacking or some sort of disorder obstructed their planned delivery.

Meanwhile Agnes, who lived in a religiously 'mixed' area, was grieving over the break-up of her new romance with, what was for us, the rarest of creatures – a Protestant boyfriend. Their relationship ended abruptly when members of his own community threatened him for dating a Catholic. I never got to meet him.

A loving, sisterly gesture and a teenage romance between a Catholic and a Protestant: both thwarted. Given the extraordinary circumstances in which we were living, there was nothing remarkable about either of these happenings, despite how much they were to be regretted.

Fri, Jan 21

Went to school as usual, not a bad day. There was a 'fashion show' at lunchtime, given by the Form 4s for the Fancy Fair.

Big explosion at Workman's on Springfield Road, 18-year-old soldier killed on Border. Soldiers were out in the street again tonight, sat there for more than 2 hours. Apparently, they had broken in to the White Fort Inn, wrecked it and arrested 9 men. Shooting and whistle-blowing all night.

Stayed with Suzette tonight – soldiers were going up and down all night and I began to get jittery … It's away after 1 o'clock at the moment and I am dying with sleep.

Sat, Jan 22

Decided to go to Derriaghy but the car refused to start, so we spent the afternoon pushing it up and down the street in the pouring rain and we were the centre of everyone's attention. The 2 big anti-internment marches at Magilligan and Armagh went off quieter than expected, although there was rioting at Magilligan.

Brilliant pictures of army brutality on TV. There's to be an investigation into the picture

*where soldier kicked a man – lying on the sand –
in stomach.*

Sun, Jan 23

*The seven men who escaped from the Maidstone
only crossed into the Republic last night. 2 more
anti-internment marches today – minor trouble
after both.*

*I spent the evening at what was supposed to
be studying but I simply wasted my time doing I
don't know what and I'm no further on with my
revision. Soldiers up snooping around Fruithill
again tonight.*

*I'm just after applying to Stewarts Supermarket
at Derriaghy for a job on Saturdays so must keep
my fingers crossed from now on.*

Mon Jan 24

*We all slept in so I decided only to go to school for
half a day. By the time 12.00 came, I decided to
stay off full day!*

*Spent the afternoon supposed to be studying
but I got none at all done, simply wasted my time.*

*Today, I'm wearing the jeans which I dyed blue
yesterday with my shortie jumper and, for once, I
feel that I look well. The only snag is there's no one
here to see me!*

*The 7 men who escaped from the Maidstone
are in Dublin today and gave a press conference –
all very amusing.*

I can't think of anything else to write tonight, (3 explosions today, no one seriously injured) – just shows what a boring day it has been.

I'm really fed up at the moment and wish something big would hurry up and happen soon.

~~~

I longed for a fall of the thick, white snow which the weather forecasters were predicting, to dispel the dinginess of our cityscape and relieve the tension and tedium of our existence. But despite the chill wind and the plummeting temperatures, the grey laden skies obstinately refused to yield.

The violence and disorder continued unabated. Around a dozen people were shot dead or killed by explosions in the first few weeks of the year; anti-internment protestors persisted in defying the government ban on marches and parades, and clashed violently with the police and soldiers, while the security forces continued to hunt for the elusive Maidstone escapees.

The tense, turbulent and brutal way of life to which my friends and I were becoming accustomed distinguished our existence from that of 16-year-old girls in every other city in Britain and Ireland. The growing threat from the IRA, and the security measures brought in to counteract it, paralysed our movements. There was more upheaval and unrest in my home town than in any other European city at that time, yet I complained that my existence was 'boring' and wished that 'something big would hurry up and happen soon'.

Tues, Jan 25

Back to school and I don't seem to have missed very much. Ma Murphy had been over to complain about John and Aidan talking to 'bad boys' who stone the army etc., because soldiers were up the street.

Mammy and Daddy went down to Granny's. When Mammy came home she began discussing France and where I'd get work. She said she would make sure I got there and she would give me money. I felt like hugging her.

Mrs Gordon came up and told me she'd enquired about jobs in the Bank Buildings – I have to go down on Saturday. Went to bed in high spirits, thankful to be alive!

Wed, Jan 26

Usual drag at school. Afterwards, I went up to the library and wasn't what you would call in the best of form getting home. I hardly spoke all evening except to give off about not getting out at night. Selfish.

Suzette sent home from work. She has conjunctivitis so that's the end of the nurses' disco for us.

IRA were hard at it today – 16 explosions – Belfast, Newry, Newtownabbey and Castlewellan, where a man was killed planting a bomb.

Thurs, Jan 27

Bitterly cold day – arrived in school, hair blown all over the place and a drip on my nose! We aren't getting half day tomorrow as I had expected. Very disappointed. I still haven't any revision done for tests and I don't care!

Two policemen were killed today in Derry. 16 explosions during the night. Tonight, there were five huge explosions one after the other – loudest ever, our very house shook.

I couldn't do my Maths tonight and I sat and cried, feeling sorry for myself. But I feel terrible, fed up, in depths of misery. Went to bed at 9.45, I'm so miserable.

Tomorrow's Friday, thank God. Maybe I'll go down to Bank Buildings on Saturday and beg for a job. Keep fingers crossed.

Fri, Jan 28

Went into school hoping for a half-day, due to the feast of Saint Thomas Aquinas. When Sister Virgilius asked for a better way of celebrating than one day off, we suggested 2!

Went over to the Co-op with Mammy after school, came home and watched the news – a policeman was shot dead while fixing his car on the Oldpark Road.

Lots of soldiers around tonight – more soldiers arriving and security being tightened for Derry march on Sunday.

Sat, Jan 29

We were up early. Mammy, Daddy and the boys went to Dunmurry and bought me a new waistcoat. I was really pleased.

I rang the Bank Buildings in nerves and asked about a job. Swiftly told by some snotty creature to write first and I <u>might</u> be considered for an interview.

Decided again to do some studying but Suzette arrived up, naturally, got none done.

Went to bed late. Snowing.

NICRA protest in Dungannon today went off considerably peacefully – turnout of 600. A few CS gas canisters, petrol bombs and rubber bullets fired – but that's normal here!

~~~

'*... that's normal here!*' The rumble of a distant explosion, rattles of gunfire, street riots and a steady succession of funerals – that was our life in West Belfast through the winter of 1971 and the early weeks of 1972. But as the snow that I yearned for finally began to fall, in the last weekend of the longest January I could remember, everything was about to change.

From 30 January onwards, thousands of ordinary nationalists, like my family and me, suddenly became afraid that we were all in the line of fire. Events would leave me scared to go to bed that night, and ashamed of myself for writing, just six days earlier, that I wished '*something big would hurry up and happen soon*'.

CHAPTER 2

'Sure there will be serious trouble.'

I only ever saw my father cry once. A few months after internment was introduced, my aunt in Sligo asked him to send her a letter describing life in Belfast at that time. Kathleen, like the rest of my mother's family, watched in horror from a safe distance in the Republic as the violence in the North escalated.

My father took up his usual position at the round, teak table in the corner of the living room where he liked to write when the younger ones had gone to bed. He wrote all evening, stopping only occasionally to relight his pipe or stretch his legs. When he finished, he pulled his armchair up in front of the fire, topped up his tobacco and began reading the letter aloud to my mother and me.

He read with passion, recounting in detail the destruction, disruption and unrest which were starting to envelop our lives. As he recalled how a defenceless teenager was snatched by soldiers just yards from our home on Internment Day, beaten severely around the head with batons, and then flung into the back of a Saracen armoured car, my father broke down, unable to read any more. He was mortified. I was shocked. At sixteen, I had no idea how to deal with such raw adult emotion.

A few weeks later, on the bleak, last Sunday in January 1972, I tried to come to terms with seeing many adults cry as the violence of Bloody Sunday was visited upon the people of Derry.

Sun, Jan 30

Got up early because of everyone going to Cooley. I decided to stay at home with Jim and Aidan. Mammy and Daddy didn't get going till late – there was a bomb on the M1 and it was closed. Stopped and searched four times.

I spent afternoon supposed to be studying but couldn't settle. Big NI Civil Rights Association demonstration and march planned for Derry – hoped it would go off ok.

However, in tears, we saw the 6 o'clock news. Paratroopers shot 28 people at it – 13 DEAD, including young boys. The army came on and told lie after lie, accused people of being bombers and gunmen.

Terrible pictures on TV – army bending down to take aim at men and boys fleeing from shooting, shooting them dead in the backs. Italian reporter called them murderers. Father and son fleeing, hands above head – both shot. Boy and girlfriend – shot girl, boy went to help her and they killed him.

I've never been so heartbroken and hopeless in my whole life before. Everyone full of hatred for army. Sure there will be serious trouble.

My mother and father entrusted me with the care of my 12- and 10-year-old brothers, Aidan and Jim, while they went to spend the afternoon with my grandparents across the border in Cooley. As the evening closed in around us, my brothers and I watched in frightened disbelief as the television news reported that the army had shot dead a number of people at an anti-internment march in Derry.

We watched marchers fleeing in terror, others tending to the dead and injured where they lay and the then Father Edward Daly waving a bloodied, white handkerchief as shots rang out in the background. By the time it was dark and the unofficial death toll reached thirteen, we were convinced that we would never see our parents again. We were terrified that the army might kill them too. All we could do was wait and peer anxiously through the darkness for their approaching headlights, praying for their safe and early return.

They refused to believe us at first when we ran out the front door as soon as the car pulled up and told them how many innocent people had been killed. 'Calm down. Calm down. One at a time. Now, what's happened?' Reunited as a family, we gathered in front of the television and watched the harrowing scenes of bloodshed and grief.

Despite being only 75 miles away from Belfast, I had never been in Derry. My sense of it was of a poor, grey, grim-looking place where the Troubles had started. We had driven through it a few times en route to Donegal but had never stopped there: across Craigavon Bridge, over the River Foyle, out the Letterkenny Road, and minutes later, across the border into the Republic; 'God's Country'. By the end of Bloody Sunday, the Bogside was being spoken of around the world.

Within hours of the six o'clock news, I – a young, relatively un-politicised nationalist – and thousands like me all over Ireland were sharing the disbelief, sorrow and anger of the people living in those previously unfamiliar Derry places: Rossville Street, William Street, Glenfada Park and Westland Street.

Six of the boys who were killed were just a few months older than me. The march they walked in was similar to the one which my father and uncle had joined four Sundays earlier. The Paras (Parachute Regiment), whose members gunned down the innocent men in Derry, were on duty in Belfast at that time too. I realised that being young and innocent afforded no protection. My father warned us grimly that there would be awful trouble after Bloody Sunday, worse than anything we had seen before.

Violence erupted in nationalist areas around Northern Ireland within hours of the Derry shootings, making me afraid to go to bed. My father refused to have any lights on upstairs because there were soldiers everywhere – in the gardens and on the street – and they'd be jittery, he warned us, after the day's events.

I lay in my bedroom in the eerie darkness, listening to the gunfire outside, some of it in the distance but much of it very near. Ambulances and fire engines wailed through the night and an army helicopter droned on and on and on. Unable to sleep, I peeped out the side of the bedroom curtains and saw the orange glow of at least half a dozen huge fires lighting up the sky.

There were reports of protests and demonstrations in parts of England, New York, Norway and Australia. I was scared.

However, I also knew that I was witnessing something tragic but momentous.

Mon, Jan 31

In a very tense atmosphere, went out to school. Normal till 11 a.m., then rumours of bombs etc. began and parents from Andersonstown came down to collect their daughters – because of the rioting and no buses.

School was in sheer chaos – almost everyone went home. Finally, at 1.45, Sr. Virgilius called Assembly and we were <u>all</u> sent home because fear of what was to come was so strong. At the hospital, hijacked lorry was in flames, so was Falls Road Co-op, and the Broadway cinema.

Not a sign of a soldier – all too scared. When we reached the barracks, we were greeted with jeers from the military of 'Why did you have to walk girls? Ha, ha, ha!' It took me all my time to restrain myself from saying something to those British bullies and thugs.

Hijacked lorries in Fruithill, barricades set up. We went over to see remains of Co-op, Lipton's supermarket etc. Still smouldering – a terrible sight.

Tues, Feb 1

I was very doubtful as to whether or not I should venture into school. Finally, at a quarter to 10 I decided to go, after the four boys had been sent home and their schools closed, because of shooting.

Got a lift down – no buses – only to find hardly anyone at all in. In my 3c class, 18 people were absent.

Buses came back on but two were hijacked and so, at 3.35, we set out walking. Frankie and Eleanor got lifts, Lizzie and I had to walk – and what a walk!

As we passed Beechmount, a hundred or so boys waited for the army, armed with bottles, stones, petrol bombs etc. and let fly as we passed because a Saracen had arrived. Soldiers jumped out and we fled up the road – Liz and I in front, followed by the rioters, then the soldiers!

At Donegall Road, lorry set on fire as we passed and then more Saracens. Dived for cover. At Whiterock, everyone got free ice-cream from hijacked lorry, then we got a lift home. Shooting all night. Army up and down trying to dismantle barricades. One soldier killed.

Wed, Feb 2

NO SCHOOL – TAOISEACH DECLARES DAY OF NATIONAL MOURNING FOR 13 DEAD.

Really was mourning. Went to 10.00 Mass, the church was packed. Requiem Masses all over province.

Listened to the funerals of the 13 dead on the radio and I just couldn't restrain myself from *weeping continuously as the 13 names were read out, giving ages – as young as 16, as old as 41, a father of seven children.*

The weather suited the atmosphere – torrential rain all day, dark and stormy. On the radio even the reporter, who was also in tears, commented on how the sun broke through the clouds as the coffins were placed in the earth.

However, Andersonstown's hooligans were soon at work. By 2 o'clock, army had been attacked several times, and Christie's wallpaper shop had been burnt down. Caroline Records shop was burnt down last night. Man shot dead by the army in Ballymurphy, cars hijacked for barricades. Liz's birthday – went up to her house for a while.

～～～

Dignified, respectful mourning turned to violent rage. Protesters in Dublin vented their fury by burning down the British Embassy. In Andersonstown and on the Falls, hordes of youths went on the rampage, attacking the army with anything they could lay their hands on, hijacking vehicles and laying waste to local businesses.

Soldiers stood on every street corner along a tense Falls Road as we made our way to school. Public transport was of course withdrawn. The roadway was strewn with riot debris and with the charred remains of makeshift barricades and burnt-out cars. An acrid smell hung in the air as shops, which had been set alight by petrol bombers a couple of days earlier, still smouldered along our route.

Within a mile of our home, rioters petrol bombed shops,

a cinema and supermarkets. 'Caroline Records', where my brother and I had bought our first music 'singles' two Saturdays earlier, after our parents purchased the family's first record-player, was burnt to the ground. Being a young romantic, I had bought 'Softly Whispering I Love You' by Congregation, while John opted for America's 'A Horse with No Name'. It was our first and only opportunity to shop at the store.

Thurs, Feb 3

Once again, there are no buses on the road. Walked to school and arrive late. A lot absent. Reports came in of trouble up in Andersonstown again and shooting at Divis Street. Four gunmen were shot by the army, although apparently not dead.

Mammy and I walked round to the shops after school. Army Saracen pulled up beside us and in soldiers' idea of a joke, poked their rifles at us through the slits in the side. Mammy nearly collapsed with fear.

Christie's and Caroline Records both smouldering ruins and all other shops on that side are closed (except Brian's) because the electricity supply had been affected by burnings. Using candles.

Most shops were open again after yesterday when there wasn't even one sweet shop open. All had closed – and black flags hung from all houses.

~~~

Within the space of a week, the world we knew had begun to collapse around us but our exam date was immovable, despite our pleas for mercy. Belfast may have been burning, but the Troubles stopped at the entrance to the school.

The rate at which events were deteriorating meant that none of us could predict how and where we might be when our A-levels actually came around in a year's time. We no longer had any interest in our 'mocks' and we resented our principal Sister Virgilius' insistence on 'business as normal'. It seemed that the Dominican sisters, cloistered behind the solid red-brick walls of our nineteenth-century convent school, simply 'refused to recognise' the Troubles.

Every morning, we passed in single file through a narrow, black, wrought-iron gate in the six-foot-high stone wall which separated the school from the chaos on the Falls Road. A row of ancient, towering, horse chestnut, beech and sycamore trees shielded six hundred teenage girls, in maroon-coloured uniforms, from the mayhem outside. The wall enclosed our five-storey, red-brick school, its lawns and cherry-blossom trees, its tennis courts and hockey and camogie pitches. At lunchtime and after class, solitary nuns, in their cream Dominican habits, passed silently and serenely along the leafy corridor formed by the trees, fingering their rosary beads, and rapt in prayer.

When we managed to arrive in time for morning assembly, the nuns appeared to show no interest in whether we might have had to walk a couple of miles to get to school that day. They didn't openly acknowledge that we had possibly run a gauntlet of rioters and burning vehicles on the way home the previous evening. They seemingly made no allowances for the impact that a night-time backdrop of shooting, bin-lid banging, sirens and army helicopters might have had on our studying, nor did they blink when dozens of girls were recorded as absent during the morning roll call.

Sometimes, when the 'boom' of an explosion shattered the soporific boredom of a lesson, the teacher would pause for a few seconds while we tried to work out the direction from which the sound had come; we would use any excuse to stop class. The girls nearest the windows might be given a moment to check for plumes of smoke but, almost immediately, our noses were back to the grindstone.

My schoolmates and I seized on the prevailing turmoil to try to escape the daily drudgery of classes, homework and revision but we were granted no respite. The pressure to achieve academically was relentless and the staff – religious and lay– were unstinting in their commitment to the demands of both timetable and syllabus. The regimented school day, the focus on exams and the insistence on full uniforms were the only constants in our otherwise turbulent lives. School provided us with a rare but secure anchor in a very unstable world, but the wisdom to see that eluded us in Lower Sixth.

Mother Laurentia, a severe but saintly old nun, who squinted out at us from under her wimple through round, wire glasses, repeatedly warned us that if we didn't settle down and apply ourselves to our work we would 'end up working on the buttons counter in Woolworths'.

Secretly I would have been happy to take a part-time job anywhere – even in Woolworths – if it helped me to get out of Belfast and away to France that summer.

Fri, Feb 4

Had to walk to school again today, still no buses and we're unlikely to have any for quite a while.

Our first test is this afternoon. Eleanor, Oonagh etc. got hold of last year's O-Level paper from which, they guessed, our essay would be taken. They prepared an essay during their free class and, sure enough, they got it on the paper. However, 'muggins me' decided to be honest to myself and as a result, found the exam to be very hard-going.

Walked home again after it – we're getting great exercise these days thanks to the Catholic boys of Falls Road and Andersonstown. Mrs McGlade is in a terrible state. Peter is arriving – with two English fellows – on the boat at 7 pm, to march in Newry.

Sat, Feb 5

Suzette was up banging at the door at 10.30 this morning while we were still in bed. Came up to see if I would go to the pictures this afternoon. Said I would. We went to see 'Soldier Blue'. It was good but not to the extent that I had expected.

Mammy and Daddy went down town. This is the first time Mammy has ventured into town in months.

Still not worried about the tests, even after the disaster that Spanish was. Met the two 'groovers' Peter McGlade brought home. In spite of their unkempt and bedraggled appearance, they were both very nice fellas!

Sun, Feb 6

Daddy has almost definitely decided not to go to Newry march, although very reluctantly.

Huge number – 60,000 people – turned up. Not as much as one stone thrown, a massive display of union and discipline. A great success. However, 26 summonses have been issued to SDLP people and others who marched.

On the Frost Programme tonight, during an interview with Protestants on the Shankill, John McKeague says he calls 'Bloody Sunday' "Good Sunday". One regret is that there weren't twice as many killed!'

~~~

John McKeague's comments stunned me, even though the loyalist leader was already well known for his extreme anti-Catholic views. I was incredulous that someone purporting to be a Christian could not only utter such venomous and sinister words but also revel in the deaths of so many innocent people.

It was the first occasion when I was directly exposed to such raw sectarianism. I was shocked to discover that the grief and outrage, which the murder of thirteen innocent people provoked in homes like mine, were not felt equally across Northern Ireland.

Mon, Feb 7

Didn't get up until late due to the exams not beginning till 1.00. Today we have French.

No one is in the slightest bit worried about these tests for some reason. As Sr. Virgilius told us last week, there is so much tragedy and despair around about us, irrelevant things are soon put from our minds. We are more concerned for our lives than for exams.

French was very difficult – made a mess of the paper but don't really care.

Notices were distributed around school today telling us not to come in on Wednesday but to join in 'D-Day' i.e. Day of Disruption, or as it will be in Andersonstown, Day of Destruction!

Did some revision for English and RK tonight and I'll be going to bed after writing this. No buses today. P.S. Very important – internee escapes from long Kesh!!!

Tues, Feb 8

Buses <u>still</u> aren't on the road yet, so had to walk to school for RK exam at 9.30. It was really funny – we couldn't do it all and we couldn't even 'waffle' the way we always do in RK tests.

Spent lunchtime trying to learn quotations out of 'Antony and Cleopatra'. The result? Complete confusion when I tried to write them out during the test.

We tried to get Sister Virgilius to close the

school tomorrow during the tests because of D for Disruption Day. Day of <u>peaceful</u> disruption. Schools were asked to close – but we didn't.

On the way home, we were threatened by three boys, if we didn't close! Therefore we all decided not to bother going in. Seem to be no definite plans for tomorrow's disruption.

～～～

'Intimidation' was as good an excuse as any for taking a day off school. D-Day was organised as a peaceful protest against internment, with the organisers calling on the public to disrupt normal life as much as possible – by staying away from work and school, closing businesses, attending rallies and picketing RUC stations.

St Dominic's kept its doors open, offering education as always, but I stayed home, wanting to be part of the new 'excitement' that was sweeping through our community. There was a thrill about being warned to stay at home, even by a handful of teenagers the same age as ourselves. Children and teenagers, myself included, were excited to be playing their parts in what was by now a very adult 'game'. We all wanted to show our anger and register a protest – however minor – at what had happened in Derry. I was no longer complaining that I was bored.

Wed, Feb 9

D-Day.

Schoolchildren from St Malachy's and Bearnaghea walked to City Hall. Other schools closed early. Aidan joined in a sit-down protest addressed by Paddy Devlin over at the Busy Bee.

Reports of people in Newry going to the GPO, tendering £10 notes to buy 1p stamps – and queuing up to find out if it was necessary to have a permit to grow gooseberries or keep a billy-goat!!

John said the people of Fruithill were traitors – we didn't protest for the internees. He and Aidan blocked the doors of kitchen and living-room to protest against not being allowed to protest!

Rioting broke out in Turf Lodge. Boy of 14 shot (seriously ill) by army – said they fired 'on a gunman.' All shops on the road closed. At Rathcoole, a man was shot while shooting at policemen – seriously ill, too.

Did 7 hours revision tonight for Applied Maths. I feel as sick as anything. I'm dreading these Maths, sure I won't do well. 3 nail-bomb explosions tonight, Falls Road. Chairman of Community Relations Board resigns – Maurice Hayes.

Thurs, Feb 10

Set out walking for school again, then got a lift with Mrs Gordon.

Did some more maths revision before school. Too late. Did the exam, I have definitely failed – only got one sum out of 6 done. However, I'm not the only one in that position.

Walked home. Had hoped to go down town but no buses – and I've no intention of walking down that road again. Might tomorrow.

No tests tomorrow so I didn't do a pick of revision. Watched Winter Olympics on TV and read for a while. Intend to go to concert in Methody tomorrow night – depending on situation. First time I'll have been out in months.

Fri, Feb 11

No exams at all, therefore I'm off all day. Didn't surface till about 11 o'clock. Walked round to the shops with Mammy and treated myself to a new mascara, 25p. Bought cream buns, just to get fat!

Mammy went off to work. I was left alone in the house and for a change, I didn't really mind. Washed my hair, Eleanor rang me and I rang Vera. Fixed heel on boots, darned school cardigan, washed few things and did other footery odds and ends.

At 6.30, Lizzie called down and we all met in Oonagh's. Frankie, Vera, Lizzie, Oonagh and I went to Methody and waited for Eleanor, Mary-Clare and Peter – they'd been off having, as Eleanor said, 'a wee drinkie-winkie.' Eleanor was supposed to meet a friend of Peter's but alas, he was sick. Concert was brilliant – a gorgeous fella there, all fancied him, called Gordon 'X'?

〜〜

Around that time, I was hanging by my fingertips to the edge of the 'in' crowd, the girls who – emboldened by the example of older brothers or sisters – weren't as fearful as I was and acted and looked older than their sixteen or seventeen years. I listened with envy to tales of their romantic trysts. I listened with a mixture of wonderment and disapproval as they boasted about their drinking exploits while my closest friends and I observed our Confirmation pledges to abstain from alcohol until we were 18.

As an only daughter, with no older trail-blazing siblings, I opted for the low-key, safer nights out and derived a vicarious thrill from hearing what the braver girls got up to. I could have counted on one hand the number of social outings I had during that winter but their rarity made me treasure them. We used to flock to the events which local schools occasionally organised: concerts where young aspiring rock musicians – usually the trendiest current or former pupils – flaunted their talents and impressed their peers. Such occasions gave sheltered girls like me a welcome excuse to 'slap on' some make-up and get dressed up.

My parents weren't strict, commanding rather than insisting upon obedience. 'I trust you,' my father would say, shifting responsibility for proper behaviour onto me. He and my mother left me in little doubt that, at 16, licensed premises were out of bounds. I wasn't on my own. Hotels, pubs, clubs and restaurants had become popular targets for republican and loyalist bombers, with the result that many nervous adults avoided them too, both in the suburbs and in the city centre.

Trips to 'the pictures' offered occasional diversions and early 'home times', although we avoided the big city-centre cinemas because of the risk of car bombs. The growing number of bombings and night-time shootings meant that even the simplest outings – like a visit to a friend's house – could be a logistical nightmare. Every expedition had to be planned thoroughly, approved by parents and meticulously choreographed so that lifts to and from home were confirmed. A thousand questions accompanied every request to be allowed out for an evening: 'Where are you going?', 'Who's organising it?', 'Who else is going?', 'How are you getting there?', 'What time is it over?', How are you getting home?', 'Where are you going to stand to get your lift?' Often it wasn't worth the bother.

In early 1972, Queen's University Students' Union became our Mecca; the one place which promised the excitement, normality and feeling of being grown up that I longed for. Being under age, we only gained admission a couple of times that year when 'someone who knew someone' signed us in. But it gave us a taste of what normal teenage life was surely like elsewhere and showed us what we were missing. It was only three miles away from West Belfast, but a world apart.

CHAPTER 3

'Blitzed, strife-torn corner of the earth.'

Sat, Feb 12

Daddy had to go to a meeting to represent the Citizens' Defence Committee with other businessmen etc. In afternoon, we decided to go to Lisburn where Mr Craig was having a rally of the new movement he has created, 'Ulster Vanguard'.

I got a new pair of shoes – suede – and I think they're lovely. Turned on the heater in my room tonight, planned to do Maths revision. However, I couldn't be fussed and turned it off again. Spent night watching television.

Mrs Gordon came up and we all sat and had bowls of vegetable soup. Daddy and Mammy gave me a long, interesting and 'wise' lecture on getting married and the risks involved. Made me feel I wanted to be a spinster – I don't think!!

~~~~

I was an ordinary 16-year-old living in extraordinary circumstances. Our lives had been turned upside down and yet, closeted in my bedroom night after night, I was beset by the same concerns as many adolescents the world over: would I be afflicted with teenage acne like so many of my classmates? Why hadn't I been born with straight instead of curly hair? Why were my breasts not as developed as those of lots of my friends? Would I ever have a boyfriend or would my physical shortcomings stop me having a teenage admirer, husband or children?

In my earlier teens, with no prospect of romance on the horizon, I used to worry that my parents wouldn't live long enough to see me married. By the spring of 1972, as violence tightened its stranglehold, I added the absence of a social life to the list of obstacles blocking my path to true love.

My mother and father had no cause to caution me about not rushing into marriage. I had never even come close to being asked out on a date, let alone 'going steady' with anyone. My all-girls school afforded me few opportunities to become acquainted with members of the opposite sex. My world was small and intimate, revolving around my family, St Dominic's and a small circle of friends and companions. The escalating violence provided me with a distraction from what I considered to be an otherwise boring and mundane existence. I struggled to stay focused on my schoolwork and, like everyone else, began to adjust to the new 'normality'.

By the middle of February I was accustomed to walking to and from school, to having my homework interrupted by the sound of explosions or gunfire, to listening to every news bulletin that I could, and shopping well away from the city centre. I expected my father to go out to meetings a couple of nights a week, to spend hours on end writing at the living room table, and that neighbours would call to our home at all hours of the day and night, in a way they had never done before.

Sun, Feb 13

Daddy going to annual Civil Rights Association meeting. Shock news of new proposals for settlement here announced in Sunday Times – later denied by Heath, probably true.

Body of unidentified man found in Fermanagh, sack over head, shot. Did Maths revision in case we get test tomorrow. Went over to shops at 9.30 with Mammy. The road was really eerie – not one street light, due to power cuts or else riots, no shop lighting and no people. Glad to get home.

500 attended Northern Resistance meeting and march in Enniskillen, therefore broke ban on parades <u>again</u>!

Mon, Feb 14

No St. Valentine cards – didn't really expect one.

The buses are back, a joy to see them. Place almost back to normal, boys don't even stone troops now – IRA have threatened them!

Soldiers in grounds of our school this morning – apparently a bomb scare. We didn't even get outside. Ironic.

Got English results – nearly died when I came 1ˢᵗ. Unbelievable. Shock no.2 came in RK, when Sister V said that my test and three others were good. I came 1ˢᵗ again – 89%. Agnes seemed stunned and so was I.

Took half day because Jim and Paul are off school. Hectic afternoon – the dog knocked down the plant holder and ran off with the plant!

7 bombs in town, no injuries. Man found shot yesterday turned out to be a soldier (lived in Dublin).

Maths test tomorrow because we didn't do it on Wednesday – can't win. Frankie rang – I FAILED Applied Maths.

Shrove Tuesday, Feb 15

Pouring rain and very dark. As usual, we slept in.

Spanish papers weren't corrected. Sister Virgilius said she thought my answer on existentialism was excellent – in fact it was all guess work! I was scared stiff going in to Applied Maths class – but she didn't say anything about my test, so I didn't worry. Saw my mistakes – carelessness. Spent free class preparing for Maths exam, rest of school sent home half day. Only 8 idiots left to do Maths – were told we could do them at home if we wanted! Not too bad.

2 bombs in town – Sawyer's and an engineering works completely wrecked.

Had piles of greasy, sugary pancakes for tea – lovely. Had made up my mind not to open a book tonight – kept my word and opened nothing except this diary.

Ash Wednesday, Feb 16

One of the coldest and most miserable days I have come across this winter. Into school as usual. Had

Blitzed, strife-torn corner of the earth.'

intended going to 8.30 Mass but wasn't there in time. Got French marks – 55%, hope to get Maths and Spanish marks tomorrow.

In spite of going to bed fairly early last night, I am exhausted today and decided to go even earlier tonight. However it is now 11.15 and I'm still up.

Wrote to the Bank Buildings about a job – keeping fingers crossed.

Last night was a relatively peaceful night – 5 men shot by IRA for stealing, only one seriously injured. Bomb in tyre manufacturer's in Belfast this afternoon.

Spent night by the fire trying to keep half warm, frozen all night.

Newsflash: soldier killed by shooting and gelignite bomb on M1 near Lisburn. Man hooded and shot dead in Derry – probably IRA job.

On that miserable note, get into bed.

Thurs, Feb 17

Didn't bother to go round to Assembly – too tired and fed up. Got Maths marks – 58% – terrible disappointment, had (though I hate to say it) expected more. Liz and Frankie got around 80%. No Spanish results.

I looked like a wreck today – white face and black rings under my eyes – decided to go to bed early but didn't go till 12!

Didn't keep my Lent resolution either. Didn't go to Mass, too lazy and tired. Have decided to go *every second day instead.*

Daddy's birthday tomorrow and then he's off to Edinburgh on Monday, shall miss him. (Haven't bitten my nails for 3 days now, must keep it up).

Man shot in Derry was 45-year-old Catholic UDR man. A callous murder. Soldier killed was 18 years old. 3 bombs in town, no serious injuries, thank God.

~~~

Lent had just begun but my commitment to my resolutions was already wavering. Belfast, in the spring of 1972, was no place for self-sacrifice and mortification.

The weather was unremittingly dreary and my exam results were neither as good as I had hoped nor as impressive as they would have been in the past. The Applied Maths test which had turned out so badly for me was only a 'mock' A-Level but I had *never* failed an examination before. I hated the subject with a vengeance; nevertheless, the news of my failure – delivered so gleefully by one of my 'friends' – left me shattered and humiliated. There appeared to be no prospect of me getting away from Belfast, and the IRA was slowly but surely cranking up the pressure.

Traditionally, the six-week period before Easter inspired an attempt at self-denial and we saved the sweets that were given to us or bought with our own pocket money. On St Patrick's Day, mid-way through our period of penance, we feasted on a congealed mass of Fruit Salads, Black Jacks, Drumsticks and Toffee Logs, scoffing the remainder on Easter Sunday. Five months before my seventeenth birthday, I decided I was too grown up for such childish observance and opted, as the nuns exhorted us, to do something positive and worthy like going to daily Mass instead. My resolution – like my resolve – was short-lived.

Life was generally depressing, my self-discipline was shaky but mothers and fathers seemed to be made of sterner stuff. Remarkably, the wheels of family life kept turning and parents went about their business, not just in my home but in the majority of homes across Belfast, as a new normality established itself.

Every weekday morning, my father left home just after eight o'clock and made his way by whatever means of transport was available – bus, black taxi or on foot – to his desk in Churchill House in the city centre. At midday, my mother set out for the part-time job she loved; looking after dozens of West Belfast's most deprived three- and four-year-olds. Operating from a prefab on the Upper Glen Road, she and her colleagues supplied these innocents with paper and chubby crayons; 'playdough' made up daily from flour, water and dye; storybooks and sand – and shielded them for four hours from the brutality outside. Across the city, despite the unrest, shopping was done, houses were cleaned, children were sent to school and church, and to doctors' and dentists' appointments. Meals were cooked and pancakes were served up on Shrove Tuesday.

The disturbing prospect of my father being sent to Edinburgh within a matter of days to attend a three-week Post Office training course unsettled me. I couldn't remember him ever being away from us before, other than on the rare occasion when he and my mother might have spent a night in Dublin, and I was worried about what might happen while he was gone. I wished he didn't have to leave us.

Fri, Feb 18

Daddy's birthday. We haven't bought him anything yet but we'll get him something before he goes to Scotland.

Three MPs – Unionist Phelim O'Neill, Independent Tom Gormley and Bertie McConnell – join the Alliance Party. Their first 3 MPs, doing well considering their party was only established last year.

Daddy went to a meeting of the Citizens' Defence Committee tonight – Annual General Meeting – and was nominated as the new Press officer. All pleased with himself. Came home about 12 and then went down to Gordon's.

Couple more explosions down town – no reports of anyone being injured.

~~~~

I proudly shared my father's delight when he told us he had been officially installed as the CDC press officer. The role was entirely voluntary and the organisation's decision to acknowledge the time and effort he had selflessly devoted to it since early in the Troubles was no more than he was due.

He often quoted the assertion by the eighteenth-century Irish political thinker, Edmund Burke, that, 'All that is necessary for the triumph of evil is that good men do nothing.' Like many other decent men and women who cared passionately about what was happening to their community, he was trying to steer it away from the abyss into which we appeared to be heading. We adjusted our family routine to allow him to incorporate new 'political' activities into his already busy days.

On the nights he was free from meetings, he lit his pipe and took up his customary position at the living room table. Surrounded by newspapers, files and folders he began writing speeches, sending letters to newspapers and drafting press statements.

Many adjourned SDLP or CDC meetings reconvened informally in our living room, or members who had missed a gathering would drop in to be updated. It wasn't unusual for our neighbours, the Gordons and McGlades, to arrive at our front door as late as midnight, especially if a major incident had been reported on the late night news. My mother, always at the centre of these impromptu get-togethers, provided supper and refreshments, while the chatting and speculation continued into the early hours of the morning.

Sat, Feb 19

Slept in for a while and Aidan brought my breakfast up to bed because, he said, I would be helping him with his French next week – sort of takes things for granted!

Mammy, Daddy, Paul and I went over to the shops – at least the ones which remain! Stoning troops etc. – usual practice for a Saturday afternoon.

I made the tea and watched the Cliff Richard Show. Fairly peaceful day.

Sun, Feb 20

We went to 10 o'clock Mass. Daddy goes off tomorrow, therefore he and Mammy making the best of each other. Watched 'A Tale of Two Cities' with Dirk Bogarde – too much! Went for a drive down to the docks to see where the Ardrossan boat sets out from, however everywhere is closed up.

Had birthday party (belated) for Daddy and then went out to shops later with Mammy. We bought piles of sweets for Daddy. I carried them home, only to discover that there was a hole in the bag. Had to re-trace our steps back to the shop, along the deserted, unlit road. I'm sure we looked really peculiar!

Mon, Feb 21

Got up, knew Daddy leaves today for Edinburgh. Decided to take half day or at least get out early. Came fourth in Spanish, 64%, very surprised.

Came home at half two, taxi came at half three and we arrived at the docks for the quarter past four boat. Very dismal scene, dull and cold. Said goodbye to Daddy, soldier beside us leaving his young wife – she and Mammy both in tears. Waved goodbye to Daddy and to the soldier on the boat. Picture of loneliness.

Came home, feeling lonely and scared of what could happen.

Got home to hear that four men were killed when their car, carrying a bomb, blew up. 6000

rounds of ammunition found in St Rose's School.
14-year-old boy found on the way to his home in
Ardoyne – dead from gunshot wounds.
Daddy rang at half eleven to say he had arrived
safely, thank God.

~~~

I doubt if I had ever been in a more cheerless, dispiriting place than Belfast docks that February afternoon. A chill wind blew up the Lough as my father hugged each of us in turn and assured us it wouldn't be long till he was home again. I tried not to cry as he walked up the gangway before waving to us from the deck.

As the Ardrossan ferry pulled away from the quayside, leaving my mother, brothers and me huddled together in the cold, the departure of my father felt like a bereavement. He was only going one hundred miles across the Irish Sea to Scotland but we could not have been sadder if he had been setting sail for America instead.

I felt more vulnerable and exposed than ever before. He was the 'man of the house', our provider and protector, my mother's 'other half' and the person best placed to give me answers about what was happening in our city. I snuggled into his side of their double bed that night and slept there with my mother who was now on her own, caring for my four brothers and me. I counted the nights until he would return.

My father's ship was scarcely out of Belfast Lough when reports came through of another five violent deaths. Twenty-four hours later, six civilians and a Catholic padre were killed when the Official IRA bombed the headquarters of the

Parachute Regiment in Aldershot. My father wasn't gone a day but already I was filled with foreboding.

Tues, Feb 22

Got up at 8.15, had slept with Mammy. Lonely going out without Daddy. Into school, bunked off first two classes. Bored and depressed.

Got a lift home. Very tense atmosphere, soldiers were everywhere and firing rubber-bullets everywhere.

14-year-old boy, who was shot accidentally, was buried today. Scuffles after the funeral.

Then news came in of an explosion at Paratroopers' Headquarters, Aldershot – 7 dead, 17 injured – IRA reprisal after killings in Derry. Brutal attack – 5 women, 1 man and Roman Catholic padre killed.

Daddy rang but couldn't 'say anything' over phone from Scotland.

Wed, Feb 23

We slept in until we were wakened by the sound of two bombs – a good start to the day!

Were at Albert Street mill. Had a long wait for buses due to traffic diversions.

The four men who were killed in the explosion in their car were buried today, therefore there weren't any buses but we got a lift home. Firing rubber-bullets etc. in all roads and directions.

Really feather-headed today – went to the

bother of carrying two library books, which I hadn't even finished reading, into school, intending to go to the library – only to discover they aren't due back till Friday!

Daddy rang – they were given a free phone-call home. He spoke to everyone for ages. Felt like a reunion – wish he were home again.

Thurs, Feb 24

Had a uniform inspection at 2 o'clock. Half the school look like tramps these days, wearing coloured coats over their uniforms for safety in mixed areas.

Suzette was up to see me, watched Top of the Pops. Did NO homework. I washed my hair and rang hairdresser to make an appointment for getting it cut tomorrow. I look like 'the wild man from Borneo', according to Mammy.

Had a postcard from Daddy, although he didn't ring us. As usual, Mrs Mc Glade was up.

The only circumstances in which St Dominic's pupils were exempted from wearing full uniform was when 'showing their true colours' might put their lives in danger. Otherwise, the uniform rules were as strictly enforced in our grammar school on the turbulent Falls Road as they would have been in the finest young ladies' colleges in England.

Staff lined us up regularly to examine our attire: white blouses, striped ties, maroon gym-frocks or skirts, and blazers of the same colour with the Dominican crest and motto, 'Veritas', emblazoned on the breast pockets. We were made to wear brown, leather sandals indoors, ensuring that the polished, wooden convent floors were protected from the dirt and grit carried in on our shoes from the world beyond the wall.

Teachers inspected our skirts to make sure they were no shorter than the modest regulation length, although we hitched them up to the limits of decency as soon as we passed out through the school gates again. One of the few benefits of being forced to walk home was the chance it afforded to come face-to-face with the boys from St Mary's, making a similar journey in the opposite direction. Such fleeting encounters were eagerly anticipated.

For reasons of foolish vanity, I envied the girls who lived in North Belfast and who passed through Protestant areas to get home. The uniform rules were relaxed for them, allowing them to wear fashionable, colourful coats instead of the staid, shapeless Dexters which were inflicted on the rest of us. By covering up their distinctive maroon uniforms, they concealed the fact that they were Catholics.

Feb 25

Teachers were all writing out our reports which are due out on Monday – an ordeal I am not looking forward to!

At lunchtime, someone told us that the town centre was in chaos – bombs and bomb-scares everywhere. Queen's Arcade was blown up, Malone Golf Club and music shop in Wellington Place.

After school, I went to get my hair cut – terrible delay on buses afterwards due to explosions etc. but I stood and waited because I was too tired to walk home.

At end of local news, report came in that the Minister of Home Affairs, John Taylor, had been shot and very seriously injured in Armagh.

Wish Daddy would ring or was here to discuss it. It must be terrible for him not to be able to express his feelings to anyone of kindred sympathies.

Sat, Feb 26

Glad to get a lie-in for the first time this week. Got up at about half ten, after having breakfast in bed from Jim and Paul. Got the dinner ready and went through the usual procedure regarding the news on Saturdays – 12.55 news, 1.00 news and 1.30 news. Condition of John Taylor still unchanged – very ill.

No reply yet from Bank Buildings – have given up any hope of getting a job there in summer.

No word from Daddy – probably out enjoying himself.

We went out to the shops – fellas stoning the army. One 12-year-old was sitting with a lovely transistor, tuned in to the army station and was able to tell the 'stoners' when the army were in their area – really funny!

Mrs Gordon came up, I did some homework.

~~~

Our evenings lost their focus, no longer shaped by the time my father arrived home from work, his schedule of meetings or the other demands on his time and company. I missed his reassuring presence about the house – hearing what he made of the day's events – and I watched the clock every night, willing him to ring us. The longer he was away, the more I wished he was home. As the death toll grew steadily, so did my fear of what might happen before he returned.

An ominous new term had crept insidiously into some politicians' vocabulary and into the media coverage of Northern Ireland. No news or current affairs programme was complete without a reference to the inevitability of the 'Protestant backlash'. I had no idea what 'backlash' meant, or what form this impending threat would take, but with all the talk of imminent civil war, I was old enough to be afraid.

The word 'backlash' started to haunt me. It leapt out at me from the television, radio and every conversation I overheard at night when neighbours called in to spend time with my mother. What frightened me most of all was that people were no longer asking *if* the backlash would happen, but *when*. For the first time since the Troubles began, I was beginning to be afraid that we might all be killed just because we were Catholics.

Sun, Feb 27

Went to 11 Mass, came home, had dinner, did some homework.

There was 1 bomb this morning – Monarch

Laundry, Donegall Road. Northern Resistance march in Derry went off peacefully. Condition of John Taylor is still unchanged.

Daddy hasn't telephoned us since Thursday night. I wish he would. We feel awfully cut off when he doesn't, perhaps he's sick. Anyway, he may ring later.

Spent evening doing homework and trying to keep awake. I must write to Passport Office tonight, just in case I manage to go to France.

Mon, Feb 28

Heard an explosion in the afternoon – Wallpamur and Isaac Agnew's – both blown up, becoming very frequent nowadays. Extremely boring day.

Daddy isn't due to ring until tomorrow night – beginning to miss him very much. Watched 'Panorama', all about 'Protestant backlash' – terrifying.

Went to bed very late and then sat up and wrote a French essay. I'm convinced I'm not wise!

On the late news, hear that two Catholics – 1 on the Springfield and 1 in Woodvale – were shot tonight and are seriously ill. Could be the start of the backlash.

Tues, Feb 29

Into school fairly early but by the time we reached second class, I could hardly keep my eyes open. Went to the dentist in school and he said I was ok.

There were another 7 explosions today. By the time daddy comes home from Edinburgh, he won't even recognise the city any more.

Daddy rang tonight – sounds very homesick and says he's really looking forward to getting back to this blitzed, strife-torn corner of the earth! Tried to do some homework but I just couldn't settle.

CHAPTER 4

'Two months to bury our dead.'

Wed, Mar 1

It is a gorgeous day, for March anyway. Aidan arrived home from school in a white science coat and no trousers! Indecent. He was accompanied by his science teacher – had spilt acid over himself and burnt through his trousers.

Mammy was going to go into town but there were a couple of explosions and this deterred her, naturally.

Did my homework and I'm still miles behind in English notes etc. Get them done at the weekend, if I'm lucky.

~~~

As winter turned to spring, there were very few Catholics in Belfast who were not fearful for the future. The 'Protestant backlash' was on everyone's lips but I had no clear idea what it meant. Would hordes of loyalists invade our area and burn us alive in our beds? Would carloads of sectarian assassins drive up and down our streets spraying our houses – and us – with gunfire?

Struggling to make sense of newspaper and television reports, I was too scared to contemplate what might happen to us if this vague concept – the backlash – materialised in the form of tens of thousands of armed, trained and uniformed UDA and UVF men. There weren't enough IRA men to protect the entire Catholic population; besides, the IRA seemed more intent on fighting the British Army and blowing up buildings in town.

I wondered if it would be like August 1969 all over again, when hundreds of Catholics were burnt out of their homes by Protestant mobs – 'Paisleyites' – and whole streets, within walking-distance of where my father grew up, were razed to the ground. The memory of standing on the Andersonstown Road on a sunny summer morning, looking at a vast pall of black smoke hanging over the Lower Falls, was still fresh in my mind two and a half years on. The sight of beleaguered families making their weary way up the road, with their last remaining possessions piled onto trailers and open-back trucks, would always stay in my memory. They were generally referred to as 'refugees'. I prayed it wouldn't happen again.

As my mother and I watched yet another programme about the backlash and the growth in Protestant militancy, I realised that I didn't know any Protestants. Not even one. All my friends were Catholic and we lived in a huge and expanding Catholic part of the city. My parents, grandparents, aunts, uncles and cousins were Catholic as were the regular callers to our house like our friends the Gordons and McGlades, and all our other neighbours. I attended Catholic primary and secondary schools, and my teachers were of that same religion. I played hockey against teams from Protestant schools when I was younger but the only non-Catholics with whom I was otherwise familiar were the often hostile, bitter and aggressive unionist spokespersons who featured on television programmes.

In the 1970s, roughly two thirds of the population of Northern Ireland were Protestant but almost everyone in Andersonstown – around 40,000 people – was Catholic. The only exceptions I knew of were the Martin family who owned a 'farm' across the road from the back of our house.

To call it a farm was to afford it more status than it perhaps deserved. It was really just a very large field, right in the middle of the busy, built-up area that comprised Lower Andersonstown. The Protestant owner kept a peacock – the most exotic, beautiful and, to us, inaccessible creature we had ever seen. Its distinctive, screeching call would draw us to the back window, where we'd watch it strut vainly across the field in the direction of our house, puffing out its dazzlingly blue chest, and fanning its magnificent turquoise and green tail with its thousand golden 'eyes' in full view of our kitchen.

We never got any closer to the splendid creature, nor did we ever get to know – or even meet – the people who owned it, even though they lived only the width of a field away. They occasionally kept pigs and a few horses too. When the horses ventured close to the wire fence which separated the field from Kennedy Way, local children – including my brothers and I – would gingerly feed handfuls of grass into their big, chomping, whiskered jaws. That was as close as we got to meeting our Protestant neighbours or any Protestants at all.

Fri, Mar 3

Didn't get all my homework done and so, had to bunk English Lit and Spanish Conversation to do my English.

Really fed up these days so, as soon as Vera said she was going to Queen's, I decided to take a chance on getting in. Went with Vera, Valerie, Lizzie, Jackie and Tom. Had a fantastic night, got piles of dances, never enjoyed myself so much before and didn't come home till a quarter to 2. Good job Daddy isn't here!

When I got home, Mammy told me a fellow had been arrested at the top of the street, Mrs Gordon got caught in an explosion at the bus depot and an 18-year-old soldier was shot dead on Cliftonville Road.

This city is definitely getting worse. Just wait each day to see who will be the next person killed.

Sat, Mar 4

Woke very early in spite of late night last night. At 7.30, heard a large explosion. Turned out to be on the Lisburn Road – a man was killed by RUC while planting bomb (18-year-old from Cavendish Street).

Went down to Bank Buildings for a job interview. Town was crawling with soldiers, searching and insulting everyone who came from direction of Falls Road. In the afternoon, Auntie Jo, Uncle Jim and family arrived.

A 3-7lb gelignite bomb exploded in the Abercorn Restaurant, had 300 people in it. 2 killed, 136 injured, 27 seriously, (had arms, legs, eyes removed).

I don't think I have much chance of getting the job – will know by Monday week.

Daddy rang – very bored and homesick.

~~~

There but for the grace of God … The Abercorn Restaurant was in the city's main shopping thoroughfare and was on the familiar, well-trodden route linking all the shops my mother and I loved to visit: the elegant Robinson & Cleaver department store, with its sweeping marble staircase; Anderson & McAuley's at the foot of Castle Street, for 'style' and dressmaking materials; the staid Bank Buildings where I had been trying without success to get a part-time job; and Littlewoods, which my father frequented for its Cheddar cheese and fresh fruit.

Mothers and daughters, and dozens of shoppers like us, would stop in the restaurant to rest weary limbs and draw breath during Saturday afternoon outings. It was usually packed but my mother and I were always content to queue as long as we got our weekly treat: a prawn open sandwich when the weather was warm and sunny, or Chicken Maryland with delicious banana and pineapple fritters when it was cold. If we weren't having lunch, we'd indulge ourselves with their exceptional Lemon Meringue Pie. I used to be intrigued by the plastic Tupperware container that the waitress only had to shake to produce the lightest fresh cream I had ever tasted. We would stash our bags under the table – just as, it transpired, the bombers had done – and review our purchases or plan the next stage of our shopping expedition.

Sickened and bewildered, I listened to details on the evening news of the two women who had been killed. I watched the black-and-white pictures of more than a hundred bloodied, dazed, dust-covered shoppers being helped or carried away from the wreckage.

I felt queasy at the realisation that had it not been for my early morning job interview at the Bank Buildings – a couple of hundred yards from the Abercorn – and the visit by my aunt and uncle, we would probably have gone into town and almost certainly to the restaurant.

The two innocent, unsuspecting women who were killed there that Saturday could just as easily have been us.

Sun, Mar 5

We all got up at 10 – all 12 of us – and went to 2 different Masses. House was absolutely chaotic with all the cousins going mad.

Listened to the 1.30 news – all about 'Abercorn disaster', and talk of civil war and Protestant backlash. Terribly frightening.

We were out in the back garden with Uncle Jim and Auntie Jo when suddenly there was a terrible burst of machine-gun fire. We all ran into the house, really thought we were being shot at. Turned out to be at Finaghy Road North – no one injured.

Granny O'Callaghan came up and we played republican and Civil Rights records for her. She's *getting more and more lively every day although she's <u>84!</u>*

Mon, Mar 6

This is the beginning of Daddy's last week in Edinburgh and Mammy is beginning to get a bit panicky over how little change we've made to the house since he went away!

I'm waiting for the post every day now for a letter from the Bank Buildings, to let me know about the job – although I was told not to expect to hear from them till at least next Monday.

Told that a nun had died in school, we therefore can expect to have either Tuesday or Wednesday off. Very mercenary attitude but I'm really getting fed up with school.

More explosions in town. Hear that there's to be a march in Andersonstown on 19th March.

Everybody talks now about Protestant back-lash. Hope they wait till Daddy's back!

Wed, Mar 8

A nun in the convent died on Monday and so we have no school today because of her funeral. Got off to a lazy start by lying in bed. Helped Mammy to paint windows and doors – really hard work – to give Daddy the impression that we were working the whole time he was gone!

News at 4.30 that another UDR man had been shot dead. UVF issued a threat this morning that

for every member of the security forces killed, they
would kill 10 Catholics and 1 priest – and it would
take us 2 months to bury our dead!

~~~

The UVF threat chilled me to the bone, making me feel utterly helpless, vulnerable and frightened. The prospect of it taking 'two months to bury our dead' conjured up images of mass murder and mass graves. I wanted to scream out loud to someone, to anyone who would listen, that my four brothers and I, my parents, our neighbours and friends, were innocent. We had done nothing wrong. We had neither bombed nor shot anyone and yet the UVF was threatening to kill us all. It was terrifyingly evil and unjust.

Their threat resurrected John McKeague's horrifying words a month earlier when he said that he regretted there weren't twice as many people killed on Bloody Sunday. I could not fathom the loyalists' hatred and struggled to rationalise their desire to punish innocent people like me when we had done nothing wrong.

Thurs, Mar 9

I'm still sleeping with Mammy, Daddy comes
home tomorrow. She thought she was taking flu
last night and suggested I stay off school today.
Naturally, I didn't object! I got up, got the boys out
to school and looked after Mammy although she
was more tired than sick.
Mrs Gordon came up and I was painting a window
when news came on to say that there had been an
explosion in a house in Clonard Street. Everyone

immediately presumed – after the UVF threat – that it had been caused by them.

However, the Provos had been making a bomb in the house and it went off. 4 men killed, their bodies were blown to pieces. Co-op in town blown up.

Fri, Mar 10

Daddy is due home at last, although the three weeks went much faster than we had expected – so much happening here in Northern Ireland to keep one occupied.

Came home straight from school to see him – Mammy had the house sparkling – but he was away to leave a fellow he met on the boat to the Derry train, because he was a stranger in Belfast.

He came home and dished out the presents – Tartan scarves, which now have a political significance here. However, Mammy said nothing. Since he went away, 28 people have been killed!

My father doled out the presents he had brought from Scotland to his five expectant children. The bags of crumbly, pastel-coloured, sickly-sweet Edinburgh Rock were devoured, as was the tin of Scottish Shortbread; but the cosy, colourful tartan scarves were quickly hidden from sight.

A 72-hour Provisional IRA truce was due to begin within hours of my father's return. In the nineteen days he had been away, almost thirty people had been killed: women shoppers, cleaners, a policeman, British soldiers, UDR members and

IRA men. 'Tartan gangs' had begun to make the headlines. These denim-clad loyalist youths, usually in their mid- to late-teens, had adopted tartan scarves as a symbol of their Protestant Ulster-Scots identity, the colours denoting which part of the city they came from; they were linked to the UDA and Ulster Young Militants. With their trademark scarves tied around their necks, they marauded in packs up to a hundred strong, striking terror in the hearts of isolated Catholics unfortunate enough to cross their paths.

None of us wanted to hurt my father's feelings by telling him that the tartan scarves he'd brought home from Edinburgh were the last thing that any young Catholic in Belfast would now be seen wearing. He would find out soon enough.

Sun, Mar 12

Mother's Day. Got up, cleaned around and then we all went to 11 Mass. Came home and got up to date with 'happenings round about' through newspapers.

After dinner, went up to do my room. It's a really beautiful day – so bright and peaceful. Pity it wasn't so peaceful every day. Provos seem to be observing their truce.

Young woman (24) was killed by Official IRA bullets which were fired at army and missed. First incident for the past 47 hours of peace.

Mon, Mar 13

I heard the postman leaving a letter, I rushed out of bed, I was sure it was from the Bank Buildings, but it wasn't. I've given up all hope of getting the job, seeing as they haven't written to me yet.

Another Monday – back into school. Siobhan asks me to go to Dublin with her on Thursday or Friday. I'd go anywhere at the moment to get out of Belfast and into a half normal place. Mammy allows me to go and so, I intend doing so. Excited.

Beautiful weather at the moment and I'm praying it will last.

Tues, Mar 14

Pouring when I set out for school. Had decided to bunk French Conversation – hadn't my homework done for it. Madame was very angry because so many girls are attending French Conversation so irregularly. If I do it again, I'll get into trouble.

Tomorrow is to be a Day of Prayer for Peace.

The fourth man who was killed in the Clonard Street explosion was buried today. Mammy and the boys all arrived home very late today. I was getting very worried about them.

Wed, Mar 15

Came in to school with Oonagh, then met Siobhan. Said they were definitely going to Dublin tomorrow and I could have a lift. I was really thrilled and we spent lunchtime making out plans on how best to enjoy ourselves.

In the afternoon, I had to supervise 1F for Sister Joan – and even she knew about me going to Dublin. Word certainly gets around in the convent! I felt sick as anything this afternoon and didn't feel like going to Spanish so I bunked it.

The weather is really beautiful – praying that it remains so.

Today is Day of Prayer for Peace here, continuous Rosary in school. Tonight told Auntie Margaret over phone I was going to see her in Dublin.

2 soldiers killed in explosion, Grosvenor Road.

~~~

I jumped at the opportunity to escape from Belfast for St Patrick's weekend and a short phone call to my mother's warm and fun-loving sister Margaret, who lived in Dun Laoghaire, on the south side of Dublin, secured me a place to stay.

The prospect of celebrating the feast day of Ireland's patron saint in the capital rather than in the North thrilled me. People all over the Republic would be enjoying the day as a national holiday. I could look forward to celebrating being Irish – proudly and in public – with thousands of others. People would carry the Irish tricolour openly through the city streets, free from fear of attack. We would enjoy traditional Irish music being played in the open air and we could tell strangers that our names were Siobhan and Eimear without feeling nervous about being Catholics.

St Patrick's Day celebrations in Belfast at that time were low-key, with few people being foolish enough to flaunt their 'Irishness' outside the safety and privacy of their own homes and neighbourhoods. My parents and a few friends would 'drown their shamrocks' with a simple night's craic – a drink and a sing-song – while the pinnacle of my celebrations was a day off school; an opportunity to feast on the sweets we had gone without in the first half of Lent; and going to Mass, sporting limp bunches of wet shamrock pinned to our lapels.

A rousing rendition of 'Hail, Glorious Saint Patrick' provided the high point of the ceremony; the congregation seemed to belt out the hymn with particular fervour and emotion when the saint's intercession was invoked:

'O Come to our aid, In our battle take part.'

I knew Dublin would be different and relished the prospect of having some fun with Siobhan. Like Agnes, she lived in North Belfast, so our friendship had little chance to develop outside of school hours. In Dublin, she and I could be as Irish as we wanted to be and do the things we were unable to do in Belfast without putting ourselves in danger. I couldn't wait.

St Patrick's Day, Mar 17

I woke early and went to 9.30 Mass with Auntie M. Rang Siobhan to make arrangements for the big Parade in Dublin. We arranged to meet at Trinity College at 11.30.

Didn't get into Dublin till 12 and then I couldn't find my way to Trinity. Went round to the Ambassador and watched the parade from there

– it was fantastic, musicians, flags, Americans – although I didn't meet Siobhan.

Came back to Dun Laoghaire, then Siobhan rang and we decided to go to the pictures. Met her at the quays at 5.30, had our tea out, wandered around and went to see 'Airport' and 'Madame X' – they were great. Had a brilliant night. Siobhan came home to stay in Auntie M's – chatted till 2!

Sat, Mar 18

Siobhan and I exhausted after last night's exploits – didn't get up till 11 and we could hardly see for tiredness. Decided not to go to disco tonight but to go to the pictures again instead. Auntie M realized how tired we were and said she was sending us off to bed at 7!

Went out roller-skating in the street. When we came in, we had wakened up and I persuaded Siobhan to go to a dance after all. We went to bed for an hour, then went to dance which began at 10. Had a fantastic time – met piles of nice fellas. I really liked one of them. He's from Blackrock and doing engineering at university.

Uncle Paddy collected us at 1, then discovered clock is put on one hour tonight, therefore really 2. We sat and gabbled till 4.30 and enjoyed every minute of it.

Sun, Mar 19

Certainly felt the effects of talking till half four this morning. We didn't even hear the carry-on of the children (and that was something!) until Auntie Margaret called us at 11.

Set off after 4. I was dropping with sleep the whole way home. Siobhan slept the whole journey – but I couldn't get into a comfortable position.

The anti-internment rally was on here (Andersonstown) today – 20,000 at it.

I couldn't honestly say that I'm glad to be home, due to the fact that home is in Belfast. Seems even worse now, compared to Dublin.

Mon, Mar 20

Exhausted after my weekend exploits. I was going to take the day off school but Mammy wouldn't allow me! Struggled in to face another monotonous week.

Decided I'd better go to French Conversation after threats from Madame last week about the consequences if we didn't go.

Large explosion in town today – Lower Donegall Street. Provos claimed responsibility. Outcome: 99 injured, 6 killed.

Mrs McCormick came down to tell us that Prods were shooting over the Peaceline tonight.

Daddy had to go down to CDC offices to write letters arranging for transport of refugees etc., if case arises of Protestant backlash.

I went up to McCormick's and sat with Rita and Anne. Saw pictures of the victims of Donegall Street bombs on their coloured TV. Really sickening.

As a result, didn't get to bed early tonight either – although there are many people in Belfast who have much greater worries.

~~~

Rita and Anne lived just a few doors from me in a house that always seemed brighter and 'shinier' than my own. Lamps and bright lights adorned every flat surface in the long, narrow living room, illuminating every nook and cranny and making ornaments and silverware twinkle and gleam. A huge green lava lamp, which held pride of place halfway along the room, mesmerised me virtually every time I visited the house: the big blobs of green wax constantly merging, breaking up and floating away again. That night, I didn't even notice it.

Staring at me from the large television was a dazed-looking woman with bright scarlet blood streaming from her skull. All around her, people covered in dust and with their clothes in tatters, were being carried away on stretchers or being tended to on the ground where they lay in pools of more red blood. An old man was lying on the footpath – obviously badly injured – and I thought I was going to be sick.

It was the first time I had ever watched colour television. Bomb-victims' blood was a lot more shocking in full technicolour than it had ever been in black and white.

I had never been as close to the scene of an explosion as I felt I was that night and I prayed to God that I never would be. Many of the hundred or so people who had been injured in the Donegall Street blast had been running away from a bomb scare in the next street. I imagined the terror they must have endured.

Shortly after that attack, the government announced that it would no longer allow cars to be parked in the city centre because so many bombs had been brought in that way. The one which exploded in Donegall Street was 'a 200-pounder', packed into a Ford Cortina just like ours.

I despaired at the sort of place I was living in: a so-called capital city where cars weren't permitted to stop in the centre. My three days in Dublin reinforced my desire to travel further away – and for much, much longer – but I had little expectation that I would get a chance to do so. The deadline for hearing if I got the Bank Buildings job passed and I resigned myself to the likelihood that the position had already been awarded to someone else. My father told me he never believed anyway that there was a chance they would give the job to a Catholic schoolgirl.

Wed, Mar 22

Weather isn't too bad although I was still late for school. Very few in Spanish, large number playing in finals of Inter Schools Hockey League against Ballyclare. I gave hockey up in Form 3, I was too lazy to persevere with practices etc.

They drew with Ballyclare, 1-1, and share the Cup therefore for six months each. Prods weren't

*very pleasant – catcalling etc. against Catholics.
Went off in tears and according to Jackie, at a dance
in Ballyclare tonight, some of them announced
they had <u>beaten</u> St. Dominic's – couldn't take the
defeat.*

Thurs, Mar 23

*A lot of people seem to be expecting some
announcement of Peace initiatives from
Westminster today. Faulkner over (in London)
all morning and was called back a second time in
the evening. Mammy and Daddy set out for Aunt
Alice's – being very courageous*

*Shock announcement that transfer of [control
of] security to Westminster is expected and, if
so, Faulkner and his <u>whole</u> Cabinet are going to
resign. Therefore – Direct Rule.*

*Daddy refuses to believe that I heard this, until
he hears it himself on TV. Great anxiety all night,
everywhere. There's going to be an announcement
at 11am tomorrow – everyone is praying Faulkner
will resign. Too good to be true!*

Keep fingers crossed.

～～

As events came to a head, I was thankful that my father was
no longer in Scotland. We needed him with us for whatever
was going to happen. Speculation about imminent political
reforms – including the phasing out of internment – fuelled
the sense of excitement but underlying it was a deep anxiety
about the possible repercussions.

The last week in March drew near and my father was called to more and more CDC meetings. Each night before his return, my mother would busy herself seeing my youngest brothers off to bed and making supper, while trying to hide her anxiety. As I tried in vain to overhear what was being discussed, my father and maybe one or two other committee members would update my mother and a couple of neighbours on the latest developments, chatting in hushed tones into the early hours of the morning over endless cups of tea. When I asked him what was going on and why there were so many meetings, he told me ominously that they were trying to get things organised for refugees 'in case anything happens'.

The militant leader of Ulster Vanguard, William Craig, threatened to set up a provisional government if the Prime Minister, Ted Heath, tried to introduce changes to which unionists were opposed. Less than a week earlier, Craig had told a rally of 60,000 people that it might be their 'duty to liquidate the enemy' if the politicians let them down.

I was scared, and convinced, that we – the Catholic population – were the enemy he was referring to.

CHAPTER 5

'The glory of the Lord.'

Fri, Mar 24 ANNOUNCEMENT OF DIRECT RULE

Into school, where everyone is waiting announcement of Heath's initiatives at 11 o'clock. Even Sister Virgilius has supplied a transistor, for people to listen to in library.

We're not really surprised – after last night's speculation – when Direct Rule is introduced. Everyone is thrilled at the thought of Faulkner and his other colleagues 'getting the boot!'

We were allowed out of school early in anticipation of Protestants causing trouble – a lot of them had walked out of work – all feel betrayed by Mother England!

Ah! Daddy is thrilled – walked in after work and announced he had 'seen the glory of the Lord!' Never thought he would live to see end of Faulkner and Unionism. We had a party in the house to celebrate, while two thirds of the country is mourning and one third is rejoicing.

Daddy got phone-call from Tom Conaty and was asked to go on 'Frost Programme' tonight. He went but couldn't say a word due to his job!

~~~

The end of the Stormont regime was something most nationalists never dreamed they would see and was the only occasion – apart from the Day of Mourning for Bloody Sunday – that I can remember 'politics' being allowed to interfere with the school routine.

When the senior girls heard the Prime Minister announcing to the House of Commons, in plummy, sonorous tones, that he was suspending the Stormont Government for its refusal to transfer control of security powers to Westminster, we cheered aloud. Political ingénues, one and all, we were reared on stories of religious discrimination, gerrymandering, second-class citizenship and Stormont as a 'Protestant Parliament for a Protestant people'. We believed that the announcement marked a new beginning for our generation. Tempering our youthful elation, though, was an apprehension fuelled by the whispered mutterings of the adults around us that a high price might be paid for the demise of Unionist domination.

In the early seventies, graffiti was plastered on almost every wall along main roads in working-class areas: anti-RUC slogans, anti-British ones, some blatantly anti-Catholic, and others railing against the IRA or loyalists. One particular piece however, on a long, stone cemetery wall which I passed daily on my way to school, stood out above the rest in its profundity: 'Is there life before death?'

Journalists and photographers, who were dispatched to Belfast's 'war zones', loved that piece of bleak, street philosophy. On the day Direct Rule was announced it captured the sense of elation and expectation, curbed with intense anxiety, prevalent in nationalist areas. My father was chomping at the bit to share both his delight and his concern when he was invited to take part in London Weekend Television's popular 'Frost Programme', but being a civil servant he was obliged to keep his views to himself.

My parents reserved their celebrations for later that night when neighbours and friends gathered in our house, hardly daring to believe that within days fifty years of Unionist domination would be brought to an end. On television that night, Edward Heath spoke of 'a new start ... a chance for fairness, a chance for prosperity, a chance for peace, a chance at last to bring the bombings and killings to an end'. The same evening the BBC informed us that 88 people had been killed since the start of January.

I allowed myself to dream that the IRA would end its bombing and shooting campaign, loyalists would stop their attacks on the Catholic population and the army would be returned to Britain. I dared to imagine that after nearly three years the Troubles might finally be over and Belfast would be a place where I wanted to stay.

My dream was short-lived and I learned, not for the last time, that what one community hailed as a tremendous breakthrough, the other regarded as a devastating loss. An announcement by the Vanguard leader, William Craig, of a two-day general work stoppage in protest at Heath's action immediately had us stockpiling supplies of bread, milk and candles. We waited anxiously to find out the extent of unionist opposition to Westminster's decision.

Sat, Mar 25

The first time I regained consciousness was 11.30 and there wasn't a sound. Everyone was still asleep as a result of last night's jubilations.

I feel terrible – headache and sore glands, Mammy keeps harping on about what I look like and that doesn't help matters! After lunch, she, Daddy, Jim and Paul go to Aunt Alice's – scared to go out at night. Aidan in bed sick (I ought to be there too).

Watch news, SDLP accept peace initiatives. Still haven't got over shock of Direct Rule!

Boy (17) shot dead in Ballymurphy last night.

Watched the Eurovision Song Contest – Ireland came second LAST! Luxembourg won, doubt if I'll get up tomorrow.

~~~

The Northern Ireland government had been suspended, we were a day away from mass walkouts and unprecedented unionist demonstrations but it took the Eurovision Song Contest to really stoke the fires of rivalry and national pride. Patriotic fervour seldom burned as strongly as it did when we were gathered by the television waiting nervously to see whether the UK would give Ireland any votes – and vice versa.

In March 1970, 'Dana', a sweet, innocent-looking, 18-year-old schoolgirl from Derry's Bogside won the competition for Ireland and we were convinced the Troubles had put Europe on our side. By the end of the 1972 contest, with Ireland's entry languishing towards the bottom of the results table, we were quickly disabused of that notion. Not only had the UK 'slighted' us, so had nearly every other country in Europe.

Vicky Leandros soared to victory with 'Après Toi' for Luxembourg and I went to bed disgusted and humiliated by this double 'snub'; it was the first and only time that Ireland's entry was sung in Gaelic.

Sun, Mar 26

Mammy made me stay in bed this morning and I wasn't in need of much persuasion. Aidan was in bed too and apparently Suzette is in bed with the same thing I have.

Mr Craig's Vanguard strike is due tomorrow – everyone wonders what effect it is going to have on us all. We're all storing up pints of milk – there'll be no milk or bread etc.

I'm not in a very good mood – feeling sorry for myself and am not getting enough sympathy, as I would like from Mammy and Daddy.

Mon, Mar 27: BEGINNING OF VANGUARD STRIKE

The first day of Craig's action against Direct Rule. Got up early in case of cuts in electricity. We were ok.

Terry came over to get her hair done by Mammy but the second she lifted the hairdryer, the electricity was cut off. Mammy went down to see Mrs McGlade, and we were cut off again. Boys all sent home from school because of no heating or light. (I was still off sick).

Craig had a crowd of 25,000 at City Hall today and over 200,000 walked out of jobs. Really terrifying, effect they have on province – all brought to a complete standstill.

We were cut off again after tea. Mammy and Daddy went down to Granny's to see Panorama.

Michael Smith, John, Suzette and I played cards by candlelight – pity the company wasn't more interesting.

Everywhere is in complete darkness.

Tues, Mar 28: LAST DAY OF STORMONT PARLIAMENT

Craig's Vanguard strike is still on today and, when woke at 7.30, we were cut off from electricity, therefore had tea – made last night – out of a flask, for breakfast.

Cut off till 10.15. Had dinner but were re-cut off at 1.30 until 4.45. Did some English notes because I wasn't allowed to go to school today. Went down to Mrs McGlade's for a cup of tea when electricity came back on.

After tea, we made apple-tarts but as soon as we had them ready for the oven, power cut off again – and we were left with nothing to do but twiddle our thumbs. At the moment, we are sitting watching some experiment John is doing, by candlelight. Very romantic! Don't know when we'll be 'back on'.

Very tense atmosphere all over – no life

anywhere. Will probably go to bed if power doesn't come back.

100,000+ protestors at Stormont's last fling today. Day of celebration for us though! Terrified of backlash!

∽∿∽

Hardly a cat stirred outside as we sat in the dark on the first night of the strike with the candlelight flickering on our playing cards. My mother and father lit a coal fire before setting out on the 50 mile journey to my mother's home in Cooley where – in the safety and stability of the Republic – electricity was guaranteed and they could follow the latest political developments on television.

The living room was warm and cosy and melted butter trickled down my fingers from the slices of thick white bread we toasted over the glowing embers. It was the sort of novelty we usually enjoyed but instead I was absolutely petrified. In the unaccustomed silence and eerie darkness, I caught my breath with every strange noise as I imagined UDA and UVF men outside the house.

The spectacle of tens of thousands of Protestants walking out of their jobs that morning and taking to the streets frightened the living daylights out of me. The ease and speed with which the protestors had succeeded in bringing industry and commerce to a standstill – leaving us with no bread or milk deliveries, no buses and worst of all, no electricity – shocked and terrified me. It reinforced an awareness of how vulnerable we were to the vagaries of the North's unionist workforces.

Over the next forty-eight hours, as nationalist euphoria at the abolition of Stormont began to dissipate, we had no choice but to heed the ominous warnings and threats emanating from militant loyalist quarters. I was forced to acknowledge that if anything was going to precipitate the Protestant backlash which the Catholic population had been dreading, this was it.

The rumours which were circulating, about thousands of loyalists preparing to take to the streets to fight, suddenly assumed a greater and more terrifying credibility. *Tens* of thousands gathered for mass rallies and protests, brandishing new red and white Ulster flags; virtually overnight, these had replaced the Union Jack as a symbol of a newly-energised and more militant loyalism. I began to wonder if we were heading towards civil war.

It was at times like that, my father reminded us, that we should count ourselves lucky not to be living in 'flashpoint areas' like Short Strand or North Belfast, where Catholics were surrounded and outnumbered by Protestants. For the first time, I appreciated the foresight and wisdom of my Falls Road-reared father and valued his knowledge of Belfast's political geography and its prejudices. I realised how blessed we were that when he married my mother eighteen years earlier, he set up home with his new bride – a relative newcomer to Belfast – in a quiet and secure nationalist area. My father enjoyed mimicking an ad which ran on television around that time, urging viewers to 'get the security' of some building society or other around them. When it came on our screens he would joke that we were lucky to have 'the security of the ghetto' around us.

I had always assumed that ghettos were places in America where poor, black people lived in awful conditions. I was shocked when, at my father's prompting, I looked the term up in a dictionary and saw it defined as part of any city where people from 'a particular disadvantaged, minority group' lived. I realised he hadn't been joking at all and that although we had a lovely four-bedroomed home, with trees and a garden, we *did* live in a Catholic, nationalist ghetto. I started to thank God for it every night and prayed for those who weren't so lucky.

My father would become particularly exasperated when he heard studio 'experts' on national television discussing the Northern Ireland conflict as a war between Catholics and Protestants. He patiently tried to explain to me the nuances and deep-rooted causes of our historic problem: the difficulty of reconciling a people belonging to two different cultures and identities.

'It's about unionism versus nationalism, loyalism versus republicanism,' he said, 'not Protestants against Catholics.' I appreciated the subtle distinction but remained terrified of the Protestant backlash. It was very difficult to do otherwise, especially in light of the newspaper cuttings I had pasted into my scrapbook in recent days: '25,000 Protestants expected for mass protest at City Hall', 'Protestants in shops, offices and factories left work at 10.00 a.m.' and 'A Protestant extremist gang is believed to have been responsible for the shooting incident in County Derry early yesterday morning'.

Despite my father's admonishment, I was viewing our Troubles in terms of 'them' and 'us'.

Wed, Mar 29

Aunt Alice and Josephine came up for their annual Easter visit, laden as usual with Easter eggs etc. They're very kind and have had some harrowing experiences lately, living in dread of Protestant backlash.

Horrible, blustery, depressing night. Nothing of any interest has happened today – I should be thankful.

Oh! Faulkner and his Cabinet resigned officially – 3 cheers!!!

2 explosions – bomb disposal expert (39) killed.

301 people killed since Troubles began.

Thurs, Mar 30

Went over to the shops and Mammy went to work. She came home – had been caught in a 3-hour-long gun battle between army and IRA.

8 explosions today.

After she came home, we went over to the Holy Thursday Mass in the church. Daddy was already in when we got home – had bought our Easter Eggs. I got a childish pleasure out of this. Drove Daddy down to CDC meeting after tea.

Heard that a woman – mother of 10 – had been shot dead in crossfire in the estate. Watched film but then heard fierce gun battle out at Casement Park – will know result tomorrow. (302 killed since Aug '69.)

~~~

The mother of ten, Martha Crawford, was yet another innocent woman in the wrong place at the wrong time. Less than three weeks previously, the Official IRA accidentally shot dead a 24-year-old mother down the Falls Road when they fired at soldiers and hit her instead. Three weeks before that, a woman in her late sixties was killed in similar circumstances, also at the bottom of the Falls.

The more often that 'ordinary' people became victims, the more I was conscious of my own vulnerability and that of my family, friends and neighbours; people like my father's elderly aunts, Alice and Josephine, who lived near the Springfield Road, a short walk from one of the 'peace-lines' – those ugly, towering, corrugated iron walls, topped with barbed wire – which ran along Belfast's sectarian interfaces, keeping Catholics and Protestants apart from each other.

The two genteel old ladies were both well into their seventies: one tall and angular with grey curly hair and beady blue eyes; the other smaller and stouter with dark brown eyes. They were the last survivors from a family of five unmarried sisters and one brother, my grandfather. Both women retired from working in England to rejoin their sisters in the family's small terraced house in the Lower Falls, close to their beloved Clonard Monastery and in the shadow of one of Belfast's industrial landmarks, Mackie's Foundry. Their home was literally within a ball bearing's throw of the foundry which, since its establishment in the late nineteenth century, had employed generations of Protestants making machinery for the textile industry, and armaments during the Second World War.

The huge, red brick factory towered menacingly over their home, blocking their view of the sky, and the workers' shift patterns dictated the women's movements. As they grew older and more frail they had a horror of being caught on the street – shuffling along with their shopping bags or walking their old black and white collie, Bonzo – as Mackie's disgorged its workforce at the end of a shift. They particularly dreaded the sound of the factory horn on days when the IRA bombed the city centre or killed members of the security forces; on such occasions, it wasn't unusual for droves of Mackie's workers to stampede along the Springfield Road, sometimes smashing windows and exchanging vile sectarian abuse with anyone in their path.

As the winter of 1971 turned to the spring of 1972, there were many nights when the two old ladies didn't bother to undress at all. As gun battles raged between the army and the IRA on the streets outside, or Catholic and Protestant crowds clashed along the interfaces between the two communities, they would sit up all night in the darkness, praying that they would survive to see the morning.

My great-aunts were fiercely independent but they had willingly taken refuge in our home, in August 1969, when Protestant mobs burned Catholic houses to the ground just a couple of streets from where they lived. As fear of a Protestant backlash escalated, they packed two suitcases with their clothes and most treasured possessions, and stashed them under their beds, ready to flee if necessary.

As more and more people became victims of paramilitary and state violence, I reluctantly accepted that you didn't have to be 'involved' in anything to be killed. I preferred not to dwell on such things; if I had, I would never have left the house.

Alone in my bed at night, though, it was hard to stop such thoughts preying on my mind. Since the start of January, around 100 people had been killed – an average of more than one a day. What happened to Mrs Crawford could just as easily have happened to my mother; she was caught up in the same ferocious gun battle on her way home from the nearby pre-school playgroup where she worked. She was angry when she got in but counted herself lucky to be alive. So did I.

Good Friday, Mar 31

Not a very nice day. After breakfast, the whole family (excluding Tito) went out to Derriaghy and Lisburn. I purchased a bra for myself (95p) and I was raging because Mammy didn't pay for it. She bought Aidan shoes, a shirt and an anorak – must admit, though, I do fare better on the whole than the four boys put together.

We went to the Good Friday ceremonies. I felt awful – had a splitting headache and felt down in the dumps. Came home, had tea and went up to my room. I really felt browned off with the family.

Felt I'd love to go away for a couple of months and get my head showered. Mammy and Daddy were giving off to me because I was in a huff but I couldn't help it.

Peaceful day. Provos get rough reception after killing Mrs Crawford yesterday.

Sat, April 1

April Fool's Day. Mammy not well, I bought her 10 daffodils, cost me 20p. Jim and Patrick went to Musgrave Park and came home with armfuls of daffodils, free! I was raging.

Went over to Confession – an ordeal I'd been dreading but got over it successfully.

Quite an enjoyable day – bomb down town. Had great fun in kitchen with Mammy and Jim carrying on, throwing pieces of raw chicken around!

150lb bomb exploded in a coffin in a hearse in Church Street.

Easter Sun, Apr 2

Exhausted after Midnight Mass. Mammy cross because Jim and Paul breakfasted on Easter eggs before going to 8.00 a.m. Mass and as a result, broke their Communion fasts.

At 12, set out for Cooley. Stopped 3 times by Army – Paras.

Had dinner. Auntie Briege was there. Left her out to convent in Dundalk, then watched the Easter Rising commemoration parade. Imperial Hotel for afternoon tea – very pleasant.

On way home, stopped again by Army.

Easter parades passed off peacefully here. Provos were jeered by women of Andersonstown – they have lost a lot of support since killing Mrs Crawford. Delegation sent to Sean Mac Stíofáin to have them removed.

Easter Mon, Apr 3

Everyone still off work and school. Had a light lunch because Mammy has decided we will live and dine in luxury today and will have 'dinner' at 7.

Daddy, John, Aidan and I went down to the cemetery to watch funeral of Mrs Crawford. Heartbreaking sight, to see her 10 children marching behind her flower-covered coffin. Soldiers all took up positions of standing to attention, removed their caps and saluted as the coffin passed. Publicity stunt – 100s of photographers there.

Went down to see the republican plot which is filling up very quickly (too quickly for anyone's liking). Met three women, each with a husband or son buried in it. Tragedy of life in Belfast.

Had late dinner, really enjoyable.

～～

John was nearly fifteen and Aidan had just turned thirteen when my father brought the three of us to Martha Crawford's funeral. Going to the funeral of someone we didn't know personally was an unusual and sad way to spend an Easter bank holiday but in Belfast in 1972 it didn't seem odd at all.

'Imagine if that was *our* Mammy!' Aidan whispered to me, as the coffin was slowly driven past us.

Mrs Crawford's grief-stricken children gathered beside the freshly-opened grave. They were crying, holding each other's hands, looking scared, with their heads down. Everybody was staring at them.

Like most people, I was gradually becoming inured to tragic death. The news of a killing would rapidly be overtaken by the story of another atrocity. Within days – maybe even hours – the latest victim would be relegated from the front pages, to be remembered only by their grieving loved ones.

Occasionally, however, the circumstances or exceptional brutality of a particular death would resonate across the whole community, far beyond the home and street where the victim lived. The Holy Thursday killing of Martha Crawford, which left ten young children inconsolable and without a mother, was one such incident.

Mrs Crawford, who was only 39, was making her way home from a local shop when she was shot in the head by a stray IRA bullet, fired during the final stages of a three hour gun battle with the army. It was neither voyeurism nor unseemly curiosity which drew thousands of mourners – including my father, brothers and me – to her funeral. My father took us to show solidarity with the bereaved and to make a stand against violence – a community united in sadness and in anger, desperate to see the killing stopped.

When we got home from the cemetery, my mother had the table laid out for our 'special dinner' and it was like Christmas all over again: turkey, stuffing, creamed and roast potatoes. I couldn't help thinking how different it must have been in the Crawford household.

Perhaps it was because it was Easter and my head was still full of images of Jesus on the cross; maybe because it was a holiday time when those children should have been enjoying Easter eggs and having fun; maybe it was because Mrs Crawford was an ordinary mother and left behind ten orphaned youngsters. Whatever the reason, the memory of that heartbroken family returned to my head unbidden for many days.

Wed, Apr 5

I cleaned the house although I was really fooling that I was doing work – too tired to put my heart into it.

I listened to Official IRA pirate radio and stuck some articles into my scrapbook until 6 o'clock. Watched TV then went on a Cook's tour around Belfast with Mammy and Daddy. Up the Shankill to see if there was any sign of trouble after last night, when a 500-strong Protestant mob stoned police and army patrols.

Toured through Ballymurphy – conditions there are shocking.

Thurs, Apr 6

After doing the dishes and tidying the living-room – while the boys seemed to be doing nothing! – I asked Mammy if I could go into town for the first time since Mar 4th. The reply? I could go if I wanted to and could stay there!

Mammy said I had a cheek getting up late and then wanting to go out. I was furious and took it out on her for the rest of the morning but went to the doctor's with her in the afternoon. Went on a Cook's tour all over Ballymurphy again, due to bomb in a car at Beechmount. It exploded at about 9 o'clock

Watched TV – Scarman Report out today (in our favour).

Fri, Apr 7

Today is really the last day of the Easter '72 holidays – really flew past although I did nothing at all exciting during them. Will be glad to go back to school on Monday – can't be more boring than this! 3 IRA men killed, own bomb.

Sat, Apr 8

Up early for the dentist with Mammy. Were home again after 11, but everyone was still in bed – so ructions followed!

We left to go down town, I in the hope of getting a new coat or 'strides'. However, Mammy didn't even mention these and bought herself a new coat and dress. They're lovely.

A bomb went off in the Europa Hotel while we were in Robinson & Cleaver's – nearly blew it down – and us too!

I went down to McGlade's tonight – anything to get out of the house.

~~~

The school holidays dragged on interminably and I was sick and tired of being confined to the house. I hadn't been in the city centre since 4 March – the day on which the Abercorn Restaurant was bombed – and common sense should have told me to stay at home. But, after an absence of five weeks,

I was impatient to get back to the big shops to track down a pair of navy trousers – the trendy 'strides' – that I coveted so badly. I hounded my mother until – weary of my petulant behaviour and probably against her better judgement – she eventually relented.

We were in the city centre no more than an hour when the ground trembled and I waited for the plate glass shop windows to come crashing in around us. Visions of the Abercorn and Donegall Street bombings flashed into my mind as we froze momentarily and braced ourselves for what might come next. On this occasion, the massive bomb was a one-off. The area around the hijacked lorry in which it was placed had been evacuated and no one was hurt.

By April, our shopping became functional rather than recreational and, with an odd exception, was confined to the new, small retail developments that had begun to flourish in the safer suburbs. Our special 'girls-only' Saturday outings – the bonding sessions which mothers, daughters and sisters took for granted everywhere else in Britain and Ireland – slipped beyond our reach. Occasionally, though, the lure of the bigger shops or a lull in the bombing campaign would override our instinct for self-preservation. We would take a chance.

More often than not, an ear-splitting blast, the reverberation of a nearby explosion, an order to evacuate a street or a shop, or a loyalist 'Tartan' gang tearing through the main shopping thoroughfare shouting anti-Catholic abuse, would send us fleeing home prematurely, our plans for a day out thwarted.

When an alarm went off in a shop like C&A or Marks and Spencer, we surged forward in panic like everyone else in the store, ignoring the security staff's pleas to stay calm, to walk rather than run. Every man, woman and child would run for their lives – literally – regardless of the advice.

My mother would grab my hand, I would grasp hers, and we would push and shove like everyone else, trying hard not to break into a panic-stricken run, wishing our legs would go faster, hoping – praying – that we would get away before a bomb might go off in the shop behind us. With my head pounding as if it was about to burst, I would pray that we weren't heading straight into the path of another device, primed and hidden in one of the cars parked in the street outside.

My father invariably, and understandably, worried about us when we went on those expeditions. 'What are you going in for?', 'Do you really need it?', 'Have you not got something else you could wear?' he would inquire. By the time we arrived home, often later than intended because of some sort of disruption, he would be standing at the front gate anxiously watching for us.

Why did we run such risks, exposing ourselves to such danger and inflicting such worry on my father? Whatever her fears for her own safety, why on earth did my mother – and others like her – bring her 16-year-old daughter into such a perilous environment? Why did I – an intelligent teenager who was well aware of the prevailing menace – badger my mother to take me shopping the way I did?

My mother worked heroically to make our depressing, abnormal lives as normal and enjoyable as possible, even if that meant a shopping trip, fraught with danger, to placate a demanding daughter. Every day, women like her – to all appearances unremarkable and unexceptional – fulfilled their mothering roles valiantly, keeping family life intact while their communities were being ripped apart by republican, loyalist and state violence.

Schoolgirls like me forged ahead with the urgency, selfishness and impatience of youth. It was easier to 'whistle past the graveyard' and delude myself that these awful things were not really happening, than to think we might be blown to pieces or felled by a bullet any time we crossed the front door.

CHAPTER 6

'My nerves are shattered'

Mon, April 10

Back to school – only good news was the fact that I might be going to see Coleraine University on Thursday – I hope so.

We got half day – a bomb at Beechmount on the way home and all traffic was diverted. Spent quiet, peaceful afternoon doing nothing although I should have done the work I had planned to do during the holidays.

Mammy wouldn't go to Dunmurry to get me my strides when she came home from work and I was furious. Started to sulk but realised I was being selfish – so planned to put it off till tomorrow. Keeping fingers crossed.

Tues, Apr 11

At break-time, I was sent for by Sister Clare – I'm <u>definitely</u> going to Coleraine on Thurs.

Came home after 4 – Jim and Paul told me that Mammy said I had to be ready to go out to Dunmurry for my new trousers. I did so but, today above all days, Mammy didn't get home till after 5 p.m. because of shooting in the estate. I was furious and cursed the IRA!

Decided not to do any homework, I'm getting worse.

Wed, April 12

I feel as though I've been back at school for two months instead of two days!

Looking forward to my journey to Coleraine tomorrow. We were all briefed in detail by Sr. Virgilius after lunch today, about the do's and don'ts of going on a school trip. Same rules as we have heard a hundred times already.

Thurs, Apr 13

Up early to go to Coleraine University. Anne Mulvenna collected me in the car at 7.45 and we arrived at the station far too early. We felt really embarrassed, and like a pack of queers, going around in our uniforms, being herded by Sr. Eusebius.

Had a brilliant day and met piles of nice people. Have decided to study Social Administration. I'm delighted to know what I'm going to do, for once! Had great carry-on on the train coming home – got as far away as possible from Sr. Eusebius and had a brilliant time with the boys from St Malachy's etc.

Terrible day of bombings – 28 in 24 hours, everyone thought we were heading for peace!!

~~~

Being selected by the nuns to travel to the New University of Ulster's Open Day was the first official and reassuring confirmation that, despite a few hiccups, I was performing to my teachers' satisfaction and was regarded as 'university material'. Third-level education had been my ultimate objective from the day I started St Dominic's in 1966, back when no one could have foreseen the devastating way our society would soon implode.

By the time I was preparing for my A-levels, I was starting to question whether my education had any value at all. I had no idea where or what I wanted to study. The relentless toll of death and destruction made long-term planning seem overly optimistic and, on the worst days, quite ridiculous.

The invitation to the Open Day at Coleraine suddenly forced me to acknowledge that despite the ongoing mayhem, it was time to think seriously about my future. Within a few months I would have to make choices that would shape the rest of my life. The one thing I had already decided though, was that the north coast town of Coleraine would *not* be my campus of choice.

Four years after opening, the New University of Ulster remained mired in controversy. In 1965, thousands of protestors had travelled to the seat of the Unionist government at Stormont to demonstrate their opposition to the decision to build a new, third-level institution in the small, predominantly unionist town of Coleraine, instead of in Northern Ireland's second city – overwhelmingly Catholic and nationalist Derry.

I was desperate to gain some insight into degree options and university life and was delighted by the prospect of my first trip to the North Coast. But I would have been just as keen to go anywhere else, as long as it guaranteed a day out of school and away from Belfast.

Fri, Apr 14

I intended bunking Spanish conversation class for the second time but just as I walked out of the 'new wing' corridor, I bumped head-first into Mrs White. It was the first time she ever used that way for coming to class and it was just my luck to bump into her!

On the way home, the whistles started to blow in the estate. Soldiers were around – started firing rubber-bullets so I ran for my life.

Peeled the potatoes for tomorrow and then went in to watch Marx Bros. on T.V. Really hilarious – haven't laughed so much for months.

Sat, Apr 15

Everyone got up in fantastic moods and we decided to take off for Cushendun. By 1, we were on our way – visited Cushendun, Cushendall and Ballycastle. The scenery, and peace, was really beautiful, so different from Belfast. Had our tea in McBride's Hotel, a remnant of Daddy's youth.

On way back, at Monagh Road, stopped by a crowd and told to get home immediately. Army had shot the OC of the Official IRA, Joe McCann, and there was serious trouble.

Fellow shot dead by Protestants in Ardoyne.

Start of a night of trouble, with shooting, burnings and riots most of the night. Look with dread towards tomorrow.

Sun, Apr 16

There were 3 soldiers killed by the IRA last night in retaliation for shooting of Joe McCann.

Rioting all night all over the city. Rioting continued today – 5 buses burnt in Turf Lodge, so we'll have no more buses for goodness knows how long!

Tues, Apr 18

Buses still aren't on and the leader of the 'Stickies', Joe McCann is being buried today.

Had a 'fight' with Mammy before going to school – she said I had to take half day and come home at 12.15. She collected me, Eleanor and Ana half way home. I wanted to go to the funeral but she wouldn't let me – I was raging and <u>bored</u>.

Something happened to put a sudden end to my ennui. Sitting at the front with Suzette when Mrs McGlade came up to say there was something wrong in Kennedy Way. IRA man with gun in McGlade's garden. I nearly collapsed. He'd made his way down from McCormick's. His comrade warned us to stay away from the back garden. However, he didn't open fire, thank God.

Shooting all night – my nerves are shattered.

The arrival of unseasonably warm weather and brighter, less frightening evenings inspired my parents to take my brothers and me on our first visit to the wonderful Glens of Antrim. A day spent tramping along forest paths, climbing over fences and trudging along the rugged and majestic Antrim coast road left us exhilarated and exhausted, as we drove back into Belfast. My head was still filled with the wonder of the waterfalls we had seen thundering down the rocky gorges in Glenariff, when my father braked to a sudden halt.

A blazing, double-decker bus and two hijacked vans barricaded the road a couple of hundred yards in front of us, while crowds of men and youths – some with scarves wrapped tightly around their faces – milled about. On one side of the road, teenage boys were smashing paving stones into fist-size pieces; others were stacking petrol bombs into milk-crates.

As my father struggled to negotiate a three-point turn, and the rest of us craned our necks to see what was happening, a group of men ran towards us, waving us down and yelling to get out of the area. Two of them pulled their scarves away from their mouths just long enough to thump the roof of the car and shout at us that the Paras had shot an Official IRA leader, Joe McCann, and killed him.

Violence erupted throughout nationalist areas as tales spread of McCann's exploits in defence of his community and against the British Army. First-hand accounts and urban myths were intertwined, and by the day of his funeral – one of the biggest ever seen in Belfast – Joe McCann had become an iconic figure, brutally hunted down and slain. I had never heard of McCann before that sunny Saturday afternoon and yet, three days later, I was demanding to attend his burial.

Given his awesome reputation, I was amazed to learn that he was only 25 years old when he was shot. When the first photographs of him appeared, I was even more impressed to discover that he was a dark, handsome character with chiselled features. A week later, I pasted an article into my scrapbook from one of the Sunday papers, describing him as a 'Che Guevara figure who could use either a gun or political argument to bring about change'.

I treasured a black-and-white postcard-sized tribute to McCann – a photograph captioned 'Joe McCann: The Irish Revolutionary', positioned above the lyrics of 'Big Joe', to be sung to the air of 'Joe Hill'.

From Creggan Heights to Lower Falls,
From Turf Lodge to Ardoyne,
Where workers fight and organise,
Says he, 'You'll find McCann',
Says he, 'You'll find McCann'.

As an impressionable 16-year-old schoolgirl, I was fleetingly seduced by the dangerous 'glamour' of an Official IRA man who became a legendary, republican working-class hero in death.

Wed, Apr 19

Got up at 8.15 and began to walk to school. The weather is absolutely beautiful – the temperature is away up in the 70s – I'm nearly sick with the heat and don't know what will become of me when I go to France!

125

Sr. Virgilius is away on retreat and the whole school is going wild. Everyone outside at every opportunity to get the sun but we were chased inside twice by Mother Laurentia. Mrs Gordon came up tonight. Shooting all around us, really terrifying. UDR man killed today, 2 bombs. Rioting.

Sat, Apr 22

We all got up quite late – becoming quite a habit every Saturday. No one was in the mood to go away anywhere, as had been planned.

Mammy and I went into town. Boys played football. I got a new red raincoat which I quite like – I can't be definite yet. Came home in a black taxi – buses aren't on yet.

A Special Branch man was seriously wounded by shooting in Newry. 12 internees released.

Sun, Apr 23

Got up late, all in rotten moods and I knew a row was inevitable. It came after Mass, with the usual 'weeping, wailing and gnashing of teeth'. Then as if by a miracle, someone mentioned going to Cooley and everyone agreed. Inside half an hour we were on the road.

A cousin of Mammy's arrived and invited us to his chicken farm on Sunday fortnight! Stopped a couple of times on way home by the army.

Fairly quiet day i.e. 2 killed. An 11-year-old boy

dies days after being hit on the head by a rubber
bullet and a 73-year-old farmer shot. No bombs.

~~~~

Cooley was a magical and mystical place, only fifty miles or so south of Belfast, but the nearest thing I could imagine to Tír na nÓg – the most famous 'Other World' in Irish mythology. If my beloved grandparents had had it in their powers, they would have packed up our belongings in the spring of 1972 and moved us permanently from Belfast to Cooley; lock, stock and barrel. In phone call after phone call, and every time we visited her, my grandmother pleaded with her eldest daughter to leave the city.

The place of my mother's youth offered us everything that Belfast didn't: freedom, fresh air, open spaces, mountains, streams, myths and legends. According to Irish folklore, my namesake Eimear stormed its hills in pursuit of her fickle lover, the Celtic warrior, Cúchulainn. Legend has it that at the age of 17, he single-handedly defended Ulster from the onslaught of the forces of the warrior Queen Medbh of Connaught, in an epic battle called the Cattle Raid of Cooley.

We picnicked in the hills around the legendary 'Long Woman's Grave' and added stones to the ever-growing pile on her burial cairn. I delved into clusters of luscious green ferns to pluck bluebells and shy primroses to bring home. As youngsters, we chased imaginary leprechauns among the ruins of the seven-hundred-year-old King John's Castle in medieval Carlingford. We swam and splashed in the sea at Shelling Hill; the long, deserted, shingly beach lay just a short drive along fuchsia-lined country lanes from my grandparents' home.

As we swept up the long, hedged driveway, my father would honk the car horn to announce our arrival. Immediately, my granny – loving and small, with white curly hair, twinkling eyes and a constant smile on her face – would appear at the kitchen door, often in a wrap-around apron and with her hands covered in flour from the bread she was making, to welcome us to safety.

As the tantalizing smell of her home baking wafted towards us from the huge range in the kitchen, we went in search of our grandfather; invariably, we found him bent over a spade in the huge field in front of the house, digging out potatoes, turnips, cabbages and carrots for us to take home. He would take off the felt hat that he wore to shield his bald head from the elements, then wrap us in huge bear hugs and rub his stubbly day's growth against our cheeks to hear our delighted squeals.

Over the first cup of tea, served with home-made bread and jam, and apple tart or fresh cream sponge, the talk always turned to politics – flippantly at first: 'What are you going to do with that big fella Paisley?', 'When are you going to leave them to it and come down here to a civilized place?'

My father was often irked during those conversations by the Southerners' perception of the Free Presbyterian leader, Dr Ian Paisley, as a harmless figure – 'The Big Man' or 'The Doc' – someone to be mimicked and joked about. 'He's no laughing matter in the North,' my father would reprimand them gently. Subdued by my father's sombre tone, they would resume their conversation and allow it to meander in another direction.

As the children drifted away to find more exciting things

to do – to collect warm, freshly-laid eggs from the henhouse or gather rich pungent watercress from the crystal-clear stream at the bottom of the drive – my grandfather, father and any of my aunts' husbands who were there got down to the serious business of 'men's talk': the endless political analysis and speculation about what would happen and when.

At six o' clock, silence was compulsory. We waited as first the Angelus – the daily devotional prayer to Our Lady – and then the news and Gaelic sports results were broadcast from the bulky, brown, Bakelite radio, high up on a shelf in the corner of the living room. It was our cue that the day was at an end.

My parents listened anxiously for news of any violent incident that might affect our long journey home. My grandfather would already have packed the boot of the car with sacks and boxes of fresh, home-grown fruit and vegetables to sustain us when we returned to 'the black North': always potatoes, as well as a selection of carrots, turnips, cabbages, onions, lettuce, blackcurrants, rhubarb and gooseberries – whatever was in season.

Hugs, kisses, and heartfelt – often teary-eyed – pleas from my grandmother would follow: 'Would you not stay the night?', 'Why do you stay in that place?', 'Why don't you pack up your belongings and move down here?'. The only explanation was that Belfast was where we belonged. It was what we knew. It was home.

After every visit, we set out for the city physically and mentally revitalised by Cooley's magical recuperative powers. Within minutes of leaving, my mother took her rosary beads from her handbag, to be greeted with groans from the boys and me squeezed into the back of the car. Amid fits of the giggles and rows over not having enough space, we took it in turns to recite the five decades of the rosary, praying that we would get home safely.

Once across the border into the North again, we braced ourselves for encounters with soldiers with blackened faces manning checkpoints on dark, country roads. We approached unfamiliar Protestant townlands in trepidation, imagining loyalist gunmen or renegade members of the security forces lying in wait for an innocent Catholic family.

My youngest brother began to associate a particular wooded hill on the right-hand side of the M1 motorway outside Belfast with the final leg of the homeward journey. As soon as that hillside came into view, he would mutter, from the back seat of the car, 'Stink-bombs Belfast', expressing what all of us were thinking.

Mon, Apr 24

Buses are back on again after 1 week's absence.

Another glorious day – came home and got into summer clothes, although I had to put on a heavy cardigan after tea.

I was interrupted about 10 times by Aidan while I was doing my homework. He was doing (supposed to be doing) French and Maths and I ended up doing half of them for him. My temper finally exploded, Mammy sat in the living room listening to my outburst and then took it all out on me! Couldn't restrain myself from crying bitterly for the rest of the night.

*I wouldn't speak to anyone (Daddy at CDC).
I was sulking and went to bed at 12, still without
speaking. Will get the rounds of the house
tomorrow!*

*Heard a huge bomb somewhere and saw smoke
rising after it.*

Tues, Apr 25

*Swallowed my pride after last night. The huge
bomb we heard at 11.30pm was at the Telephone
Exchange in Cromac Street (200lbs gelignite).*

*I even went to French Conversation class …
too much! It was a beautiful day, although the sky
was overshadowed by a huge pall of black smoke
from a warehouse, blown up at dinner-time, in
Northumberland Street. 14 internees out today.*

*After tea went to Aunt Alice's with Mammy.
Daddy went on down to CDC – we didn't leave
till 11.30. The news was that there were 6 soldiers
shot and a mob of 300 Prods beginning to attack
Catholics in East Belfast.*

*Came home as quickly as possible – and my
lullaby on getting into bed was another bomb
somewhere!*

Wed, Apr 26

*The weather wasn't as nice as it has been for the
last couple of days – good things can't last forever!
Decided to go to see 'Love Story' with Frankie.*

Was speaking to Lizzie about France – she still wants to go, so I'm praying the letter giving this the go-ahead comes soon. Sister Karen said she would do her best to get us jobs for the summer (for July), so I'm hoping there too.

Went to see 'Love Story', wept a bit, but the film was rather disappointing – an anti-climax to build-up it had been receiving. Suzette up for a bit but didn't stay long.

I'm getting ready for my outing with Mr McLaverty tomorrow, it should be good fun. Leaving at 9.30 from school.

Thurs, April 27

Had almost forgotten about going on Mr McLaverty's trip! Into school 9.30, but we didn't set out till after 10 – flat tyre had to be changed and goodbyes said to nuns.

Arrived in Downpatrick, visited two churches, walked along the towpath at side of Quoile River, crossed from Strangford to Portaferry on ferry, and then went for lunch in Mr McLaverty's bungalow. Set out for home at 3.30 – bored stiff listening to his yarns! Arrived in town after 4 and went for a scout round the shops, then home.

Watched the splashdown of Apollo 16 into the Pacific and then came up to bed at 9.00pm! Now – at 11pm – I'm writing this.

22 internees out, Mammy wants me to take day off tomorrow to go into town.

~~

The elderly man whom I regarded as boring was Michael McLaverty, one of Belfast's most distinguished and best-loved authors. Once a fortnight, the writer and retired school principal, came in to our A-Level English class and did his utmost to teach literary criticism to a largely unappreciative class. Literary criticism seemed irrelevant, as did the whole of my A-Level curriculum, as I grew more and more pessimistic about the future.

I watched television, fascinated as American astronauts returned safely from their latest trip to the moon. On our side of the Atlantic, Belfast continued to be ravaged by centuries-old divisions of culture, religion and territory.

In its relentless onslaught against the security forces, the IRA had killed almost three dozen soldiers and policemen since the start of the year and seemed intent on blowing the commercial heart of Belfast to smithereens, with reckless disregard for civilian casualties. In separate incidents in recent days, UDA gunmen singled out two young Catholic men in North Belfast and shot them, for no reason other than their religion. Loyalists were fighting running battles with the army and police force they purported to support and thousands were rumoured to be joining an armed Protestant militia. Was this the way a civil war started? I was too terrified to acknowledge that it might be.

Fri, Apr 28

I decided to take Mammy's advice to stay off school and go into town with her.

After listening to the news – there was serious rioting between RUC and Tartans last night in

E. Belfast – we headed for town. Met Daddy at 10.30, then got Mammy a dress in C&A.

A bomb exploded in King Street while we were in town, so we came home as quickly as possible…

Sat, Apr 29

Woke to the feel of Macauley's dog, Mac, licking my face – the boys had brought him upstairs! Got up at half eleven, as did rest of the family.

Fairly peaceful night. Great talk about the existence of an armed, 10,000-strong Protestant militia. Terrifying thought.

Mammy and Daddy went to a nursery to get shrubs. At 3 p.m. Jim and I went down town to try to get me a pair of trousers, unsuccessfully.

I was glad to get home due to the presence of Tartans and Paras everywhere. Cause? Rioting between RUC and Tartans in E. Belfast again. Hope it continues!

2 shot. 16-year-old boy (Protestant) seriously ill. Baked all night for Mammy's concert tomorrow night …

Heard on news at 12pm that Tartans and army were at it in E. Belfast. 6 RUC men injured and 5 Tartans arrested. Catholic pub burnt.

8-year-old girl shot dead in crossfire. 17-year-old seriously ill. Man seriously ill – shot coming out of a cafe.

Sun, Apr 30

Mrs Gordon came up last night to see if anyone would collect for Rebuilding of Bombay Street, so John, Daddy and Aidan set out to 11 Mass to do so. Spent the afternoon making sandwiches and decorating buns for Mammy's concert tonight

At 6.30 she left, all dressed up and, I must add, looking very well. Mr McCormick said she looked 'like a wee girl of 25.' Daddy went too with Mr Gordon at 8 p.m.

News that there was serious rioting again on the Newtownards Road etc. – Great! Not Catholics for a change (see how long that lasts).

Daddy and Mammy came home at 1.30. No key – so they had to climb in kitchen window!

<hr>

Of course my heart went out to the small, vulnerable Catholic minority who lived in East Belfast, under the shadow of the Harland and Wolff shipyard. But, as the type of violent unrest which usually characterised nationalist West Belfast took hold of predominantly Protestant parts of the East, I was smugly satisfied.

Over the course of a weekend, loyalist mobs had tried to impose 'Tartan Rule' in areas on the other side of the River Lagan – fighting running battles with police and soldiers, and attacking houses, pubs, shops and anything else that came into their line of fire. Almost 30 people were taken to hospital.

What mattered most to me was the welfare of my nearest and dearest – my family, friends and neighbours first of all – and then the rest of my community. If there was going to be trouble anywhere, I was happier to see it break out in alien East Belfast, where I had never set foot, rather than in already beleaguered Andersonstown. 'Out of sight, out of mind,' I thought, in the same way people across most of Northern Ireland regarded the trouble in my part of the city. Vast tracts of rural and coastal Northern Ireland remained virtually untouched by the Troubles and their residents were understandably content that the violence stayed at arm's length.

As Belfast cowered under the growing threat of widespread violence, my parents restricted their socialising to their own snug living room or to the homes of friends nearby. The friendships which developed over gallons of tea, plates of home baking and – when the going got especially tough – glasses of whisky and gins and tonic, were deep and lasting.

I often headed upstairs to bed reluctantly, envious of the adult camaraderie I was leaving behind. My parents and their friends, secure in one another's homes and with their offspring in safely for the night, unwound for a few hours: exchanging gossip, comparing anecdotes and enjoying homespun 'craic', until the sound of gunshots or another explosion would drag them back to reality.

At other times, after a particularly gruesome death or multiple killing, the atmosphere was sombre, verging on wake-like. From the kitchen or the upstairs landing, I strained my ears to eavesdrop on the grown-ups talking about the likely consequences or speculating in hushed tones about the Armageddon they feared was in the offing. I slipped into bed and prayed we would be alright.

On the very odd occasion when both my parents went out for an evening, they imposed strict instructions on us not to open the door to anyone, whatever the circumstances. I wished I had managed to stay awake to witness my mother and father wriggling through a kitchen window in the early hours of the morning, giggling and muttering respectively, after a fund-raising concert for the 'refugees'. Anywhere else in Ireland or Britain, parents who'd forgotten their key would have rung the doorbell or rapped a bedroom window. Had a knock at the door or a window wakened me from my sleep in the early hours of the morning, terror would have rendered me incapable of moving. My parents climbed through the window to spare us such distress.

Mon, May 1

Into school to hear latest weekend scandal, that some of them were 'paralytically stoned' on Friday. Disgusting!

Wrote to Marks and Spencer for a job. I hope I have better luck there than I had in Bank Buildings. No word from France about Elizabeth's place either. I hope she gets one OK.

Bomb in Carrickfergus – Courtaulds factory. 15 hurt, 1 killed.

I hope there's more trouble in East Belfast – terribly selfish, but I love seeing it away from 'Andytown'.

Tues, May 2

Went to French Conversation class. I have gone for past 2 weeks, which is really an achievement. We had a lecture from Sister Virgilius about gratitude – and the lack of it – in school, after Siobhan was rude to Sister Karen. Boring!

At dinner time, went into town with Elizabeth, got photos taken for our passports – I hope we find ourselves somewhere to go – and collected passport application forms...After tea, toured East Belfast – the scene of the weekend's rioting – with Daddy and Mammy. Still crowds of Tartans roaming the streets. Glad to be home again.

Did homework with the sound of bullets echoing in my ears. Terrible shooting, I don't know where. Daddy at CDC meeting.

~~~

The first welcome breakthrough in my hitherto fruitless campaign to escape to France came with an intervention by Margaret Gordon, the daughter of my mother's great friend. She wrote to a French family for whom she had 'au paired' a couple of years previously and asked their mother, Madame de Marignan, if they could help with hosting either Liz or me in exchange for some English lessons. It was a shot in the dark and didn't resolve my difficulty in finding a job but, as I checked the atlas to locate Villeneuve-sur-Lot, where the de Marignan family lived, I finally had some hope to cling to.

Every night as I said my prayers, imploring God to keep us all safe, I added, '... and please God, let us get to France'. Buoyed up by even a vague possibility of escape we, and other classmates who were going abroad, applied for our first passports – Irish rather than British. In the boxes where we were asked to state our nationality, we conspired in advance to write 'Irish citizen, British subject', revelling in what we regarded as our first act of defiance against the Northern Ireland state.

Sat, May 6

Surprised to hear Mammy suggesting that I should go down town to get the extra material I needed. She, Daddy, Paul and I went down for an hour and got all the necessities.

Got going at the dress, until I was interrupted to make the tea. Continued with it afterwards and got on very well. However, when I went in to show it to Mammy and Daddy, Daddy's only comment was that it was too short!!! Result? I burst into tears.

I kept on working at it till I was nearly cross-eyed at 12.15 and then went to bed, disgusted with Daddy.

Sun, May 7

Pouring rain – not a very good day for going into the country to visit unknown third cousins...

I didn't want to go – imagined I'd be bored to tears.

Arrived to be greeted by 10 children, aged from 15 to 1! Got on well after a while and explored the farm. A huge place – hatchery for 5,000 hens.

Collected their eggs after tea – 3,330 eggs collected today!

They also had a 1-day old calf, the boys had a go at milking the cows.

After tea, we had a singsong – Mr Meehan on the piano. Returned home late, at 10.30. Before I went to bed, I started to get my passport forms ready. Mrs Gordon called up. After listening to 11.00 p.m. news, I went to bed.

The disagreement over the length of my new dress had put me in a very bad mood for the planned expedition to meet our newfound 'country cousins'. I didn't consider the garment to be unsuitably short and I was sorely stung by my father's uncharacteristic criticism.

The prospect of our first ever trip to Poyntzpass – resulting from a chance encounter in Cooley with a cousin of my mother – held little appeal under the circumstances. The outing turned out, though, to be infinitely more enjoyable than I could have imagined.

The Meehan's farm lay near a tiny village in the heart of idyllically peaceful and predominantly Protestant countryside, equidistant from Newry and Armagh. I never met Peter before but warmed immediately to the big, gregarious farmer, with the largest and strongest hands I had ever shaken. He, his wife and their immense family opened their home and farm to us, treating us to what turned out to be our most carefree and enjoyable day for many weeks to come.

CHAPTER 7

'Unchristian type of satisfaction.'

It was late spring and early summer when I was forced to grow up. Convinced that the backlash I was dreading for so long had been unleashed, I confronted the terror that I might lose all that I loved. I found myself reduced to a level of bitterness where I was no better than my fellow citizens whose perceived lack of Christianity and charity I was all too ready to deplore.

I did not know what to expect one May afternoon when, instead of taking the first turning off the roundabout at Kennedy Way and driving into Fruithill, my father drove up the road behind our home. 'Rubberneckers', voyeurs, inquisitive or just plain nosey, we were drawn to the heavy plume of grey smoke appearing to rise from somewhere close to where we lived. At a quarter past five on an ordinary spring Saturday, I had no reason to feel apprehensive.

As the smoke filtered into the late afternoon sky, we drove up Kennedy Way and Monagh Road, before beginning a gradual descent down the Springfield Road. The steep grassy slopes of Divis and Black Mountain gave way to fields on our left, while the Protestant Springmartin housing estate rose up in the near distance; on the other side, the sprawling Catholic estates of Ballymurphy, Turf Lodge and Whiterock swept downwards towards Andersonstown and the Falls.

I felt sick to the pit of my stomach when I saw blue flashing lights and the remains of Kelly's public house in front of me, collapsed under the force of an explosion.

Sat, May 13

A Catholic ex-Serviceman was shot dead by Protestants at Finaghy Road North last night. 4 others injured. We went out to Derriaghy after dinner. Heard a bomb and saw smoke, apparently at top of Kennedy Way. All drove up to investigate. Reached Ballymurphy – Kelly's pub blown up.

When we were there, people were trying to clear injured people from rubble. 73 hurt. Protestants opened fire while we were still there. We fled home in terror. A barman was killed.

The fiercest shooting I have ever heard, all night – 5 people killed.

Trouble all over town – Catholics v. Protestants. Very frightening experience. I go to bed at 1, waiting for what tomorrow will bring.

～～～

There was no panic, just an atmosphere of stunned quietness and controlled calm, as the dust settled and the smoke began to dissipate. Ambulance staff, and men who seemed to know what they were doing, gently and methodically helped the injured – mostly men – from the wreckage.

My father parked the car on the left-hand side of the road and we joined the other shocked onlookers, huddled in small quiet groups, a respectful distance from the devastated bar.

Before we even asked what had happened, an elderly man shook his head, 'The Prods again. A car-bomb on the road outside.'

Kelly's – like pubs all over Britain – was packed with ordinary, working-class men, who were watching England playing Germany in the European Championships when the bomb exploded in a Morris 1100 left outside. There was no need for us to get involved. The most seriously injured had already been moved to hospital; the dazed 'walking wounded' were being gently escorted across the rubble to safety. 'God forgive whoever did it,' my mother said.

As we walked towards the car, having seen more than enough, a gunshot shattered the stillness, followed by another, then another. People started to swear and scream in terror, running for cover behind walls and parked cars. 'It's the Prods! Get down!' Even the ambulancemen dived to the ground for shelter. My father pushed my mother and me towards our car, shouting at us to get inside as shots rang out behind us.

I had never heard shooting at such close quarters and I started to shake uncontrollably as my father drove our old Cortina away as fast as he could. I could feel the blood pulsing in my head and struggled to catch my breath while my mother, her face deathly white, prayed aloud.

Gunfire raged unabated throughout the evening and we stood outside the kitchen door, listening in the black darkness. The light, night-time breeze played tricks on our ears, bouncing the sounds in different directions. Sometimes the gunfire seemed loud enough to be at the top of the road and then it would sound muffled and remote. One moment it was echoing from the left, then from the right. My brothers, scarcely into their teens, tried to guess who was firing – IRA, loyalists or army – and what weapons they were using.

The late news confirmed that *all* sides had unleashed their fury after the bombing and had subsequently been involved in the bloody mayhem. The loyalist gunmen, who opened fire while we were standing opposite the pub, killed a barman helping out in the rescue operation.

I pulled the blankets up around my ears when I finally went to bed, but still the sound of the shooting invaded the silence of my room and played nightmarish havoc with my thoughts. It was chilling to think that someone – in the UDA or UVF – had bombed a busy pub, full of defenceless, unsuspecting Catholic men, innocently enjoying a pint of beer and a football match on a Saturday afternoon. But what sort of human beings could be so crazed and full of hatred, that they would open fire on rescue workers? They were evil, cold-blooded, merciless killers, I told myself, who hated Catholics and would stop at nothing to get rid of every last one of us. The backlash. I feared they would happily shoot all of us dead in our beds.

Sun, May 14

Got up dreading the papers' headlines. Death toll from last night is 7.

Went over to Mass, the road littered with glass, bricks etc. When we came home, Mammy and Daddy decided to go to Cooley – peace there – to get their heads showered. John and I stayed at home.

I intended doing some Maths revision but didn't succeed. Couldn't settle amid shooting and bombing. Terrifying to know that there are other human beings at the receiving end.

Trouble on the Donegall Road. M1 closed. Trouble in Ballymurphy and Andersonstown.

We watched news, still hearing the shooting. A 17-year-old boy (Protestant) and 13-year-old girl (Catholic) both shot dead. Paras have moved in to clear the area. Dreading the consequences.

At 11, go to bed and pray for peace.

Mon, May 15

After the events of weekend, there are naturally no buses on. I set out walking, dreading the Applied Maths test this afternoon.

Met a woman from Ballymurphy and walked down the road with her. She told me about the fears of the people in Ballymurphy – full of bitterness towards Protestants and hatred for the army. The people there live in a different world completely to us in Fruithill.

Arrived in school at 9.10. Couldn't do the Maths test but I'm not too worried.

Walked home again and watched the news. Now 9 people dead. 1 Protestant, 1 soldier and 7 Catholics. Catholics come out worst as usual.

Bomb tonight – it turned out to be in a pub on

Sandy Row. 14 injured, not seriously.
  Should condemn it but feel an unchristian type
of satisfaction – frightening.

~~~

I wrestled with my conscience, confiding my bitterness and my desire to see Protestants getting 'a taste of their own medicine' only to the pages of my diary. Thoughts of revenge came uninvited to my mind. I would never have dared to speak them aloud, not even within the sacred confines of the Confession box. I was reluctant to even commit my reflections to paper; frightened because I knew it was utterly wrong to think that way, and fearful that I would incur the wrath of God – that something awful would happen to me or my family – for thinking such unchristian thoughts.

If my diary was going to be of any value to me, I had to be true to the desperate thoughts churning around in my head. The backlash had begun – and who in God's name was going to protect us?

I acknowledged privately that I was becoming bitter in a way I was never brought up to be. 'Love your neighbour as yourself', I had always been taught. Maybe I should have done the Christian thing and prayed to God for the strength to forgive the perpetrators. But I could not bring myself to do so and was ashamed that I didn't want to.

How could I be expected to regard as 'neighbours' the people who planted the bomb at Kelly's Bar? What sort of 'neighbours' would open fire on rescuers? And how could I spare any Christian feelings for the people who were causing such suffering to that worn out, defenceless Ballymurphy woman whom I had accompanied down the road?

I wanted the people who were planning and carrying out such deeds to be harried and hounded the way republicans were. I wanted to see someone doing something to stop them because it seemed nobody was doing anything to deflect them from their bloody assaults on the innocent Catholic community.

Tues, May 16

Slept in. No buses on but I've only French Conversation first so I'm not too worried – however, got a lift down with Tom Conaty. Spoke to Sister Karen about the job. She hasn't had an opportunity to enquire yet – patience!

Gorgeous day, so I didn't mind walking home from school. The first two funerals were today.

Came home and Suzette came up. Had dinner, watched news and did homework till 11. Full of an urge to work, so I took advantage of it for it doesn't come over me very often.

Saw a nest of 2-hour-old wrens in garden next door – beautiful wee things.

I think it was quite peaceful tonight.

Wed, May 17

IRA open fire on Protestant workers coming out of Mackies.

Sun, May 21

Army charged into Protestant barricades at 4 a.m. Met with savage combat. Serious rioting – army versus Prods. Hope it keeps up.

Body of a Creggan soldier found, shot dead by Official IRA. Serious condemnation from women of Creggan and Bogside – parading for peace and end to IRA offensives.

Helicopter was out all afternoon – Mrs McGlade kept us up to date with latest news. Rioting is continuing.

Mammy and Daddy both in great moods, I feel awful. Mammy couldn't be satisfied till – in the middle of all the rain – she, Daddy, Paul and I headed for East Belfast. Daft, looking for trouble. However, roads all closed.

Came home and saw terrifying pictures of UDA training on news. Scared out of our wits. 22,000 men trained.

~~~

I was at my wits' end, utterly bewildered by the endless killings and terrified by the loyalist shows of strength. Months earlier, I came to accept that I or anyone in my family could easily fall victim to a reckless IRA gunman or an indiscriminate bombing. If I was unfortunate enough to be cut down in that way – as dozens of innocent bystanders and passers-by already had been – the IRA would have offered excuses or explained away the tragedy as 'a regrettable accident'. But I knew I was not a specific republican target.

There was no doubt, however, in my scared, teenage mind

that loyalist paramilitaries were out to get every Catholic living in Belfast. I was petrified as I watched television news footage of tens of thousands of masked UDA men – decked out in dark glasses, camouflage gear, combat jackets and bush hats or baseball caps – marching through the streets of what was, only nominally, my city. They marched in military formation, testifying to hours spent drilling and training, and responded to commands barked at them by their leaders. They set up roadblocks and barricades in their own communities – declaring those parts of the city to be 'no-go' areas, similar to those operated by the IRA in Derry – and they threatened civil war.

I sat in my bedroom struggling to come to terms with it all, and pasted chilling photographs of these men – armed with pick-axe handles, sticks and shields – into my scrapbook.

Moderate unionist politicians were adamant that these paramilitary hordes were not representative of the majority of 'ordinary, decent Protestants'. I longed for those ordinary decent Protestants to take to the streets and protest at the killings of innocent Catholics, in the way the women of Derry and Belfast were challenging the Official and Provisional IRA. But the silent majority that we heard so much about remained just that – silent.

Mon, May 22

Last night, the late news had said that all today's bus services would be cancelled, therefore I, lazy Eimear, decided not to go to school – no intention of walking again.

A beautiful sunny day so I sunbathed out at the

front – i.e. with a Spanish book. Did 3 hours solid Spanish. Buses were put on again everywhere, including the Shankill where two buses were burned yesterday.

Suzette came up after tea. Had to be rude to make her leave so I could do more Spanish. Came down to see the news. Daddy is at meeting, Mammy is in McGlade's, so I stayed and watched TV and to hell with Spanish!

5,000 Bogsiders attended funeral of Private Best who was killed on Sunday.

Tues, May 23

Buses are back on the road for a change. I wonder how long they will remain!

Got my passport back this morning. I hope I'm still alive in August, to be able to go on holidays.

No word regarding job, keeping fingers crossed.

Huge bomb went off while we were in French, at least it caused a bit of distraction. 5 bombs today all over the town, nobody seriously hurt, thank God again. Soldier was shot dead in Ballymurphy. I've got a real sickener of the IRA and all their associates!

Suzette, Mrs Gordon and Mrs McGlade all up tonight – a busy house. Another bomb tonight, in Fountain Street. 140lbs explosives.

Wed, May 24

At ten to eight Mammy came racing into my bedroom – her face as white as a ghost. I knew something had happened but never imagined it would be as terrible as it was. Andrew Brennan was shot dead by Protestants as he drove home with his wife after being with his parents in Fruithill Park.

I nearly collapsed with shock. Stunned all day. Can't believe that they could be such brutal murderers.

They shot Andrew while his wife got out to open the garage-door. Not one neighbour came out to help his wife drag him inside. People talk about Christian Protestants!

Met Suzette after school and told her, she hadn't heard. She burst into tears and sobbed the whole way home in her Aunt Mary's car.

I just can't believe it. Police say they 'are looking for a motive'!

Thurs, May 25

Fruithill Park in mourning due to murder of Andrew Brennan. Everyone stunned, stories keep coming out of his exploits as a child … Wife is heartbroken. Married 18 months, no children …

After tea, watched mourners arriving for Andrew's funeral. Could not watch any longer – I had to go along with it. I cried in the park as coffin was carried out by brothers. Worst part of all for

> *his family – when he left home for the last time.*
> *Went to the prayers and came home.*

～～～

The official line from the police was that they were 'looking for a motive' as to why our young former neighbour, Andrew, had been killed. But we all knew – the dogs in the street knew – that it was because he was a Catholic, the latest defenceless Catholic to fall victim to the loyalist assassination squads. Why did the police refuse to name the crime for what it was – a sectarian murder? With a mixture of sadness and frustration, my father added Andrew's name to the record of sectarian killings which he had begun to compile for the CDC.

I was angry, heartbroken and most of all, terrified. Andrew was in his mid twenties when he was murdered shortly after visiting his family home, almost directly opposite mine. When he married, he moved to a quiet, residential area, not far away in South Belfast. But the area was 'mixed', and a UDA gunman was lying in wait in his garden when he and his wife arrived home that evening.

I stood at the front window of my parents' bedroom, peeping through the side of the closed blinds at the stream of people going in and out of the home where Andrew was reared and from where he was about to be buried. On both sides of the street, curtains were drawn and blinds closed, as a silent sign of mourning and respect.

Relatives, friends and neighbours – including the young men he grew up with – gathered in awkward, shocked silence for the removal of his remains to the chapel. They clustered together in small, hushed groups around the front of the house, dragging on cigarettes or with their hands stuffed in their pockets, and waited for his remains to be carried from the family home for the last time.

The cherry blossom in front of my parents' bedroom window was in full bloom, so poignantly beautiful and delicate compared to the savage brutality meted out in that South Belfast garden a few days earlier. Young men like Andrew – on both sides of the community – were being mown down every week but to all, except those who knew them, they soon became anonymous statistics in the ever-lengthening tally of deaths.

Since the weekend of the Kelly's pub bombing, seventeen people, including two soldiers, had been killed in Belfast; six of the others – both Catholic and Protestant – had still been attending school or college. I was reminded yet again that being young and innocent afforded no protection. For a long time I had kept count of every single person killed in the Troubles but the death rate had started to rise so quickly that my records were fast becoming outdated.

The Troubles were closing in on us, coming closer and closer to my family and to our door. The fear that we could do nothing to stop them – and that no one was going to protect us – was crushing.

I tried to reconcile myself to the idea that I would not be going to France. It no longer seemed important. I would happily have sacrificed my holidays for years to come for an assurance that my family and friends would stay alive and safe.

Fri, May 26

Quite a peaceful night – 1 explosion, at Moneymore RUC station. No reply from France.

We've had four replies to our applications for jobs – hope in Musgrave and Mater hospitals.

SDLP say that local representatives will resume work after 10-month 'strike' but they will not talk till end of internment.

Another tragedy struck some family today. Terrorist murderers planted a 150lb bomb in a car at Oxford Street, centre of the town, and killed 1 woman and injured 51, some seriously. Whoever did it ought to be shot!

Protestant barriers due up tonight.

Went to Derriaghy after tea. The one night I have no money, they had beautiful strides – I'm raging! Came home and wanted to go out somewhere – but I wouldn't risk it.

Sat, May 27

Big explosions on Crumlin and Oldpark Roads – 2 cinemas.

10,000 Loyalists marched through town. Paraded in uniform to military commands. They strike terror in everyone's heart.

I had intended going down town but somehow, between bombs and Tartan gangs, I don't think that I would be too safe. Instead, did some baking. After tea, came up to do my homework but couldn't do it – too hard.

Prod. barricades are up again in East Belfast.
Hope everything goes peacefully tonight.
Came to bed after 11 and read till 1. Exhausted.
Man found shot dead, Finaghy Road North –
Catholic.

~~~

Each time something particularly brutal happened, politicians and clergymen would talk about it marking 'a turning-point'. 'People have had enough,' they would say. 'It's time for the terrorists to get off our backs.' But nothing changed.

The IRA renewed its bombing of 'economic targets' after a lull of a couple of days, killing an innocent Protestant woman in the process. Masked loyalists flaunted the superiority of their numbers by marching in thousands through the city centre on Saturday afternoon. The UDA or UVF (it was irrelevant to us which group was responsible) assassinated another two young Catholic men, a 20- and a 21-year-old, within a mile or two of where I lived. I, and many Catholics like me, began to feel we had overstayed our welcome in the city of our birth.

Despite the long bright evenings, we grew increasingly nervous about going out, for fear of being sprayed by bullets fired by loyalists in passing cars. On the odd evening when I walked over to the local shops with my mother or brothers, I would be seized by an almost paralysing fear if I saw a car with four men inside, approaching us or slowing down.

A number of brave – some might say foolhardy – Catholic ex-servicemen began to sacrifice their nights to patrol the streets of West Belfast and watch out for unfamiliar vehicles.

But these 'vigilantes' were powerless to stop a UDA or UVF gang with murder in mind. In the case of the last young man who was killed, all they could do was recover his body from the side of the road, where he'd been gunned down after leaving his girlfriend.

We had no expectation that the army or the police would defend or protect us at that time. We felt we were on our own.

Sun, May 28

Mammy woke me at about 10 o'clock with bad news – a bomb had gone off in Anderson Street – a 100% Catholic street in East Belfast. Wrecked piles of houses, injured 80 and killed 6. Various accounts of what happened – army claim it was an IRA bomb going off too early. However, I believe the people of Short Strand – a UDA bomb. Prod barricades were up this weekend over there, therefore it's unlikely that IRA would risk moving bombs. Drove to CDC to offer our help if necessary.

Did some work on my scrapbook.

Late news – man killed by shots from passing car on Springfield Road. 3 bombs have wrecked city centre.

Mon, May 29

Death toll in Anderson Street bomb is now 8 – a tragedy, whoever was responsible. 4 Provos were killed in it.

I went to the library after school, I couldn't be

bothered going home early. However I didn't get home till 5.30 – too late.

We spent last hour standing outside because of a bomb scare – car parked in queer position. I got a bit nervy for the first time because of it. However, a hoax.

Tues, May 30

Lashing out of the heavens and everyone's talking about the summer holidays – what a hope! No letter from France yet. I'm beginning to give up hope of going.

There were two more Catholics shot dead last night – one in Belfast, one in Banbridge. The police are still 'looking for a motive'!!!!!

Official IRA have called a truce, thank God, but Provos refuse to budge!

School was boring, got soaked and am in bad form. Bought Mammy a card for her birthday and was all set to go to bed at 9.45, but Suzette arrived. She left at 10.30.

Watched '24 Hours' – all about the UDA. Came to bed convinced that prayer is our only hope, seeing that we haven't got a gun! They were terrifying.

Bomb inside Springfield Road barracks – a miracle how they planted it.

My assumptions about the Short Strand bombing turned out to be wrong. It had been easy to jump to the conclusion that the carnage in Anderson Street was the result of another loyalist attack; it was depressing to have to accept that the dead were the victims of an IRA bomb which exploded prematurely – yet another 'accident'. Life had become cheap.

The Official IRA announced a ceasefire, except for defensive purposes, and declared that its decision provided 'an invaluable chance to avoid sectarian civil war'. The Provisionals, in response, vowed to continue their campaign. The UDA, meanwhile, threatened to paralyse Northern Ireland.

The death toll since January soared to well over 150, an average of more than thirty people a month. The cataclysmic direction in which our communities were headed was clear to see.

Feeling frightened and vulnerable, I drifted off to sleep at night praying that my family and I would be spared from loyalist attacks. Without a means of protecting myself, I believed prayer was my only refuge.

CHAPTER 8

'All I could do was pray.'

I would have prayed for almost anything when I was sixteen, out of faith, habit or desperation. I prayed for success in my exams, new navy trousers, a summer job and someone to host me in France. Most fervently, though, I beseeched God to keep my family and me alive.

I liked to pray, curled up on my side in my single bed. I blessed myself in the cramped darkness and recited the first prayer I learned at my parents' knees: 'O Angel of God, my guardian dear, to whom God's love commits me here, ever this night be at my side, to light and guard, to rule and guide. Amen.'

I emphasised the words 'this night', for the darkness brought a special kind of dread even in a 'safe' place like Andersonstown. A few Hail Marys, an Act of Contrition, and then my concentration would wander. I forced myself to refocus for the final, desperate incantation: 'Please God, keep us all safe. Keep us safe from the loyalists. Look after Mammy, Daddy, the boys and me. Look after Alice and Josephine and all our friends. Don't let anything happen to us. Look after Granny O'Callaghan, and Granny and Granda in Cooley ...' At that point, the remit of my prayers was beyond the North, and the immediate need had passed. I slipped into sleep, if all was quiet.

On other nights, when fear got the better of me after talk of civil war, I got down on my knees and prayed on the floor beside my bed. I believed there was a better chance of my pleas for protection being answered if I made the effort to pray 'properly'. With my forehead resting on my clasped hands and my elbows on the bed, I implored God to keep our family safe. Comfortingly, I often heard the murmur of my parents reciting their Rosary aloud together, united in prayer for their five children, themselves and the beleaguered city where they had built their home.

I seldom differentiated between myself and the rest of the family. Occasionally though, I made specific mention of my father. Hardworking, middle-aged fathers like him were increasingly being picked out at random and murdered for no reason other than that they were Catholics. My mother's prayers bore him home safely night after night, her devotion to Our Lady unshakeable. If anyone's prayers protected us, they were hers.

Wed, May 31

Mammy's birthday . She got piles of cards – says everyone must think she's going to die, because of so many cards! Higher Sixth's last day but Sister V forbade them to have any fun or carry-on. Sister Virgilius's disapproval put a dampener on it.

Frankie and I had to walk home. The buses are off because of the funeral of James Wardlow (Catholic) – very big funeral. Got home at 4.45 exhausted. Definitely 8 dead in the Short Strand bomb.

Intended doing a night of homework or else Spanish revision but instead, spent night working on scrapbook. Mammy was over on the Somerton Road helping to get things ready for a coffee morning. No news yet from France. Soldier killed at top of Kennedy Way.

Thurs, June 1

Holy Day of Obligation, Corpus Christi – went to 10.30 Mass. Came home and got ready for going to Cooley. However, we didn't get away till about 12.30. Arrived in Newry and went to the market, quite a nice day.

Proceeded on to Cooley, stopped by Army at the border. The friendliest and jolliest wee soldier came over. I really liked him – pleasant – not like the usual type. They were still there coming home and recognised us. If I'd heard one of them had been shot, I'd have been heartbroken! Welsh, I think.

Got home after 8, Daddy went to a CDC meeting. Did homework. Mrs Gordon, then Mrs McGlade came up – such a house – then Mammy went down to McGlade's.

Fri, June 2

Got up this morning as usual to go to school but as I was standing making my lunch, a wave of nausea came over me. Thought I was going to pass out – Mammy nearly died! Up to bed where I stayed for the rest of the day i.e. till 4 o'clock. Got up, had my dinner, felt a lot better.

Mammy had intended going to Derriaghy but at 6 o'clock Daddy got a phone-call from CDC to say a Japanese reporter, who wanted to see Belfast, would be calling. Panic-stations! However he never turned up. Mysterious!

The phone call telling us that a Japanese reporter might want to speak to my father about sectarian killings caused quite a stir. While it was comforting to think that people so far away as Asia might be interested in something my father had to say, my mother was more concerned about having something in the house that our visitor would be happy to eat. Our home was a regular meeting-place but we were disappointed when the Japanese man didn't show up, unaccustomed as we were to such exotic callers.

Local people – friends and neighbours – visited regularly: school-friends, neighbours, friends of my parents, and colleagues from their political and fund-raising activities, as well as the odd journalist, looking – via the CDC – to pick my father's brain.

Friendships which my mother carried over from her time working in the Civil Service before she was married gradually petered out, as women became reluctant to leave their own districts or travel across the city at night. Those old relationships were replaced by cherished new bonds, forged out of a shared sense of excitement, bewilderment, isolation and fear.

A loud explosion or a rattle of gunfire was guaranteed to bring at least one of our neighbours, clutching a packet of cigarettes, to our front door before the kettle finished boiling for another of the interminable pots of tea. Tea and home baking characterised those get-togethers, as women waited anxiously for children and husbands to arrive home safely from school, town or work.

Like the *tricoteuses* of the French Revolution, they waited at the kitchen-table for news of what happened, sometimes tuning in to the crackling, intermittent transmissions from the police or army short-band radio. They offered each other moral and sisterly support, helping each other manage 'ordinary' family life in extraordinary circumstances.

Sat, June 3

Mammy wanted to go down town and so, expecting a good day's shopping, I decided to go too. However, Daddy and Jim also came and so we ended up being chased round the shops, being urged to hurry up.

Returned home having bought nothing but a file, a file refill and a Spanish dictionary – how exciting! Watched the news.

UDA marched in Derry and rioting broke out – 3 cheers!

Sun, June 4

Mammy had suggested that we might go to Cooley today – but we didn't go. Spent a couple of hours doing Spanish revision.

> *Daddy went to a meeting to discuss the setting up of barriers in Fruithill at night – but the idea was rejected (I think).*
>
> *We all went to the Corpus Christi procession in De La Salle grounds, except John – he said he was too busy to go! – this led to another row between him and Mammy. I did my Spanish till Suzette arrived at 8. She didn't stay very long once I gave her the hint that I had work to do.*
>
> *Man shot dead in shop, Carlisle Circus. Catholic.*

~~~

The Corpus Christi procession was one of the big occasions in our Catholic calendar and out of deference to my parents I felt obliged to attend it when asked. I had a sneaking admiration though for my 14-year-old brother John's chutzpah when he insisted he was 'too busy' to go.

The June event gave the children who made their First Communion that year a final opportunity to parade around in their beautiful white satin dresses, tiaras and veils or – in the boys' cases – new jackets and suits.

Proud to be Catholics, hosts of angelic-looking seven-year-olds lined up excitedly in pairs behind a posse of priests and altar boys, all in full-length, black-and-white robes. Four altar boys clasped long wooden poles supporting the corners of a white linen canopy high overhead; beneath it, attendants fastened an elaborate golden stole around the shoulders of the presiding priest. The smell of burning incense wafted from a thurible swaying from the hands of one of the altar boys and the choir began to sing 'Sweet Heart of Jesus'. As

(1) Rescue workers search for casualties in the wreckage of the Abercorn Restaurant in Belfast city centre after a bomb exploded inside it on a busy Saturday afternoon. The explosion, on 4 March 1972, killed two young women and injured more than 130 other people. (*Belfast Telegraph* archive)

(2) Oxford Street bus station where six people died on the day that became known as Bloody Friday. A total of nine people were killed and 120 injured when more than 20 IRA bombs exploded in Belfast on 21 July 1972. (*Belfast Telegraph* archive)

(3) A loyalist barricade near Ainsworth Avenue, North Belfast in July 1972. (*Belfast Telegraph* archive)

(4) On the last day of the Northern Ireland Parliament, 28 March 1972, 100,000 unionists converged on Stormont to protest at the imposition of Direct Rule from Westminster. (*Belfast Telegraph* archive)

(5) The O'Callaghan family in Cooley when Eimear was 14. Back row, L- R: Aidan, Eimear and John. Middle row: her father, Jim, brother, Paul and mother, Maura. Front row, sitting on grass: her brother, Jim.

(6) The front cover of the diary which Eimear kept during 1972, the worst year of the Northern Ireland conflict.

(7) The home in Fruithill Park, Andersonstown, where Eimear lived with her parents and four brothers.

(8) The home in Cooley of Eimear's maternal grandparents, John and Rose Murphy. Cooley, across the border in the Republic, was a haven of rural tranquility compared to West Belfast.

(9) and (10) Some of the pages in Eimear's ironically named 'Happy Days Scrapbook'

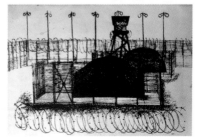

(11) Two of a series of greetings cards produced by internees during their first Christmas in Long Kesh prison.

(12) Eimear on Le Pont l'Archevêché (with La Cathédrale de Notre-Dame in the background), hours after arriving in Paris for the first time.

(13) La Domaine de Jampau, in the South of France, where Eimear spent most of August 1972.

(14) Eimear visits Villeneuve-sur-Lot during her stay in the south of France.

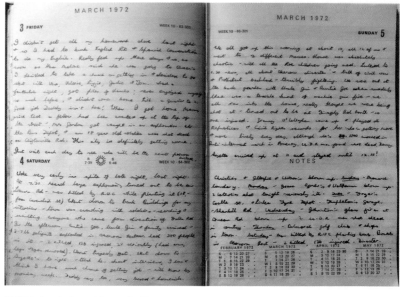

(15) Extracts from Eimear's diary.

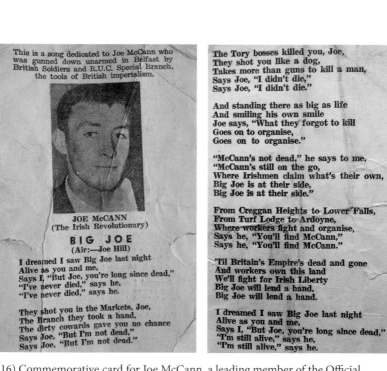

(16) Commemorative card for Joe McCann, a leading member of the Official IRA, who was shot dead by soldiers from the Parachute Regiment, 15 April 1972.

(17) and (18) Outbreaks of rioting regularly disrupted normal everyday activities. Here, hijacked vehicles burn on the Falls Road a few hundred yards below the entrance to St Dominic's School. (*Belfast Telegraph* archive)

(19) Soldiers and members of the UDA on joint patrol in the Castlereagh Road area of East Belfast in 1972. (*Belfast Telegraph* archive)

(20) A lorry carrying furniture belonging to displaced Catholic families advances towards an army barrier in Lenadoon, minutes before an announcement that the IRA ceasefire was over, 9 July 1972. (*Belfast Telegraph* archive)

the parade moved off, parents beamed with pride and the rest of us traipsed behind, intoning the rosary dutifully and joining in the hymns. With his hands wrapped in the ends of his brocade stole, the priest raised the gleaming golden monstrance aloft for veneration and led us through the grounds of the most besieged secondary school in the heart of riot-torn Andersonstown.

While I was celebrating my Catholicism – albeit reluctantly – in the 1972 procession, another man in the north of the city paid the ultimate price for his religion. His death, at the door of the shop where he worked, brought to almost a dozen the number of Catholics killed in just over a month.

Sectarian murder was now the tactic of choice for the UDA and UVF. Isolated Catholic families in religiously-mixed areas lived in terror of a late-night knock on the door, and dozens began moving from their homes. Even in an almost totally Catholic street like Fruithill, some people proposed putting up barricades to prevent loyalist incursions; such was the level of fear.

Tues, June 6

I have to ring all the class-bells today and for the rest of the week – killing me, running up and down the stairs all day! Quite a nice day – went to the library after school but didn't get any work done, so came home again after 4.15.

Aine and Patricia came down tonight and stood talking for ages. Did homework, heard a bomb and wrote to Mme de Marignan. Got a letter from her today but she didn't mention getting Elizabeth a place.

Wed, June 7

No replies from the hospitals yet about jobs. Can see me having to claim unemployment benefit in the summer to get money for France!

Coming home we were put off the bus at Andytown Barracks, by army – according to them, they were being shot at continually from Andersonstown Park and cars were being hijacked and burnt. But they let us through to walk up!

No sign of any activity but very serious rioting on Glen Road for some reason – never understand the people up there – 50 more internees got out and they <u>still</u> riot. 1 soldier killed.

Mammy and Daddy went over to Mrs E's and came face-to-face with UDA barricade. Mammy nearly conked out! She actually rang Commander of Army here i.e. General Tuzo!

Thurs, June 8

A really beautiful day. Mammy came home at 4.30, then she and daddy went down the road to get daddy medicine and stuff for his eyes. Full-scale battle when they left between John, Aidan, Jim and Paddy McGlade – I'm used to them now.

A man was shot dead while working on a building site on the Shankill Road. A Catholic, naturally – Norman Campbell.

Spent the night helping Aidan with his French for a test tomorrow – has no effect on him.

Mrs McGlade came up, Daddy at another

meeting. A 25-year-old woman shot dead tonight on Glen Road – Mrs Smith, Tardree Park. Unknown causes.

Fri, June 9

Daddy had to go to hospital for 9 to see about his eye, I had hoped to get a lift but he was too late.

Heard a bomb, third class – pub on Crumlin Road. Came home – Europa Hotel blown up and City Hall damaged by bombs in the grounds.

Watched news – UDR man was killed by gunmen when coming out of Autolite factory on Finaghy Road North.

Announcement that Provos were imposing a car curfew on Falls due to recent attacks on Catholics from Prods.

UDA are putting their barricades up tonight for some reason. Ominous – 24 hours too early. Daddy went to a meeting.

Watched special edition of '24 Hours' about UDA plan to burn Andytown, Ballymurphy etc. to the ground. Say they will take on the Army – modern arms and plenty of them. Mammy and Daddy went to Gordons'.

Shooting started. Lay in terror in bed for 2 hours listening to it.

All I could do was pray.

Sat, June 10

Expected to hear of a terrible death toll this morning after the shooting last night. However, 1 girl killed only – Catholic, 16 – Grosvenor Road.

All Prod barricades are up – no buses – town centre closed. Everyone terrified to go out. Even Daddy is scared now – sure that the threatened backlash is on its way. Next Friday, midnight, ends UDA ultimatum to Whitelaw!

Tidied my room till tea-time.

Watched news – terrifying to see UDA again.

Daddy felt hungry so Mammy and I went round for chips, ice-cream and lemonade at 10 and had a 'party.' Felt that tonight could be our last Saturday night ever.

Pray to God for peace and safety. 'Auntie' Terry rang, scared out of her wits.

~~~

Threats by sinister masked men in dark-glasses and paramilitary uniforms that they would burn Catholic estates to the ground haunted my mind for hours. Night after night, their faces and voices loomed at me from the television screen, threatening to bring Belfast to a standstill. Scarcely a night went by when I didn't hear shooting somewhere, usually finding out nothing more about it unless someone was killed.

I suspect it was Dutch courage arising out of shock that propelled my mother to protest to Army HQ in Lisburn about the UDA barricades which prevented her getting to

North Belfast. Belfast's religious geography made it virtually impossible to cross the city, even as an act of charity to visit a lonely elderly widow, without risking a confrontation with the worst elements of 'the other side'.

We probably had more Catholic and Protestant churches per head of population than any other city in Ireland or Britain. We had Catholic schools and Protestant schools, Catholic pubs and Protestant pubs, Catholic streets and Protestant streets. Working-class territories were demarcated by bunting and flags, and kerbs painted red, white and blue or green, white and orange, depending on whether Protestants or Catholics lived there.

As a rule, it was considered wisest and safest to stay among 'your own'. My mother and father's near encounter with masked, cudgel-wielding UDA men in North Belfast put paid to their trips to that part of the city for the rest of the year.

I was on the cusp of adulthood, no longer a child, and I struggled on my own to come to terms with what was happening. My parents gathered with friends, in our home or in theirs, and largely out of their children's earshot they mulled over the prospects of civil war, assuaged each other's fears and joked blackly about doomsday scenarios. But I had no one and nothing to turn to other than God and my diary. I was convinced that prayer was my only resort. If I prayed night after night, someone 'up there' must eventually hear my pleas and keep us safe. *Was this civil war?*

Sun, June 11

Serious trouble last night between Protestants and army. Great to see it.

Decided to go to Cooley to get away from it all. Arrived eventually after army road-blocks, marches etc. Lundy cousins from Dun Laoghaire were also there. Had a very enjoyable evening, spoilt only by the thought of what we were returning to face in Belfast next week when UDA ultimatum expires!

Got home to hear of fiercest gun-battle ever in Ardoyne/Oldpark. 4 killed.

Army were very 'Catholic-minded' – Paras rescued Catholic families and there was great outcry about partiality from Prod side.

I felt really miserable going to bed. Listened to non-stop sound of bullets and explosions, thought of people in the middle of it – and cried.

Mon, June 12

I was surprised to find that the buses were on today after last night's trouble.

Was late again for school – I just can't manage to be early any more. At 10.30, Sister Virgilius assembled us all (Lower 6th) in the Library and gave us a lecture on punctuality etc. Said we were the most immature lot she had ever come across!

I wore my blazer today for the first time in ages. Result? It poured and I got soaked going home.

Terrible day of bombings – Derry's Guildhall

blown up and 4 or 5 other places too.

Hundreds of Catholic families have been forced to flee their homes through intimidation – great coverage on radio and TV, although no consolation to the victims …

Tues, June 13

Paul's 8th birthday. He was thrilled at being so old! I was too tired to go to French Conversation class, so I bunked it.

Sat out sunning ourselves at lunchtime. The weather is really beautiful – then we got the news that the buses are off again. Rumour that the leader of the IRA hunger strike – Billy McKee – is dead, therefore buses and lorries hijacked and burnt. Walked most of the way home and then got a lift.

Provos have asked Whitelaw to meet them in exchange for a 7-day bilateral truce – he refuses! He meets the UDA – promises them something, does a deal with them and then they announce their barricades won't go up at weekend.

We're shocked at Whitelaw – have all been sold out!

Wed, June 14

Jimmy is still sick after the party yesterday. Heard him up vomiting at 4 o'clock this morning, however I didn't get out of bed.

Fri, June 16

John was sick today – fear of Chemistry test added to sickness. I was late for school once again, as has been usual for past 2 weeks.

Mammy rang Musgrave to see if there was any possibility of a job for me – too late. Lizzie says there is a possibility of jobs in Churchill House (Post Office) – pray that it's true.

On the way home, we were put off the bus at the barracks – apparently 'they' were hijacking everything in sight. ONE car had been taken!!

2 policemen were shot and very seriously injured in Kennedy Way – first report said they were dead. Gunmen escaped. Granny rang to tell us once again to pack up and leave! Catholic man shot dead – UDA.

~~~

As the UDA continued to ratchet up its deadly pressure on the Catholic community and the IRA carried out a second gun attack near our home in a couple of weeks, my grandparents begged us again to leave Belfast. Despite their infrequent visits to the city, they were well enough acquainted with its geography to know that Kennedy Way ran along the end of our garden.

My grandparents fretted constantly about us. My parents in turn were anxious about each other and my brothers and me, and prayed for our safe arrival home every time we went out. I watched the clock for my parents' return every time one of them left the house. I was scared for my own future, sick of the never-ending cycle of bloodshed and fear.

As my mother assured my grandmother by phone that we were safe, I pasted yet another story from *The Irish News* into my scrapbook: 'The Protestant mob drove into the top end of the 100 per cent Catholic street, hurling petrol and nail bombs. The terrified people rushed into the street and soldiers carried screaming children to safety ...'

I went to bed tormented with thoughts of what we could do if something similar happened to us. It wouldn't happen, I told myself, because we weren't living cheek by jowl with huge numbers of Protestants. But if the unthinkable *should* happen, I calculated, Cooley was the nearest place we could go and that was more than fifty miles away.

I wondered what would happen to my parents' jobs if we had to flee. Would we lose our home in Fruithill? Would we be accepted into new schools and be able to keep up with the classes? Would we be like the families I read about, left with nothing but the clothes they were standing in?

Many of the families forced out of North Belfast fled to Andersonstown or even further out, to Lenadoon. The 'lucky' ones were divided between relatives; others settled wherever they could, sometimes in new houses which weren't fully built and were still without water, electricity, even roofs. I appreciated again how lucky we were, in my father's words, to have 'the security of the ghetto' around us.

Mon, June 19

Beginning of our last full week at school this year. Time has really flown.

Had our maths test. I was really dreading it – however, it wasn't too bad, only I made a mess of it as usual. Freezing cold day – had our lunch in the huts, too cold to sit outside.

Miss Murphy didn't turn up for French class but then arrived during our <u>free</u> class and took us. I was furious – all for the sake of education!! Frankie came home with me, called in to get a French book and then Suzette called – she's off till Wednesday.

Big moves on the political scene today. Political status – although not with the tag – is granted to prisoners. Day 36 of hunger-strike. Daddy thinks I'll be able to get a job in the Post Office – I hope so!

Tues, June 20

Daddy called me dead early i.e. at about 10 to 8, to write the letter of application for the job. There was no notepaper etc. last night and so, I had to be content with a piece of CDC notepaper cut in half! Wrote it out – careless and untidy – Daddy was in a hurry.

Tomorrow is Midsummer's Day and it is freezing cold and wet.

No news from France yet. Hope to get Post office job – pray I will. Piles of homework, worked solidly until 11. I look like a ghost. Haven't all my English done but I don't really care. Near the end of term.

Wed, June 21

No letters. I'm tired waiting. Got into school quite early for a change. Too cold to sit outside and yet it's the longest day of the year. Investigation on news into the bad weather – worst for years.

Pouring coming from school – to crown it all, no buses (as is very common nowadays), due to the funeral of man shot in Leeson Street by IRA.

Rumours of truce by Provisional IRA – no firm announcement yet – keep hoping.

Thurs, June 22

I got up quite early in expectation of a letter from France or else from the Post Office – no luck! Beginning to give up hope of getting away.

Dreading the second Maths test. My dreads were certainly well-founded – the test was terrible! I'm sure I, and most of the others, have failed. Boring afternoon, came home at usual time.

Soldiers at Andytown Barracks were waving to everyone, therefore realized that IRA must have called a truce! They have – beginning Monday at midnight. However, have four days before this! All night – discussions on the subject on TV.

Did <u>no</u> homework. Daddy at meeting.

Terrible shooting, therefore clear that 'they' aren't easing off till the truce comes.

Sun, June 25

Mammy told me at 1.30 a.m. last night that she would be going to Dundalk today, therefore when I woke I didn't know whether it was true or I had only dreamt it. However, it is – going to Ballymascanlon Hotel to represent Women's Voluntary Service Group with Mrs Gordon etc. Went at 1p.m.

Incessant shooting to be heard all day long – up in Lenadoon – IRA and army having their final fling, 700 rounds fired in 70 minutes, but no soldiers hit.

Expected Mammy home early therefore, when at 12 o'clock she still hadn't arrived, I was nearly out of my mind with worry. She came in at a quarter to 1, had got lost because of a detour in Newry. I came to bed, relieved.

Mon, June 26

Last day before IRA truce – end to violence, we hope.

Into school, watched a film Sr. Emmanuel gave us. Out of 89 Lower 6ths, 51 were present. Got 71% in Maths test – I'm very pleased.

No news from France, I'm off the idea now of going – anti-climax!

Came home from school early – John had a bit of a party for his birthday – just the usual family business.

*Watched Panorama (about us), and news.
Went down to Suzette's, watched news and '24
Hours' (about us). Not off to a very good start –
terrible day of bombings and raids.*

Girl from school on arms/bank raid charge.

*2 soldiers and 1 RUC man killed, and 1 civilian
killed.*

~~~

The Secretary of State, William Whitelaw told MPs that he
prayed the ceasefire would be 'a starting point to the end of
violence'. I pasted his statement into my scrapbook hoping,
although not yet convinced, that my prayers were being
answered.

As the clock counted down towards the start of the
ceasefire, I failed to feel the sense of elation I had anticipated.
The killings continued literally until midnight, bringing to
nine the number who died since plans for a ceasefire were
announced. I prayed that events the following day and
afterwards would raise my spirits.

Tues, June 27 – Day 1 of Truce

*Got letter from France – nearly prayed my heart
out before opening it – good news! Lizzie can go
to France! Raced into school to tell her. Brilliant!*

*Do no Maths in school. Holiday atmosphere
beginning to creep in – only about half of the school
are in these days. After tea, went up to Elizabeth's
to help her write a letter to France, stayed there
till 10.30.*

> *Came home and watched programme on Ulster.*
> *Went to bed at 12.30 and did some homework*
> *which I didn't bother starting earlier.*
>
> *It's great to be able to go to bed in peace i.e.*
> *knowing there'll be no trouble all night. Apparently*
> *people in Lenadoon, Clonard etc. are feeding army*
> *with cigs, beer (from a hijacked lorry), playing*
> *football with them – and put a Tricolour on a*
> *billet!*

~~~

I couldn't decide which was more mind-blowing: an Irish tricolour hanging off a British army billet or the prospect of flying off to a foreign country and a whole new world. Madame de Marignan, who lived at Villeneuve-sur-Lot in the south of France, had responded generously to the recent approach from her former 'au pair', and our neighbour's daughter, Margaret Gordon. She and her family were willing to host me – a complete stranger – for the month of August, in return for some housework and casual English lessons for her children. She also promised to try to make a similar arrangement for Liz. After all the months of praying and waiting, of frustration and despair, my friend and I would be going to France and doing so against the backdrop of an IRA ceasefire.

I told my mother I needed new clothes for going away. I wondered what the weather would be like and whether I would be able to understand people speaking French. I couldn't wait to hear French accents and see French men in the flesh instead of in films and on television. I suddenly regretted staying away from so many of my Conversation classes.

I thought about the graffiti on the wall down the Falls Road: 'Is there a life before death?' At long last, I could answer 'Yes!'

CHAPTER 9

'Too good to be true.'

My elation at the start of the IRA ceasefire lasted only hours, fading first to muted optimism and then utter desolation, as loyalist paramilitaries failed to respond positively to the republican gesture. I was politically naïve and war-weary, too obsessed with my France 'project' to think through properly how they were likely to react.

Dressmaking became one way I had of coping with the bad days. Sewing whiled away the hours and diverted my attention, albeit temporarily, from the savagery on the streets. It gave me an excuse to listen to my favourite Radio Luxembourg DJs – Kid Jensen and Tony Prince – in solitude and quiet, and it stopped me wondering what poor unfortunate was being dragged into a car, before being beaten, hooded and shot. It helped keep the vicious world of guns, cudgels, masks and barricades at bay while allowing me to cut, shape and perfect a garment of which I could be proud.

I withdrew to my bedroom and sewed like someone possessed, until my back and shoulders ached from hours spent hunched over my sewing machine or crouched on the floor cutting out pieces of fabric. Eventually, when my eyes were too strained in the bad light, I called it a day and climbed into bed.

Experience should have taught me that the loyalists would rear up in anger if they suspected the government of having done a deal with republicans: if 'the other side' had won a concession, then 'our side' must have lost something. This mind-set, shared by both sides of the community, stymied many political advances. I subsequently waited in fear and resumed my sewing as the fantasy I dreamed up around the ceasefire turned out to be no more than that.

Wed, June 28

Pouring rain all day today again – not looking very good for us getting off on our holidays tomorrow. Went down to watch Form 3 sports, got soaked. Came home early, as Siobhan rang the school bells 20 minutes earlier than usual – messing!

Daddy came home to say there's NO possibility of a job in Post Office. Just cried – don't know where I'll get the money now. (Flights available on Aug 4, in case I still go). Watched TV and read – no homework to do.

Mrs McGlade was up, watching '24 Hours' – about us. UDA barricades are going up <u>permanently</u> on Friday – could lead to terrible trouble. I pray it won't.

Mammy says that she'll give me the money for France. I want to get it myself.

Sun, July 2

Granda rang – saw the news etc. and wanted us all to go down to Cooley. At 12, we decided to go – whole family, in and away. Auntie Jo and new baby, Shane, were there. Went down to Carlingford Pier – the weather is really glorious.

When it came to leaving to come home, Auntie Jo decided to take Jim and Paul to Navan with her for a holiday – so 5 remaining in family came on home.

When we got home, heard that 3 more bodies had been found, shot dead – 2 Protestants and 1 Catholic, i.e. 5 killed (shot) this weekend, 2 Catholics, 3 Protestants.

Sewed until after 12, making the suit and then came to bed.

～～～

I pressed the foot-pedal harder and felt the motor's vibrations run through my fingers as I fed the pink denim material ever faster under the hammering needle. I cut, pinned, tacked and sewed, losing track of time but not forgetting to switch from Radio Luxembourg to the BBC for news bulletins.

I was looking forward to wearing my new suit as I wandered without a care around a distant French town called Villeneuve-sur-Lot. But, with my only remaining job prospects dead in the water and the UDA setting up dozens of barricades and no-go areas in the city, I despaired of ever doing so. While I kept my hands busy, I tried to empty my mind of the sense that our society was self-destructing.

My two youngest brothers jumped at the chance of a

spur of the moment holiday in County Meath and gleefully waved us goodbye before setting out from Cooley with no extra clothes and no other belongings. Their impromptu departure meant that as the rest of us headed back to Belfast, on the first weekend of our school holidays, my parents had two fewer children to worry about.

Mon, July 3

Great to know I don't have to get up for school for another two months!

However, the terrible news greets us that 2 more Catholics were murdered last night i.e. 7 killed in past 48 hours.

House very quiet without Jim and Paul. Mammy left me off at Malone Road to go and meet Elizabeth at Queen's and book flights for France – but no student cards available, so have to wait till Thursday.

Went around town, then came home and did some sewing.

Daddy went to CDC. Big confrontation between 2,500 UDA and 500 soldiers, over putting up more barricades – however avoided battle by meeting Whitelaw.

Tues, July 4

Second day of the holidays and it is pouring rain – not off to a very good start. Mammy decided to get her hair cut, didn't persuade me to get mine cut <u>yet</u>.

> *I had to meet Daddy in town at half twelve to compile a list of information on the <u>27 Catholics</u> who have been killed by sectarian murder squads since January this year. Met him, went to 'Irish News' and went through back-dated copies.*
>
> *Did some baking for Mary Holland, the 'Observer' reporter, who wants the information Daddy and I collected. She left at 10.30 p.m.*

~~~

My father was meticulous as he morbidly catalogued the killings of innocent Catholics. He was energised by the prospect of having a reporter of the standing of Mary Holland – a well-known and highly respected commentator on Northern Ireland affairs – coming to our house to interview him. The loyalist bloodletting was increasing steadily and, by the first weekend after the IRA ceasefire, we were almost afraid to turn on the morning news.

From my 16-year-old West Belfast, Catholic perspective, the UDA and UVF were going about their ghastly deeds with impunity. The police – to the exasperation of fearful Catholics – continued to trot out the ludicrous line that there was 'no apparent motive' for what we knew to be sectarian murders. When the former Unionist Prime Minister, Brian Faulkner, was asked at a news conference about the 'unexplained' killings of Catholics, he dismissed outright the possibility that a Protestant backlash was under way. But the steady stream of funerals to Milltown Cemetery testified otherwise.

I met my father at the top of Royal Avenue – the main thoroughfare through Belfast city centre – having rejected my mother's recommendation to get my hair cut. For as long as I could remember, my thick curly hair was a bone of contention between us. It defied the laws of gravity but, throughout my teens, I pigheadedly insisted that, given a chance, it would eventually grow downwards instead of upwards and out.

My father and I walked past boarded-up windows and bombed-out buildings to Donegall Street and the offices of *The Irish News*. There, behind a high, oak, L-shaped reception desk, a small team of women dealt with a steady flow of people submitting death notices and classified ads. The tall narrow windows were covered with opaque, self-adhesive plastic film to protect staff from shards of flying glass in the event of an explosion. The sombre front office was deprived of natural daylight and relied instead on electric bulbs, even in the height of summer. It was difficult to imagine that the office looked any different from when the newspaper was established at the end of the nineteenth century.

My father asked for six months' back copies of the paper and the thick, bound volumes – cataloguing stories of death, destruction, division and occasional hope – were laid out on the counter before us. He divided the names of more than two dozen loyalist victims between us and, for the next two hours, we pored over the circumstances of their deaths, adding to or amending the accounts my father had already compiled.

It was a depressing and wearisome task but the fact that a quality, London-based newspaper like *The Observer* finally wanted to hear our community's story spurred my father on. It ensured that when Mary Holland was ensconced with him for three hours in our sitting room that evening, she received a thorough and accurate briefing on every one of more than two dozen killings.

Thurs, July 6

After not bothering to find out yesterday if student cards were available at Queens, I find myself faced with a problem – Eliz. will be out all day and I have arranged to meet her at 3.15. I don't want to go now because I rang this morning and there aren't any cards.

Sewed all afternoon, got my suit finished – it's lovely.

Mammy and Daddy had a brainwave – Aidan is going away on Saturday, so she, Daddy, John and I should go to Donegal! Too good to be true!

Fri, July 7

Mammy decided to go to Cooley to leave some clothes there for Jim and Paul, to be collected by Auntie Jo. She had day off from work and Daddy decided to take half-day. I don't want to go. Announce that Tito is to be brought too, so I definitely decide to stay at home. They all went off after 1. I sewed all evening and then made myself a big plate of chips for my tea.

Mrs E rang, warning me that there would be trouble at Lenadoon tonight – true enough!

Sixteen Catholic families – put out by Protestants – are trying to move into houses vacated by Prods, but are forbidden to do so by UDA. Discussions with army – big confrontation avoided but 16 families homeless. Protestant shot dead in Cavendish Street.

Sat, July 8

After breakfast Aidan got ready to go to Kildare – set out for de La Salle at 1, stayed there till 2.

Went on a tour of Lenadoon, stopped by the Fianna – with a rifle – then went out to Derriaghy for messages. After tea, tailed some gooseberries and then did sewing.

Watched late news – permanent UDA barricades should go up tonight.

400th person to die here since 1969 died today – a Catholic (12th person murdered this week) – shot from passing car a couple of days ago.

~~~

I didn't detect any panic on my parents' part – more an unspoken relief that there would only be four of us at home instead of seven. My youngest brothers' sojourn in Navan was extended and Aidan was also prepared for dispatch to the Republic with a group of classmates from the De La Salle boys' school. The suggestion that the rest of us should go to Donegal had seemed too good to be true – and it was never mentioned again.

The time I spent helping my father with his 'record-keeping' concentrated my attention on the brutal attacks being carried out on defenceless members of my faith.

The plight of wretched families caught up in the housing controversy at Lenadoon, and left without a home to call their own, appalled me. An IRA gunman shot dead an innocent Protestant man in the street next to my school and brought to a dozen the number of men killed in the North in just over a week.

The death toll soared. As nerves frayed and speculation mounted about impending trouble, the eyes of West Belfast and further afield were trained on the sectarian cauldron of Lenadoon. It was patently clear after just a week and a half that the ceasefire was not going to deliver the happy, carefree summer of which I had been dreaming.

CHAPTER 10

'The inevitability of civil war.'

The night before my seventeenth birthday I retreated upstairs to my bedroom around eleven o'clock and, upset by the day's events, tried hard not to cry. Three of my brothers were safe in the South and my parents, glad to have the company of some neighbours, were speculating grimly – over cups of tea and glasses of whisky – about civil war.

Sun, July 9

Mammy going to Dundalk – she didn't call me for 9 Mass as I asked. I was glad – went to 11 with John and Daddy. Wore my new suit – I admit myself that it's lovely!

4 men shot dead (3 Protestants, 1 Catholic) last night – i.e. <u>16</u> this week. After dinner, there was a 'call to arms' by the Provisional IRA on Radio Saoirse. They were going to force the 16 homeless families into the empty houses in Lenadoon, in spite of army.

Went up at 5 with Daddy to look. 2,000 rioters started storming army post, and army returning with rubber-bullets, CS gas and water cannon. Shooting started and announcement is given

*out that TRUCE IS OVER. Fled. New bombing
campaign to start!*

*Mr and Mrs Gordon and Mrs McGlade
assembled in the house when Mammy came home
after 11p.m., stayed till 1.*

*8 bombs in Derry and Belfast tonight – bad
start for Twelfth week.*

*4 killed by Army in Ballymurphy, including a
<u>priest</u> and a 13-year-old girl. Shooting all night.*

~~~

Like many people in West Belfast on that glorious Sunday
afternoon, I was curious about what would happen when a
number of Catholic families, intimidated from their homes
elsewhere, tried to move into houses allocated to them in
Lenadoon – houses previously occupied by Protestants.

An announcement on the IRA's pirate radio station left
listeners in little doubt that a final showdown was imminent
but, while the sun blazed from a cloudless sky and the
ceasefire remained intact, I had no reason to be any more
frightened than usual. Determined not to miss out on the
possible 'excitement', I jumped into the passenger seat beside
my father when he announced that he was driving up to
Lenadoon, a mile or so from our home, to see events for
himself.

The size of the crowd took me by surprise. The area
was buzzing, teeming with photographers and reporters –
including some I recognised instantly from television – all
clearly aware that something 'big' was about to happen.

As we walked downhill, I caught sight of the soldiers for
the first time and was overcome by a sickening feeling of

dread. Scores of them – fully-armed, carrying shields and in riot gear – blocked the entrance to the avenue where the Catholic families intended to take up residence. Hundreds of local people – some carrying sticks, hurleys and metal bin-lids – escorted two lorries laden with furniture as they were being driven slowly but steadily towards the Army lines.

Chaos erupted as missiles were hurled and soldiers responded with baton charges and rubber bullets. Shots rang out, a male voice roared that the ceasefire was over and the crowd split in two: one group staying to pelt the soldiers with bricks and stones; the other running for our lives, out of our depths in a pitched battle.

Nine hours later, and two hours after I turned 17, I could still hear gunfire raging in the near distance. Around 6,000 shots were fired in West Belfast that night, in the fiercest gun battles the area had ever experienced.

I struggled to fight back tears as I stared at the new, dark pink denim suit hanging on the front of my wardrobe. Night after night I had toiled over it painstakingly in anticipation of wearing it in France. I wondered whether Mass in St Agnes' chapel that morning was as far I would travel in it.

My bedroom floor was littered with scraps of pink material, paper-patterns and thread ends. On my last day at school I had carelessly dumped my uniform, books and files wherever they fell and was left with nowhere to sit other than on the bed. I knelt on the floor, amidst the clutter, listening to the unremitting gunfire and looking at the backlog of depressing cuttings I had yet to paste into my scrapbook.

'Situation at its worst since 1968', '12 dead since IRA ceasefire', 'Civil war warning in London', '4 shot at weekend', and so on and on and on. As I passed through the living room on my way to the kitchen for a glass of water, I overheard the adults mentioning 'bloodbath' again; the term, with its chilling connotations, was cropping up more and more often in their casual conversations. After kissing my parents goodnight, I went back upstairs, curled up in bed and cried.

Mon, July 10

(6 killed overnight, 12 bombs in Derry and Belfast).

My birthday. At first I was scared to get up in case everyone had forgotten my birthday – however, got a card and promise of a camera from Mammy and Daddy, card from Agnes. Suzette forgot completely about it but I don't care.

Poured rain all day – depressing weather and depressing news. Everyone, high up and low down, talking about the inevitability of civil war!

After tea, Daddy said he had planned to bring Mammy, John and I out to Greenan Lodge to celebrate my birthday – but 'due to wartime situations' beyond his control, we couldn't go.

Stayed in house bored sick. Suzette came up but all she did was complain about how bored <u>she</u> was.

Truce irrevocably over. All looking to civil war.

~~~

In the grand scheme of things, my birthday was of little importance except in so far as I could celebrate still being alive. The news headlines on my 'Happy Birthday' morning were that ten people had been killed since Saturday night – all of them in Belfast – and the gun battles were continuing.

Given what was going on all around us, I could not have faulted my parents if they had forgotten the date. Not only did they remember my birthday, they promised to buy me my first ever camera – 'to take away with you,' they said – insisting that I should press on with my plans regardless.

'Don't worry about us. We'll be alright,' my father assured me selflessly, probably not believing it himself, but pointing out that nothing had happened to anyone belonging to us so far. I prayed more fervently than ever that it would stay like that.

I began to try to convince myself that of course my family would all be safe, that God wouldn't let anything happen to them. The prospect of flying to Paris with Liz in four weeks' time, being let loose in the most romantic city in the world and then travelling southwards by train, exceeded my wildest dreams. I fought to keep my excitement in check in case something awful happened to thwart our plans.

Tues, July 11

Got a card from Auntie Kathleen (+£1). Shooting echoed around us all morning – easy to see and hear that truce is now over!

After dinner, John and I went over to Queen's – called in to see Elizabeth where she's working and then booked flights for August 8!!!

John, on his own, had been up watching the assembling of the barricades at Derran Pass. IRA in full force, with pneumatic drills etc. Definitely, a barricade mentality exists here – tonight UDA barricades up, tonight IRA barricades up, and army has barricaded off the city centre.

Notes: More bombs. Catholic found shot dead at Carlisle Circus. Another man (Protestant) dies from gunshot wounds from Sunday. Boy (17) shot dead at Suffolk. Catholic no-go barricades up. Catholic schoolboy killed, also Protestant man.

Thurs, July 13

Daddy was too tired to go into work, therefore he stayed off. Decided to go out to Greenan Lodge for my promised dinner. Had a huge feed, it was gorgeous.

Beautiful day. Had intended to go off somewhere for the day however, due to intense military presence in the area, decided to go on a tour of Suffolk and Lenadoon.

Supposed to be a meeting in La Salle School about re-housing the homeless – all fell through. Five families living in La Salle – put out by Protestants.

Came home and had our tea but I was too full to eat!

Desperate shooting at 11. Thought I was being shot at – IRA up the street shooting into Kennedy Way.

~~~

I celebrated the beginning of my eighteenth year three days late when my parents deemed it safe to venture to a hotel near where we had fled in panic when the ceasefire broke down. The area was still crawling with army patrols but after passing through the barrier designed to prevent car bomb attacks, my parents, John and I eventually got to enjoy the 'chicken-in-a-basket' for which the hotel had become popular, along with desserts and a big pot of tea.

A check on my finances confirmed what I suspected: I was broke. I had already spent £1.90 on a passport application and photographs, and I needed new clothes for wearing in the continental heat. I worked out that if I stayed in France for just over three weeks as planned, I would need around £20 spending money. The £1 from my godmother in Sligo was very welcome but as to how I would find the other £19, I had absolutely no idea.

My parents loaned me the £21 for my plane fare and I promised to pay them back at Christmas, provided we were all still alive.

Fri, July 14

Daddy is back at work today and Suzette is still in Dublin. Decided to go to Lisburn to get John shoes. After travelling 8 miles to Lisburn, found that none of the shops were open – all closed for the Twelfth, <u>still</u>. Went to Woolworth's – the only shop open – and then came home.

Went to shops on Andersonstown Road, however car conked out – left in the embarrassing situation of having 3 men – one of whom is high up in the IRA, according to John – pushing us. Got car started and came home to strawberries and ice cream – summer is definitely here!

Talks going on concerning army presence in Lenadoon, and homeless families.

Soldier shot dead (Lenadoon). Another one, shot after c'fire collapsed, died too. Soldier killed Ardoyne gun-battle – 3 men killed (2 IRA).

Sat, July 15

St Swithin's Day and it is a glorious day, 77 degrees F! Hope it lasts. Itching to get out since I got up, however washing breakfast dishes, dinner dishes, bed-making and baking all came first.

Daddy at CDC meeting – came home 'carless' – hijacked at gunpoint. Through various contacts, it was returned by OC of 'A' Company, Provisional IRA – second time lucky.

Went outside and sunbathed with Mammy, Daddy and McGlades. Suzette came over with a belated birthday present.

Uncle Denis had heard about the car exploits and came up too (gave me £1).

3 gunmen were sitting outside McGlade's – after a message from another car, whizzed off.

440 dead now.

～～～

The unusually high temperatures, and the near certainty of going away, dispelled the gloom and despair that previously engulfed me. Dishes of strawberries, scoops of ice cream floating in fizzy lemonade and the pursuit of a suntan distracted me from the steadily mounting death toll.

I was happy to let the soft summer days wash over me, stretched out lazily on the grass on the old black and red tartan rug, a good book propped up in front of me and my radio playing low. The gentle hum of traffic in Kennedy Way and the chirping and warbling of sparrows, blackbirds and thrushes, as they flitted between the bushes and trees at the bottom of our garden, lulled me into an easy contentment.

The violence was less oppressive, and everything – even the hijacking of our old blue Cortina – seemed more manageable when the weather was so benign. If the three masked gunmen who commandeered the car from my father had known that we pushed it home the previous day they might have been less keen to seize it.

In the lackadaisical haze of that week, I registered each successive death only fleetingly, just long enough to confirm that I didn't know the victim. I lost track of the numbers killed until, looking back through a few pages of my diary, I discovered with guilty shock and disbelief that the death toll had gone up by 40 in the space of a week – 30 of them in the five days since my birthday and nearly all in Belfast.

Sun, July 16

Arranged last night to go to 9 Mass with Suzette – however, I only woke when I heard her banging on the door at 8.50! Got up to go to 10, but others were too late so waited till 11. Went up to De La Salle school after it.

TV cameras etc. were all there and piles of refugees. Met a wee girl, Carol – brought her down to the house for the afternoon.

Sweltering hot day – stayed out in the garden and ate ice cream and more ice cream!

ALL Lenadoon families were asked by Provos to move out of the area, as a form of protest against heavy military presence. 1000s marched down to Casement Park – went over to see them – ALL ages. Have decided to stay out all night – till army go.

Brought Carol back up to school – all Lenadoon crowd there too. Overcrowding, so she came home here for the night. Mammy and Daddy up helping out in De La Salle.

Mon, July 17

Carol woke me at about 10, I was exhausted. She started to play the guitar – I could've killed her! Another glorious day.

Mammy decided to bring Carol back up to school at dinner-time, when she was going to work. Left Carol and me off at La Salle – about 2,000 in school – all 'Lenadoonians' AND refugees. Bunged out. Sat on the grass. Babies crying – tired and hot. Harassed, worn faces. Smoking cigarettes non-stop. Army won't move out, therefore people have no homes.

Came home and sunbathed.

Gunmen opened fire on army from next door – I saw them. Terrified! No one hurt, thank God. Got my arms and back roasted with the sun. Same weather forecast for tomorrow. At the moment

there is wild shooting going on. Four times I have
turned the lights out while writing this.

~~~

The air reeked of stale clothing, soiled nappies, cigarette smoke and food being prepared in the canteen. Up to two thousand men, women and children were taking refuge in De La Salle Secondary School, where we had celebrated the feast of Corpus Christi just six weeks earlier. Many of them had been intimidated or burnt out of their homes in North Belfast while hundreds of others formed part of the protest mass exodus from Lenadoon.

The air was warm and fetid. People lay stretched out on mattresses and make-shift beds, too dispirited to get up. Small children crawled about the floor, bewildered by their crowded surroundings, and hassled adults – many with crying babies in their arms – lined up in queues to register their family details with those who were trying to establish some order. My parents were there to lend a hand.

Scores of youngsters rejoiced in the fresher air outside, shouting and screaming at each other across the playing fields and enjoying the lack of order and discipline. Sullen teenagers leaned against the walls or lay on the ground. Parents and older people sat on the grass, looking stressed, anxious and beyond caring.

When nine-year-old Carol sidled up to me and told me nonchalantly that Protestants had petrol-bombed her home near the New Lodge Road in the north of the city, my heart went out to her. The little 'refugee' was skinny, poor-looking and as grubby as any child would be after bedding down overnight on an assembly hall floor with hundreds of others. Surprisingly uncowed by her violent experience, she was content to chat to strangers as a way of entertaining herself in the middle of the alien, noisy and chaotic environment into which she had been thrust.

When she told me her tragic story it seemed like the most natural thing in the world to bring her home with me. I had always longed for a little sister. Her worn-out parents were delighted when I offered to take her off their hands for a while.

I revelled in Carol's enjoyment of our home and her delight as – unfazed by the heat – she cycled up and down the garden on one of my brother's bicycles. I plied my new 'little sister' with as much ice cream as she could eat and filled a bath with warm perfumed bubbles up to her chin. Her exuberance gradually wore me down, though, and I accepted reluctantly that she had overstayed her welcome.

Wed, July 19

Mammy made an appointment for me to get my hair cut – gave me a lift down and I walked home. My hair is horrible! All short and curly. Came in and John made faces at it. In temper, I burst out crying and created a great scene.

Suzette came and asked me to go for a swim in the pool at the Hospital – did so. At 2.00, went to her room in Bostock House, changed and went down to the pool – sunbathed, swam, drank lemonade, sunbathed and swam again. Beautiful weather, great afternoon – and medical talent too much! Suzette had her tea here. Took photographs and messed about. Exercised Tito and came to bed.

Shooting.

Thurs, July 20

Mammy called me at 9 to say she was going down to Waterford Street for dress material. I intended getting up later on but the next thing I heard was her back again at 11.15 with me still in bed!

Another roasting day – 79 degrees Fahrenheit. We decided to go to Cooley after tea for a swim – nearest, cleanest beach. Daddy came home early – exhausted, after he and Mammy had spent from 12.30 to 6 a.m. this morning awake with gun-battles. Thank God, no one was killed.

Set off for Cooley, dropped Mammy in at Granny's, went for swim. Beautiful. Got home again at 11.45 p.m.

~~~

As youngsters, well before the Troubles, our summertime stays in Cooley revolved around frequent trips to the long, shingly and usually deserted beach at Shelling Hill, where we swam and splashed about in the tide regardless of the weather. Shivering after our swims and whipped by the cold breeze from the Irish Sea, we would sit high up in the long spiky grass overlooking the beach. With our sand-covered hands wrapped round mugs of hot tea, we devoured the sandwiches my mother and granny put together for us.

The only time I ever tasted rabbit was during one such delicious picnic; my grandfather killed the unfortunate animal and my grandmother cooked it, passing it off to us as chicken, amid a pile of home-grown salad and bread. It was delicious.

Freed from the grip of Belfast, my father, John and I raced across the sand on the empty beach and crashed into the sea, shrieking as the breathtakingly cold waves broke over us, forcing the air out of our lungs. I surfaced, took a gulp of the warm evening air, started to swim and washed Belfast out of my system.

Fri, July 21

Mammy gave John and me our breakfasts in bed! First time these holidays. I'll have to repay her (some time!). I broke all records then by getting up at 11. Still no more word from France – I'm really getting worried. Mammy rushed out to work – late as usual. Not a very nice day so I stayed inside to sew.

Heard a huge blast about 2.30 p.m. Thought it was the quarry until it was followed at 2 minute intervals by 21 others – all around town. Tragic results – 'Bloody Friday' for Ulster – 11? (13?) killed, 130 hurt. Provos claim responsibility.

Murderers!

I cursed the IRA and tried without success to understand how they could justify slaughtering so many people, including a bus driver, a schoolboy and two Catholic women (one a pensioner, the other a mother of seven).

I was standing by the kitchen sink, singing along to the radio and lost in dreams of France, when I heard the low, distant rumble. By that July, I was expert at recognising the sound of an explosion – of telling the difference between a car bomb and a nail bomb – just as we could distinguish army gunfire from shots fired by the Provisionals. I knew instantly that what I had heard was a huge explosion.

But another 'boom' followed within minutes, and then another. 'Those couldn't be bombs,' I told myself; there were too many of them, too close together. It had to be blasting work at the quarry on Black Mountain behind us.

It was only when I saw the tell-tale funnel of thick, black smoke curling into the distant sky that I dared to think the worst and began to panic about my father at work in the city centre. Around twenty bombs went off in the space of an hour on that busy Friday afternoon.

My father phoned from his desk in the Post Office in Churchill House to reassure us that he was safe. Oxford Street bus station, where the worst explosion happened, was only a few minutes' walk from his work. Sounding anxious, he told us he was setting out on foot for the five-mile journey home.

Bombs had exploded in all sorts of places: on bridges, in bus stations, shops, a hotel and a taxi-office; so God alone knew the best route for him to follow. Our prayers accompanied him every step of the way.

The word 'bloodbath' came into its own that day but not in the way I had visualised. For weeks, I had gone to bed in fear of a large-scale, brutal and bloody loyalist assault on the Catholic community. I never dreamed it would happen like this. My stomach churned as I watched pictures on the news of the dead and injured, and of rescue workers lifting, with shovels, what we were told were limbs and body parts. Early reports said eleven people were killed. Others went as high as thirteen and the authorities finally confirmed the death toll as nine. The initial confusion about the death toll told us all we needed to know about the carnage.

Scores of people were injured, many of them caught by flying glass and shrapnel as they fled from the sound of one bomb straight into the path of another. Two soldiers were among the dead while the others were ordinary civilians like my family and me; people from my home town, blown to smithereens by the IRA in the middle of a summer's day. My mother and I hadn't ventured into the town centre for weeks. Once again I thought, 'There but for the grace of God,' and wondered how long it might be before *my* luck expired.

I was disgusted and upset by the bloody turmoil in which people like my family played no part but from which we appeared to have no escape. I was in little doubt that some unfortunate, unsuspecting Catholic – it could be my father – would pay the price for the city centre slaughter, although the UDA and UVF needed no excuse for killing. They shot a Catholic man dead when he answered a knock on his door earlier that very morning; the following night, they abducted and killed three more Catholics – two men and a woman.

I could not imagine that I would bring myself to leave my family and go to France in just over two weeks' time.

Wed, July 26

Mammy had us all up this morning at 9 o'clock. UDA and Vanguard had threatened to cut off electricity etc. for a day of mourning for 'Bloody Friday', at 11 o'clock.

Cleaned the house down but the stoppage never materialised. I even cleaned and shampooed the carpet in the back bedroom!

Mammy arrived home early from work – at 2 o'clock – due to rioting on the Glen Road. No children arrived at the playgroup. She and I went down to the Springfield Road and Waterford Street for material. I got lovely material for a dress.

Army were in the street in full force, trying to tow away a suspicious car, met with 'opposition' and withdrew. Army back to pull down barricades at 2 o'clock in the morning. Watched them until after 3 a.m.

Fri, July 28

Had to get up early again as it was the last day before we go on holidays. Daddy is due to go on strike, half-day, for more pay. Very convenient, as we are planning on going to Cooley to collect Jim and Paul, after Auntie Jo leaves them back there.

Daddy came home at dinner time with a beautiful new camera for me – I nearly died when I saw it – a Kodak Instamatic, it's really beautiful. His strike didn't materialise.

> *Mammy and Daddy went down to see Granny O'Callaghan – she sent me up £1 – then we went to Cooley. Granny gave me £11, exact replica of a dream I had earlier – eerie! That's my spending money looked after. Jim and Paul home.*
>
> *Got into the house and were told that husband of Daddy's cousin had been found murdered.*

~~~

I had all the evidence I needed that the UDA were closing in on us. I was convinced they knew the names, addresses and movements of every Catholic in Belfast and were going to kill us all, one by one. How else were they able to find random Catholics – men like Frank Corr, and another man whose body was found alongside his – to kill so readily? I didn't know Frank Corr other than by name, but the gruesome circumstances of his death and the fact that we were connected, if only distantly through marriage, scared the living daylights out of me.

Mr Corr was a few years younger than my father and, like him, had a young family. A hurley stick, lying in the back of his car, indicated to the gang who stopped him that he was involved in Gaelic sport, and therefore almost certainly a Catholic. They beat and shot him, before concealing his body in the boot of his own car and setting it on fire. His charred remains were found along with those of another Catholic man who was picked up separately, shot and then dumped in the same vehicle. I shuddered to think about the sort of people who committed such a ghastly crime and about what else they were capable of doing.

There were still three days left in that seemingly endless,

brutal July, a month which claimed more than 80 lives, most of them in Belfast. It was small wonder that as we prepared to go on holiday to my Aunt Kathleen's house in Sligo, none of our relatives chose to avail of ours.

CHAPTER 11

'All my childish instincts'

Summer holidays were like an all-Ireland game of musical chairs. My mother's sisters, all living in different parts of the South, moved freely between each other's homes and Cooley. Sharing or swapping, all would be on the move – aunts, uncles, cousins and ourselves – but no one wanted to come to Belfast.

Most summers I couldn't wait to break free into the Republic where, I was convinced, the people were friendlier, the tea tasted nicer, the chocolate was creamier and we could be at ease in our Irishness. I would look forward routinely to my father grandly quoting Winston Churchill, 'We see the dreary steeples of Fermanagh and Tyrone emerging once again,' as we left a succession of sedate Protestant towns and villages behind us on our way to Sligo. We would be giddy with excitement by the time we reached the final sandbagged British army checkpoint at Belcoo, before crossing into the South where we felt 'at home', in a place where we were welcome. But this summer was different.

On the day we left Belfast, I could see that my father was disturbed and upset by Mr Corr's murder. On that same day, another 4,000 British soldiers flew into Aldergrove Airport, heightening speculation that the army was about to tackle the IRA 'no-go areas' in Belfast and Derry. Their deployment brought the total number of soldiers in the North to 20,000 – one for every seventy-five people – and didn't suggest that we were moving any closer to peace.

Sat, July 29

In spite of our plans to leave early we were all still in bed at 10 o'clock. Daddy went out to leave Tito at Dundrod Kennels – he (Tito) was very reluctant to go.

When Daddy came back, he had to go to express sympathy to Sheila on the death of her husband, hence he wasn't in very good form for going on holidays. Finally left at 2 o'clock.

Arrived – after a very tedious journey – in Sligo at 6. Auntie Margaret (who was also staying in Kathleen's) wasn't in – out for a swim, came back at 7.30. At 11, all children – 9 of them – sent to bed. I was sent before 12! Treated as a child. Bad sleeping conditions! Fed up already.

Sun, July 30

I was awakened by the Lundys creating a racket at 10. I was exhausted. Got up to rain and darkness at 12.

I was never so fed up in all my life before – being treated as a child, just like last night. I would love to get out but then A. Margaret announces that she is staying until tomorrow, so that the four adults can go out tonight. I vow to go out tomorrow night somewhere!

> *After dinner, in spite of the rain we headed for*
> *Streedagh – amazing fossils – v. enjoyable. Began*
> *to pour rain again. Into car and headed home.*
> *Stopped at Lissadell House and found a beautiful*
> *beach. Swam there – and turned blue with cold.*
>
> *4 adults went out for a meal and left me with 9*
> *children – mad!*

~~~

As waves crashed below us at Streedagh, a dank, misty drizzle blew in off the Atlantic but I was too mesmerised by the thousands of fossils embedded in the wet, slippery slabs of pale grey stone beneath my feet to notice the chill and the rain. I even 'forgot' to be resentful about my child-minding duties as we clambered over rocks inlaid with delicate skeletal imprints that had withstood the pounding of the elements for more than three hundred million years.

On the way back to Sligo, my father turned off into a secluded country lane where, pointing out a stately but austere-looking house hidden among the trees, he recited the evocative opening lines of WB Yeats' poem, 'Lissadell':

The light of evening, Lissadell,
Great windows open to the south,
Two girls in silk kimonos, both
Beautiful, one a gazelle.

I imagined the elegant, spectral figures of Constance Gore-Booth (later to become the famous Irish revolutionary leader, Countess Markiewicz) and her sister Eva, the poet and suffragette, standing behind the long narrow windows, as we scampered disrespectfully through the hallowed, overgrown grounds where they used to stroll with Ireland's greatest poet.

We weaved our way, knee-deep in ferns and grasses, until the woods gave way to a clearing right on the edge of a secluded bay. I sensed an almost sacrilegious thrill as I swam with my father and brothers in the ice-cold, crystal-clear water while my mother did look-out for us.

Onwards we drove – still shivering from our swim – deeper into the heart of Yeats' Country, with Ben Bulben towering imperiously above us to our left. In keeping with a long family tradition, my father slowed the car in front of Yeats' burial ground at Drumcliff churchyard and, on cue, the seven of us chanted noisily in unison the famous epitaph inscribed on the poet's headstone:

'Cast a cold Eye, On life, on Death. Horseman, pass by'. We had no idea what the inscription meant but that didn't matter. Although only a few hours' drive from home, we had been transported body and spirit into an 'other world' – famed for its landscape, history and literary tradition – unlike the city we had left behind.

I was 120 miles and a psychological world away from where thousands of soldiers would sweep in at dawn the following morning in armoured vehicles, bulldozers and Centurion tanks, to regain control of republican 'no-go areas'. I didn't know anything at all about the village of Claudy where later that same day a car bomb attack would ultimately claim nine innocent lives. Two of the major events of that appalling July washed over me, virtually unnoticed, in the distant, incessant rain of a Sligo summer.

Mon, July 31

Pouring rain again. Another miserable start to the holidays. Lundys left to go home to Dun Laoghaire at 12.30 and the seven O'Callaghans are left to themselves again. Spent boring afternoon playing dominoes and scrabble. Headed down town, visited a couple of shops and got soaked in-between times. Came home in bad form and starving.

Had tea, watched extended news bulletins about the 'Second Siege of Derry'. Played more dominoes.

Had intended going to the pictures but it was too wet. John and Aidan went fishing and got soaked. I wrote to Agnes and the French de Marignans to give final details. Notes: Early hours, army moved in to all no-go areas and took control of them all. Little opposition, however two men shot dead in Derry. Provos <u>dis</u>claimed responsibility for 3 car-bombs in Claudy which killed 6 – and injured 30 people.

Tues, Aug 1

Jim woke me by telling me it wasn't raining – however it wasn't too far from doing so. Freezing cold. Another morning passed away in bed. Weather terrible.

Decided to get out of the house – head for Mullaghmore, after a lunch consisting of 'only soup'. Boys went fishing. Daddy, Mammy and I went into bar for a drink (I had orange!).

Mullaghamore Festival starts tomorrow – begins with big opening dance, wouldn't mind going to it. Had swim – enjoyable, but nearly froze to death after it.

Went to Mrs Duffy's for afternoon tea – exactly same as two years ago. Met Lady Gore-Booth there – typical English aristocrat.

～～～

There was a limit to the number of board games I could play with my brothers before my patience at their squabbling wore thin. Had I been at home in Belfast, I would at least have had the consolation of getting ready for my trip to the south of France, now only a week away. Instead, I watched the drops trickling down the windowpanes and wished for the rain to stop.

Mullaghmore, with its air of quiet sophistication, was only about fifteen miles from Sligo. Even in the rain, the village's simple charms could coax me into good humour: the mystique and grandeur of Classiebawn Castle, where members of the British royal family spent their holidays; the old stone harbour where I waited patiently while my brothers fished for mullet, using lumps of white bread as bait; the gently sloping sandy beach where I loved to swim.

No trip to Mullaghmore was complete without afternoon tea in Mrs Duffy's guesthouse. Remembering us from our previous visits, she fussed over us like a grandmother – grouping the seven of us around two adjoining tables covered with thick, white, linen tablecloths and laid with her best china cups and saucers.

We were ravenous and devoured the dainty, triangular sandwiches, with the crusts cut off, which Mrs Duffy presented to us on a tiered cake-stand. The high point of the occasion though was the arrival of the first plateful of warm drop-scones, fresh off the griddle, accompanied by whipped cream and home-made strawberry jam. She trotted back and forth to the kitchen, producing more and more 'thick pancakes' until we had our fill.

She whispered to us conspiratorially that the woman reading a book at a table by the window – the only other person in the dining room – was Lady Gore-Booth. The romantic images which had filled my head during our illicit swim at Lissadell had been of beautiful women in long silk dresses, surrounded by all the trappings of the aristocracy – nothing like the solitary, grey-haired lady, in a pale blue twinset and fine tweed skirt, enjoying her afternoon tea a couple of tables away from us.

There was something surreal about Mrs Duffy introducing us to that elegant, urbane and unpretentious lady as 'my special friends from the North'. I was horrified to think that we might have disturbed the quiet of Lady Gore-Booth's previous Sunday afternoon or, even worse, that she might have recognised us as the gaggle who had invaded the privacy of her gardens, running through her woods to our magical evening swim. She nodded pleasantly to us, shook hands with my parents and asked if we were enjoying our stay. Thankfully, there was no hint of recognition during the brief encounter, nor did any of us mention how much we had enjoyed the dip.

Wed, Aug 2

After intending to get up nice and early for a change, I got up after Jim and Paul had left to go down town i.e. 12 o'clock. Decided to go away somewhere for the day. Couldn't all decide on one place to go – headed for Bundoran. Arrived at a little beach at end of Mullaghmore. Weather beautiful. Swam and had fights with 100s of jellyfish. After 7, headed for Bundoran. Had our tea there and went to the amusements. Revived all my childish instincts!

Fri, Aug 4

As our last days in Sligo were approaching, we decided to get out of the house and, due to the bad weather, decided to go to Donegal town. Boys fished, and Mammy, Daddy, Paul and I went round the shops. Daddy offered to buy me a ring but as I was trying one on, the stone fell off! God help Daddy, I really felt sorry for him.

Big wedding in the town – later found out that it was the wedding of the girl who had her 2 legs and 1 arm blown off in the Abercorn Restaurant explosion ...

~~~

We fitted in a final trip to the seaside at Rosses Point where the squalls of driving rain, whipping in off the ocean, persuaded us once and for all that it was time to go home. It had rained on every day of our holiday except one and yet, when the time came for us to pack our bags, no one wanted to leave. It had been so easy to forget about Belfast.

The discovery that the wedding we saw was that of one of the Abercorn victims was a shocking reminder of what we were returning to. Memories of the carnage and devastation in Belfast that March afternoon – which left the young bride maimed for life – flooded back to me. I felt more keenly than ever the contrast between the savagery of life a few hours' drive away and the tranquillity we had enjoyed all week. I began to count out the hours I would have to spend in Belfast before I escaped from it again.

Sun, Aug 6

The day we finally set out for Belfast. Cold and drizzling, in harmony with our moods.

Searched Sligo for a tin of peas – didn't realize they were such precious, rare articles! Had dinner, packed our bags and then had to clean the house. Mammy was meticulous – everything had to be glittering.

Good journey all the way to Augher. Got out for a cup of tea but nowhere was open. Sufficed with 99s. Straight home, no stops.

Plenty of military activity. Horrible sight of Belfast again. Had been an explosion in Kennedy Way just before we arrived. Boy almost killed. Piles of windows blown in – including the two houses on either side of ours – we escaped. Rioting at Casement.

Collected Tito and he was hysterical with joy.

A letter from France, for Elizabeth to go ahead!
Gave it to her, started to pack, bed at 1 a.m.!

Mon, Aug 7

A whole fuss concerned in getting our train tickets
– apparently it is impossible to do so at so late a
date. However the man, a Mr Harris – having pity
on us – gave us the tickets and we promised to
send him a card!

Home and tried to eat dinner, couldn't. Went
to Blackstaff factory and bought table-cloth etc. of
Irish linen for Mme de Marignan. We set out for
station to meet Liz at 5.15.

Had flat-tyre! Panic stations – cursing, tears
etc. Finally, arrived at station late but train also
late, thank God. Got under-14 fares and set out
for Dublin, no time for goodbyes. Uncle Paddy
met us in Connolly Station – train got in one
and a half hours late. Out to Dun Laoghaire, had
tea and went to bed. Can't sleep with excitement
about tomorrow.

~~~

The last-minute, frantic clamour to get on board the Enterprise train meant all my fretting about how I would say goodbye to my family proved to be unnecessary. Liz and I collapsed onto our seats, grateful ironically for the bomb scare that delayed our train's departure. As the porter blew his whistle and the engine chugged out of Great Victoria Street station, I decided that if I didn't see Belfast for another six months, it would still be too soon.

CHAPTER 12

'Cèpes à la bordelaise'

Tues, Aug 8

After an extremely restless night, I woke at 8. Elizabeth and I got up in a hurry – have to be gone for airport by 8.30. Getting really excited now about going away.

Arrived at airport and checked in by 10. Butterflies in my stomach. Scared at first but journey turned out to be very enjoyable. Arrived in Paris at 12.40, temperature was 89 degrees F!

Airport bus to Hotel des Invalides, passes made at us by porters. Taxi to Gare d'Austerlitz, 10 francs – our money is rapidly disappearing! Lunch. Met 2 Americans who bought us orange juice. Chatted for about an hour to them, gave us an address to visit in Arizona. Met an American chess master – the son of a millionaire.

Wandered round Paris. Took photos. Visited Notre Dame. Back for train at 9. Met chess master again and stayed with him till 9.30. Met a girl from N. Ireland. Got a carriage with 2 French fellows – dead nice but couldn't speak English. They got off at Vierzy.

Tried to sleep on carriage benches, still fully dressed. Uncomfortable but got a few snatches of sleep. Don't feel too happy on my first night in France!

~~~

The discomfort of the overnight train journey was eased only by reflecting on the glorious hours we spent in Paris. Stepping onto the tarmac at Orly Airport – a naïve 17-year-old, in navy cotton 'strides' and a navy and yellow skinny-rib jumper – I had scorched in my first blast of continental heat, hotter than I'd ever have imagined possible. It was only when I tried to buy two tickets for the airport bus to the city centre that I realised, with alarm, how little my Sixth Year French classes had prepared me for the rapid-fire exchanges reverberating all around me.

'Est-ce que c'est possible de ... de ... de ....?' I stammered and gesticulated to a dour, uniformed man in the vast, thronged concourse at La Gare d'Austerlitz. I was embarrassed and frustrated that I didn't know the words for 'left luggage lockers'.

By the time we got rid of our bags and escaped into the outside air, I was unnerved and bewildered, and my new navy leather clogs were blistering my bare toes. The onslaught of intense heat, babbling foreign voices, leering men, non-white faces, unfamiliar currency, strange new food smells and a level of traffic noise I had never experienced before, almost overwhelmed me. But it was exhilarating.

In the seven hours we spent in Paris, I was transported from the tense, monochrome world I knew in Belfast to a swirling kaleidoscope of colours and breath-taking images:

the magnificent Notre Dame and iconic Tour Eiffel; the romance of the Seine and the frenetic energy of Place de l'Étoile; elegant avenues bustling with sophisticated, purposeful men and women.

In only the time it took to kick off our shoes and savour an unadventurous 'croque monsieur' outside a café near Les Jardins de Luxembourg, I realised that there was a whole other world, only three hours from Belfast, where people knew little – and cared even less – about our violent, messy and depressing conflict.

We behaved as nature intended two 17-year-olds to behave, let loose in a foreign city for the first time. We didn't have to concern ourselves about the religious, political or cultural affiliations of the strangers we talked to. We rose above the language barrier to flirt with two charming young French men, without a word of English between them. They were just 'foreigners' and we were smitten.

By the time we stretched out – hot and fully-dressed – on hard wooden benches for the 350-mile overnight train journey to Agen, we had spent most of the £20 we each brought with us to last three weeks. Three hours into our 10-hour journey to the South West, I was jolted out of my restless slumber by a screech of brakes as the train ground to a halt in Clermont-Ferrand. Peering into the midnight darkness, through a cacophony of shrill whistles, banging doors, clanging engines and raised voices, I heard a vendor calling out, *Des sandwichs? Des sandwichs?* Disorientated and hungry, we calculated that we could just about afford to buy one crusty cheese and ham baguette between us.

Wed, Aug 9

Arrived in Agen at 7 in the morning, bleary-eyed after night of broken sleep. Slept all night stretched out on railway seats. No sign of anyone like Mme de Marignan, then a boy came over and introduced himself as Antoine de Marignan – a pleasant surprise!

Bought us a breakfast of black coffee and croissants. Elizabeth and I couldn't stop giggling – hardly understood a word he said. Brought us on a tour of Agen, then put us both on the train for Toulouse, after which I had to go on to Bayonne alone. Roasting hot day – had to stand on full journey to Toulouse.

Waited for Liz's host family in the 'buffet', however they arrived one and a half hours late. Bought us 'dejeuner' and put me on the train for Bayonne. Shared a carriage with a family of Indians – couldn't speak to them! Confusion over train's destination.

Met at Bayonne by 3 de Marignans. I couldn't understand them, they seemed giddy and I didn't like them. Arrived at their holiday house in a wood and had a cup of 'tea'. Dinner. Went to bed at 9. Not happy on my first night here. Things might look up, I hope.

~~~

Twenty-year-old Antoine was gruff and good-looking in a rural, French way. It came as a shock when he informed me that the rest of his family had left for their holiday home in a seaside town called Seignosse, in Les Landes. I had scarcely the money to cover the extra rail fare and was terrified of going on by myself. How I wished Liz was travelling all the way with me. As I settled alone into the long, unexpected, westward journey to the Atlantic coast, the confidence I had felt with her by my side quickly evaporated.

My nervousness was compounded by the overbearing high-spiritedness of the de Marignan teenagers who collected me at the station in Bayonne. 17-year-old Anne spoke little English, but what she and her older sister lacked in linguistic skills, they made up for in sophistication and confidence. As 19-year-old Marie-Joseph whisked us off in the dark – in her new, pale blue Citroen 2CV – to Seignosse 15 miles away, I found myself incapable of uttering even a single, meaningful word. Contrary to all my protestations in Sligo a couple of weeks earlier that I wasn't a child, I was feeling very much out of my depth in such an 'adult' and unfamiliar environment. I was filled with dread at the prospect of having to help these girls and their blond-haired, younger brother, Christophe, speak English in exchange for my three-week stay.

My host for my visit to France, Madame de Marignan, looked more Irish than French. She was tall and broad-shouldered, with reddish hair and freckles, and seemed to be apologising for not meeting me in Agen as originally planned. She spoke scarcely a word of English but thoughtfully offered me *une tasse de thé* as soon as I arrived in the family's summer home. I didn't know what to do when she presented a huge, white cup with no handles – a bowl – containing very hot water and a sachet of Lipton's tea with a string attached.

With the eyes of her sons, daughters and their cousins all trained upon me in the tiny white-tiled kitchen, I waited until the bowl was cool enough to lift. Then, feeling bad-mannered and self-conscious, I drank enough of the insipid amber liquid to appear appreciative. I was away from home for less than two days and already my courage was failing.

Thurs, Aug 10

Before I fell asleep, Anne told me that she and Marie-Joseph would be going to Villeneuve today. I was rather pleased to hear this, I must admit.

Had breakfast – or at least, what they called breakfast – coffee and bread.

Listened to records for a while, plenty of English ones. Then Anne, Marie-Joseph, Francois and Antoine (unfortunately) left to go to Villeneuve to look after sheep, because Monsieur de Marignan etc. are going to Lourdes.

Went to beach, very hot. Everyone went in for a swim. I made the excuse of having no swimsuit. Mme drove me back to the house for Marie-Joseph's. I made excuse of cold!

After dinner in the evening – very enjoyable, good fun – I came to bed at 9.30. Feel happier now.

Fri, Aug 11

Fierce thunder storms all night – made house shake. I was quite frightened at times. Managed to get up at 8. At breakfast, ate piles of bread, enjoyed it. Then Monsieur de Marignan, and the other aunt and uncle, whose names I don't know, all left for Lourdes. Really enjoying myself now with so few here.

Went to the beach at Seignosse again. <u>Again</u> I made the excuse of water being too cold. Came home at 6, had a shower and had a lovely dinner. Stormy.

Sat, Aug 12

Got up when I heard church bells chiming 7. Dressed, made bed and had breakfast of Lipton's tea and petit pain – enjoyable for a change. Did the dishes – consisted of washing and drying six bowls!

Went to Hossegor. Wrote postcards and posted them. Took a photo of the back of the house, started to write up my diary for last few days.

After dinner, go to swimming pool. Roasting hot. Made excuse of a headache! Had dinner, very enjoyable. Bed before 10. Storms.

PS – Mme showed me how to make and toss 'une salade' – not like home!

~~~

It certainly wasn't like home. Back in Ireland I had no hesitation in plunging into the icy Atlantic waters around Sligo or braving the Irish Sea near Cooley. In Seignosse though, on a magnificent, white, sandy beach and surrounded by scores of chic, bronzed, bikini-clad holidaymakers, my courage deserted me.

After seeing how beautifully tanned and shapely the older de Marignan girls were, I didn't have the confidence to undress before my hosts. Apart from not possessing the 'assets' required to enhance the old-fashioned, borrowed two-piece I had brought from home, I was reluctant to expose my blue-white, Belfast skin to the French public any more than was necessary. I told Madame de Marignan that I hadn't brought any swimwear with me and buried my frumpish bikini in the bottom of my suitcase where it remained undiscovered for the rest of my stay.

With Anne and Marie-Joseph gone back to their home in the country for a few days, I was able to relax sufficiently to savour my new surroundings. I became accustomed to closing the dark wooden shutters to block out the searing heat and brilliant sunshine. I enjoyed sweeping out the fine white sand and the dried out pine needles which I and the younger children, Christophe, Fanny and Aliette, carried in to the cool marble floors on our bare feet. I looked forward to the almost ritual *goûter* every afternoon: snacks of the freshest, crustiest white bread I had ever tasted; smeared decadently with chocolate spread or creamy, white, unsalted butter. And I delighted in the 'mischief' of dunking the crusts in milky, hot chocolate to soften them.

My ears gradually became attuned to the new vocabulary, the southern French accents and the nuances of the foreign language. I never quite succeeded, though, in shaking off a feeling of physical and cultural inferiority when faced with the sophistication, worldliness and 'savoir faire' of the others, especially those around my own age.

I stared helplessly at Madame, with my hands hanging

idly by my sides, when she commanded me to *fixer la salade*.
I looked in wonderment at the large glass bowl, piles of green
leaves, clumps of garlic, and bottles of golden liquid which
she set down on the table in front of me. What was I to do
with them? Back at home, a 'salad' was a delicious, colourful
array of lettuce, tomato, hard-boiled egg, warm potato salad
and ham – with a dollop of thick, yellow salad cream on
the side – which my mother laid out for our tea on summer
evenings. In Seignosse, I was at a loss.

As Madame patiently taught me how to mix a dressing
and assemble the leaves – before taking my nervous hands
and showing me how to 'tumble' the greens with large
wooden servers – I felt gauche and uncultured. I imagined
what my family would have made of such a 'salad'.

My parents and brothers often came into my head as I
lazed on the crowded beach, eyes closed against the blistering
sun. I thought about them again at night, as I lay between
cool white sheets in my shuttered bedroom with the warm
breeze rustling through the lofty pine trees surrounding the
house.

The only newspaper which came into the household, *Le
Sud Ouest*, neglected to mention Northern Ireland affairs
and no one in the family showed any interest in talking or
finding out about the subject.

As time wore on, I was relieved that no one asked me
about the Troubles. I didn't have the French vocabulary to
enlighten anyone about the situation and its complexities.
I concentrated instead on compiling a list at the back of my
diary of all the new French words and phrases I came across,
terms I didn't ever expect to use in the normal course of

St Dominic's French classes: *un ivrogne* (a drunkard), *une soirée déguisée* (fancy-dress), *un torchon* (a drying cloth), and many more.

I learned to my embarrassment that *Je suis pleine*, a direct translation of 'I am full', was *not* how one declined the offer of more food. The extent of my mortification – when Madame quietly explained to me that I had announced 'I am pregnant (or drunk)', instead of 'I've had enough to eat' – was matched only by the degree of hilarity that my innocent declaration provoked among the rest of the family.

Tues, Aug 15

Holy Day of Obligation, so we have to go to 11 o'clock Mass, here in Seignosse. Put on my pink suit and a pair of tights. Very conscious of wearing tights – everybody looks at you! Not too bad today – dull but warm.

Played games – I couldn't say anything because they were all gabbling away in French. Went out for a walk with Fanny and Aliette to try and see pheasants again but all we found were frogs.

Thurs, Aug 17

Opened the shutters on a beautiful day – great to see it. All set to go to the sea. I went to the Post Office and bought as many stamps as I could afford – still short 1.80 francs.

Sat in the sun, really hot. Decided to go to the beach at 2 – all except Christophe. Took some *courage to take off my dress. I knew I was white but didn't realise <u>how</u> white! Embarrassing! Water lovely, tried to get sunburned.*

Returned at 5. Just in when Anne and Antoine arrived on motorbike. After dinner, carried on with Christophe as usual. Watched him and Antoine playing chess. Antoine is really nice.

~~~

After enduring eight full days of blistering heat and sweaty discomfort I finally summoned up enough courage to remove my clothes and rush into the cooling, Atlantic surf in a swimsuit borrowed from Marie-Joseph.

I was starting to relax into the French way of life and Antoine's arrival that evening, from the family's home in the country, added a frisson of excitement. His reappearance confirmed my earlier impression of him being quite attractive but withdrawn. Tall and thin, with heavy features and dark, curly hair, he spoke what little English he had with a strong, sensuous French accent.

I had only spent a couple of hours in Antoine's company on the day he met Liz and me off the train from Paris. But after observing him for an evening in Seignosse, this romance-starved West Belfast teenager found herself smitten by his brown eyes, guttural tones and Gallic charm.

Sat, Aug 19

Woke up to a beautiful summer's day today, in contrast to yesterday's rain. Postman came with letters, one from Mammy and one from Daddy. I was really pleased to get them, accompanied by

£10. I nearly died but I'm determined not to spend it all. Wrote back to them immediately and posted the letter.

We all then went to the beach. Brought a picnic with us but everything we ate was full of sand. Fierce wind made everything very unpleasant. Got a bit of sunburn but nothing exceptional.

At 8, we (Mme, Aliette, Antoine and Christophe) went to game of Pelote Basque, area finals for Seignosse fête. Came home after 11, because of the cold. Went straight up to read my letters again and then bed.

Belfast, Aug 15

My dear Eimear,

We were delighted to get your two letters. Your second one was much brighter than your first and seemed to suggest that you were settling down and beginning to enjoy your visit. It was a pity you had the extra expense of the journey to the seaside house. It must indeed have left you short of cash. However, it does not matter and I am enclosing £10 in case you are short.

Things are much the same here. Two young Provos, a boy and a girl, blew themselves up trying to plant a bomb at a Cash and Carry. Fifty-six more internees were released last week, including Jim Sullivan and Des O'Hagan. An escape bid by a hundred of them was foiled yesterday when their tunnel, nearly a hundred yards long, collapsed with the heavy rain.

We had an exciting night in Fruithill with the anti-

internment anniversary march. The army blocked
it on the Glen Road, so the marchers filtered down
Kennedy Way, through our gardens, with the soldiers
chasing them hither and thither. They made Casement
Park eventually through the back of the tennis-club
and held their meeting successfully. There is a full-
scale Gaelic football match on the main road outside
Casement every night. Goal posts and all are up.

Mammy is writing to you too, so she'll fill in the
details. This is sent from the office,

Love from all, God Bless, Daddy.

Belfast, Aug 15

My dear Eimear,
First of all, Daddy and I want to congratulate you on
your Spanish. You will be delighted with the result. Got
your letters today – the first came in the morning post,
the second one at lunch hour. We are pleased to hear
that you have arrived safely and that you're enjoying
yourself. I'm sure you were tired after your journey.
Sorry to hear that you had the extra journey to pay,
but we are sending it on.

Daddy has gone to his usual meeting tonight. I
went down to see Aunt Alice and Josephine. They still
have their bags packed. Things are much the same as
when you left.

We had consternation here on Wednesday night
last. The parade to Casement Park was stopped at the
Glen Road and the whole of A'town was ringed off.
The crowd – about 2,000 – went through the Falls

Park, ended up in Fruithill and charged over our back gardens by the dozens. The soldiers couldn't understand where they'd come from.

We had a most handsome Swedish reporter running up and down the kitchen – and we locked the doors to make sure the soldiers wouldn't get through. You would really have enjoyed it, but not at the time. It was frightening.

Two more Catholics were murdered at the weekend in the Oldpark area, so really nothing has changed …

Two soldiers were killed at Casement Park today, one was the officer in charge. They are still in the schools.

There was an old man found dead on the Glen Road today. He had been there for days but died from natural causes. Six cats attacked the soldiers (sent in to recover his body) and they had to <u>shoot</u> the lot of them!

Daddy has just come in after being 'frisked' outside. He laughed at it. No more news for now. Will write in a day or so again. Give our regards to the family and thank them again for having you,

Lots of love, from Mammy, Daddy and the four gentlemen, xxx

I read and re-read the letters before putting them back into their envelopes and tucking them safely inside my diary – along with a newspaper cutting my mother had sent about the six cats being shot. I tried hard to picture the excitement there must have been as soldiers and marchers charged through our garden, and I wished I had been there.

I smiled at my mother's description of the boys as 'the four gentlemen' and I began to miss them desperately. The day the mail arrived was Jim's eleventh birthday; I pictured them all sitting down that evening to a special tea, with one of my mother's delicious home-made birthday cakes.

The postmarks on the two envelopes – as well as my parents' mention of the letters I sent when I arrived – confirmed that our exchanges had taken four days to reach their respective destinations. Our 'news' was already old and out of date but at least I had the comfort of knowing that nothing had happened to anyone close to me.

The de Marignan family, meanwhile, began preparing to return to their beloved home in the country – the impressively named *La Domaine de Jampau*. When Antoine and Marie-Joseph proudly handed me photographs of *La Domaine*, it was easy to understand their excitement at the prospect of returning there after eight weeks by the coast.

Home was a huge, elegant, old house – bathed in sunlight and situated on the crest of a gentle hill – overlooking acres of sun-parched, undulating countryside. The sunshine set the red-tiled roof and dove-grey shutters in soft contrast against the white stone walls. It looked stately and serene but, given a choice, I would happily have opted to stay in the small – and now familiar – seaside house in Seignosse.

Every night, after writing up my diary, I put a tick through the date. I had just reached the mid-point in my stay – twelve days over and another twelve to go – and became unsettled at the thought of being uprooted again and thrown into such unaccustomed grandeur.

Sun, Aug 20

A sweltering hot day, thank goodness. I've no traces of sunburn yet and we're leaving here next Thursday! Sat in the garden and nearly burned the knees off myself. At 11, we went to Mass – very long – and I couldn't understand a word of the sermon. Went to l'Étang Blanc – a beautiful place. Hired a rowing boat and Antoine, Fanny, Mme and I went out in it for an hour. Great fun, really enjoyable, then left to go to the sea – the lake was a bit too dirty to swim in.

Antoine came with us. I really like him and enjoyed his company today. Fierce wind was blowing at the sea – couldn't go in for a swim it was so cold (the water). I got sunburned all over in spite of the wind. Antoine asked me if I wanted to go to a dance in town fête. Too tired. Sat and talked, played cards.

Mon, Aug 21

A blistering hot day, hottest so far. At 10, Anne asked me to go to Capbreton with her by bicycle – she'd got a second bicycle from somewhere. In spite of the heat, we set out – eight and three quarter mile journey! Bathed and lay in the sun for a while. I sunbathed but with all my clothes on because of the fierce wind!

Came home at 5pm. Helped to prepare dinner – apple tart, but "Ma, how I miss your home cookin"– no pastry on top and what pastry there was, wasn't cooked!

Went to a corrida at 9 with Christophe, Anne and Antoine. Bullfight but comic parts with amateurs. Really hilarious, followed by fireworks display.

Tues. Aug 22

Woke up again to a sweltering hot day – all set to go to the beach and I'm actually looking forward to it for a change. Anne and Antoine to join us later on.

Went in for a swim and got soaked, surprising for me! Lay and sunbathed and the result was that when I came home at 6, I was like a lobster and could hardly move at all.

Suggestions of going out on the bicycles were made but after last night's late bedtime and the open air all day today, I was dead beat.

Had said 'no' to Bayonne!!!

~~~

I had been thrilled but virtually struck dumb when, out of the blue, Antoine invited me to take a trip on the back of his motorbike. His mother made it clear to him that she wasn't too happy about his suggestion but she needn't have worried. I was too much of an ingénue, too timid, too gauche and too overwhelmed to accept this offer of adventure.

Lying in bed that night I imagined the story I could have told on my return to school if I had said 'Oui' to Bayonne instead. I would have been the envy of all my friends as I recounted, in glorious detail, how I jumped on the back of a handsome Frenchman's motorbike, wrapped my arms tightly around his waist and sped, in glorious sunshine, twenty-five miles along the coast to Bayonne in the Basque country – and to who knows what else.

It could have been my first holiday romance but instead, I was left thinking, 'Imagine if ...'.

Wed, Aug 23

Hardly slept all night due to terrible toothache. Still hadn't gone by this morning – face numb! Beautiful day again. Have headache – can't face going out in the sun at all.

Wash clothes for going to Villeneuve tomorrow. Hoped and prayed for a letter from someone – none at all.

During dinner, and for one and a half hours afterwards, Antoine and Christophe carried on, telling me all sorts of yarns about Jampau.

Thurs, Aug 24

Anne stayed in bed late, in bad form because we are leaving Seignosse. Felt sorry for Antoine – left on his own although he says he's coming to Jampau on Sunday.

Arrived at Jampau at 12.30 – 5 letters waiting for me, including one from Sr. Karen – she's dead nice – I was delighted to get her letter. After dinner, stayed in room reading letters, having decided I no longer like the family or the place. However at 4, went out with Anne and Aliette to the plum

orchard – ate plums till I thought I would burst!
    *Then M de M came and we went to look for
mushrooms – cèpes – none, because of the heat.
Saw all his land – acres, and 250 sheep.*
    *Home is magnificent, half renovated. Beautiful
Louis XIV furniture etc. Really <u>do</u> like the family,
M de M. especially.*

∼∼∼

La Domaine de Jampau was unlike anywhere I had ever
been. As soon as our car crunched to a halt on the wide,
gravel driveway, I stepped out into the scalding midday heat
to survey the sweeping landscape. On one side, scorched
fields dotted with sheep stretched as far as the eye could see,
before disappearing in a haze of heat; on the other, row after
row of plum trees, laid out with geometric precision, bowed
low under the weight of the deep-purple *prunes* for which
the Agen area was renowned.

Monsieur de Marignan, who was small and stout with
a thick head of jet black hair, led me through heavy, oak,
double-doors into the welcome chill of a wide, dark hallway.
After the white glare of the sunlight outside, it took my eyes
a few seconds to adjust and to absorb the splendour of my
new surroundings.

Countless pieces of stout antique furniture – cabinets,
sideboards, chairs and tables – graced each of the shuttered,
high-ceilinged rooms. Ornately-framed landscapes adorned
the walls, and a rich wine-coloured brocade throw was
draped over an ancient chaise longue at the top of the
wide staircase. Madame brought me along a narrow, dark
corridor to the room I would share with Anne, and indicated

ominously that under no circumstances was I to venture any further along the narrow passageway. I felt like Jane Eyre in Thornfield Hall until Anne explained that the back of the house was undergoing renovation and was in a dangerous condition.

Not for the first time I wished my parents had been there to share the experience. They would have loved the ancient, wealthy tradition of the house, its understated elegance and the absence of vulgar ostentation.

The backlog of Belfast letters which had been set aside on a table in the hall, awaiting my arrival, reminded me that my holiday would soon be over.

Belfast, August 21

Dear Eimear,

I hope you are having a good time and the people are very kind to you. I believe from one of your letters that the food you get is not really nice but you have still got a plate of chips waiting for you when you come home.

The soldiers have moved out of 12 schools but they are still going to stay in 3 schools, one of which is our school. The soldiers have moved into 6 classrooms and are setting up temporary mobile huts for the girls. The soldiers have been digging up the tennis courts around the school and putting up high wire. The army were issued with a new riot bullet. It is made of plastic and is able to disable you.

Daddy is at his usual meeting tonight. I have just heard some more news. Because of the soldiers in our school, Brother Andrew and Sister Mona have agreed not to send us back to school.

I hope you enjoy the rest of your holiday,

Love Aidan, xxx

Belfast, August 21

My dear Eimear,

We were watching out for a letter from you at the weekend but have just got the boys' card and Jimmy's card this morning … You seem to be having a wonderful time. Make the best of it...

Things are much the same as they were here … The soldiers are in the gardens every night. Auntie May came home on Friday. I baked her some buns on Saturday night and brought them up to her, but I nearly fell over a 'blackie' in the garden and dropped the buns with fright!

Your little friend Carol came down to see us on Saturday. They have got a house but there are still some refugees in La Salle. The troops are still in the schools. Two more men were shot dead but we didn't know them …

You'll never feel it till you're coming home, so enjoy every minute of it and DON'T be buying presents. Any letters we write, we will send them to your country place in case you have left the seaside.

Thank Mme de M for all her kindness. I'll write again on Wednesday. Daddy is at a meeting nearly every night.

All my love, Mammy.

The longer I went without hearing from my parents, the more I missed them. But now, having been assured again that all was well, I wanted to settle into my new environment and enjoy the last six days of my holiday.

In the midst of such splendour and tranquillity, it was impossible to visualise conditions back in Belfast. I found it easy to imagine the smell and taste of the home-made buns which my mother mentioned and to savour the prospect of the home-made chips which Aidan had tantalisingly dangled before my senses – but I couldn't visualise British Army soldiers encamped in local schools, including my brother's. I thought about the same school when it was filled with refugees, including Carol and her family, at the start of July. I wondered what *she* would have made of *La Domaine de Jampau.*

Fri, Aug 25

My first full day at Jampau. M de M looked after me and made me my Typhoo tea – of which I took three cups, although I could hardly drink it. He asked me to give Christophe an English lesson – this I did for one hour. He was very willing to work.

I have never in my life felt anything like the heat – how I wished I was at Seignosse again. Collected plums in the orchard but due to the heat, returned and stayed in my bedroom. Male cousin (about 19) arrived – I didn't really want to meet him. When he shook hands with me, he had a certain unpleasant look in his eyes …

Mon, Aug 28

I didn't waken till after Anne started to play her transistor.

Went to a farm with Anne to get milk – half dead after it. Went on bikes, hills all the way! Roasting hot, gathered hay etc. Dead beat with the sun.

A cousin of Anne's arrived. I didn't really like her – nor did Anne! Came up to bedroom after a while and read the letters I got this morning.

Belfast, Aug 23

Dear Eimear,

Thank you very much for your birthday card. Everyone is well, including the mutt. Last night, someone broke our light. We think it was the army. I hope to see you soon.

Today a soldier was killed when his turret scout car went over a mine in Crossmaglen. Nothing else to do with the troubles has happened as far as I know, except there are some explosions here and there as there always have been. But yesterday there were nine people killed at an explosion on the border.

Well I think that's about all for now, Love Jim xxx

Even by Northern Ireland's standards, ten people killed in one day was shocking, yet I had seen no reports of what had happened. It seemed that no one in the hot, still languor of south west France was interested.

My father's as yet unopened letter would tell me in full, I expected, exactly what had happened at the border and, no doubt, elsewhere. Under such circumstances, it was difficult to begin reading the letter with anything other than a sense of apprehension.

Belfast, Aug 24

My dear Eimear,

You will recognise the inferior Post Office paper on which I am writing, but it is lightweight and very useful for Air Mail. We were delighted to get your letters and learn all the news about your visit. It must be lovely. Would they take an old fellow like myself next year, instead of a boy of 15 or 16?

The swimming in France must be lovely, from your account of it. Anyhow, enjoy it for you will have a busy year ahead. You must tell me when you get home how you find the difference between St Dominic's French and France's French.

I suppose you read about the awful tragedy at Newry Customs Post. Nine people were killed, including the three men planting the bomb. There were three Customs men among the dead.

The assassinations continue. Fr. Murphy and I were to see General Tuzo about them last Saturday. We prepared a big map showing where the killings had taken place etc. At the last minute Fr. Murphy had to go on his own but I wasn't sorry …

No more internees have been released because the bombs are going off again.

There was a very big one yesterday in Linenhall Street which caused a very big fire. Chester Park Hotel has been blown up again, also Catherwoods and several other places. So, if the bombs continue, there will be no release of internees – and if the internees are still in, the SDLP will not attend the talks in September. They also look like being a flop.

The troops are remaining in St Genevieve's School and I think parents will not allow their children to go back until they vacate it. It looks like another spot of trouble. And of course, the soldiers are still in Casement Park. There will always be trouble there. It was either a stupid decision – or a malicious one – putting them there in the first place ...

I suppose by the time you get this letter you will be preparing for home. Do not think of bringing any presents. They are too dear and too worrying, trying to decide what to bring. Tito, incidentally, was 'barking' for you and says hurry home.

Love and God bless, Daddy.

Tucking my final batch of letters into the case I had started to pack for going home, I wondered whether the time might possibly come when, apart from seeing my family, I would be glad to be back in Belfast. I doubted it.

Tues, Aug 29

Half the family took the cat to the vet. Verified that his shoulder was broken – after Marie-Joseph had flung him out the window for licking the custard!

Read in my bedroom till Mme asked me to help collect the 'prunes' with her and Antoine. This passed the time very pleasantly until 12. Was getting on great with Antoine. Had a beautiful dinner, it was a real laugh. I really like Marie-Joseph now. She was inquiring about Shetland jumpers and I told her I would get her one.

Marie-Joseph went to a Fancy Dress ball with Philippe. Gave me lovely earrings.

Wed, Aug 30

I went up to the plum orchards to 'ramasser des prunes' with Antoine and Mme. Really had a great time. Anne was up when we returned to the house for dinner, at which the threat I have been faced with materialised – 'cuisses des grenouilles'! However, they were lovely.

Had 'dîner' – a beautiful meal 'Cèpes à la Bordelaise' followed by glace d'ananas. I haven't eaten so much since I arrived.

After it, took photos. M de M gave me some to take home with me, showed me other family photos and Antoine gave me details of how to get around Toulouse. Said goodbye to Aliette and Fanny – awfully sentimental. I know I'm going to cry tomorrow. Packed bags.

~~~

When, on my second last evening in Villeneuve, Marie-Joseph appeared in a floor-length, navy velvet dress, it was hard to see her as the same girl who – less than eight hours earlier – had hurled a defenceless black cat through the kitchen window in a fit of violent rage. I couldn't believe what I was seeing and hearing as the cat, screeching for its life, flew through the air onto the path outside.

I was equally stunned when Monsieur de Marignan ushered all of us into another huge room which I hadn't been in previously and, with a flourish, produced a key to a safe concealed in a wood-panelled wall beside the huge fireplace. He opened a jewellery box to reveal a sapphire and diamond necklace – a family heirloom – which he fastened proprietorially around Marie-Joseph's slender neck.

In my three weeks away from home, my emotions were aroused and my senses inundated as never before. Sights, sounds, tastes and textures I had never experienced previously, bombarded me. For my final dinner, we gathered around a huge, mahogany table for a wonderful meal cooked by Monsieur de Marignan and subsequently served from an array of dishes and silver salvers laid out on an antique sideboard.

Rounding off the meal, I struggled to identify the flavour of the rich, creamy, home-made *glace d'ananas* which he passed around. My taste buds were thrown into confusion: they recognised it as ice cream but unlike any flavour I had ever tasted back in Ireland. Monsieur de Marignan grew increasingly frustrated, trying to describe to me, in French, what the key ingredient was. It was only after tormenting myself all evening that I finally made a connection with the tinned fruit cocktail we were occasionally treated to at home. I had never come across fresh pineapple before, let alone tasted home-made pineapple ice cream.

Thurs, Aug 31

*Antoine and others came in to say goodbye at 6.10
a.m. I was still in bed, really embarrassed as I had
wanted to say goodbye properly. After a hurried
farewell, I set out for Agen with Anne and Marie-
Joseph. With tears choking me, they saw me off.*

*After a boring one and a half hour train journey
to Toulouse, I disembarked. No one to meet me.
I waited and waited in terror, getting plenty of
suggestive looks. Finally, Lizzie and her family
arrived. At 9 p.m., half dead, headed for station.
After big row with French woman who wanted
whole compartment for her family, we settled
down with 7 others to 'sleep'. Not a hope! A wee
man fed us at 12.10 with croissants and cheese.
Blind with sleep but can't. Wish I was home.*

CHAPTER 13

'Dirty, horrible, backward, dark Belfast'

As the overnight train to Paris rattled noisily through the impenetrable darkness of the French countryside, its incessant, juddering 'chug-chug, chug-chug' lulled me into a limbo that was neither sleep nor wakefulness. A piercing squeal from one of the six cranky children squeezed in beside us jolted me out of my fitful dozing; a sudden, shrill screech of brakes as we rounded a bend startled me, sending my heart racing.

As mile after mile sped by, ugly images of Belfast flashed into my mind, shattering my attempts to reflect on my sunlit holiday. The prospect of settling into my last year of school and the miserable, dark evenings of another strife-filled northern winter filled me with dread. I couldn't wait to see my family again but Belfast was the last place I wanted to be.

The crowded compartment was uncomfortably hot and stuffy; its suffocating fug was made worse by the reek from the kilo of sweaty Gruyère cheese which Liz insisted on buying for her father at the Carrefour supermarket in Toulouse. Its stench made me feel queasy and lingered heavily around us for more than twenty-four hours, during train, taxi and plane journeys.

Fri / Sat, Sept 1, 2

After not getting as much as half an hour's sleep last night, we arrived in 'Gay Paree' at 7.00 a.m. Tried to get taxi for Hotel des Invalides, but taxi-man took us for a ride pretending he didn't know where Hotel des Invalides was. Furious – mind you, that's not surprising, considering we had no sleep.

Arrived at airport where we met Anne Diver, Kathleen McCallion, Brid Brennan and 2 Dublin girls. Had a brilliant journey home on the plane.

At Dublin, confusion over our luggage and as a result we missed the 2.30 p.m. train home. Had dinner, exhausted. Couldn't get through to home on the phone. Got 5.30 p.m. train – feel as if I'll never recover.

When we arrived in dirty, horrible, backward, dark Belfast, tried to get a taxi – but Daddy appeared on the scene with Mammy and the boys. I was thrilled to see them.

Felt guilty at having no presents – will never do it again. Gave them the bottle of wine – 'eau de vie' – nearly knocked Daddy out! Gordons came up and they had a great night – one would have thought they were all pissed!!

Came to my own bed, at last, at 1.00 a.m. Nearly died – didn't regain consciousness today until 11.30. Told that Auntie Jo and family are coming. They arrived at 1.30. After dinner, went out and collected my skirt from drycleaner's and got a new pair of shoes for school.

Did tour of Andersonstown and all West Belfast. Shocked at conditions of occupied schools. Like a war-zone.

～～～

I surfaced, befuddled and disorientated, from the deepest sleep I had enjoyed in weeks. The woodchip wallpaper, the posters on the wall and the sewing machine on the table in the corner gradually helped me to get my bearings. Familiar sounds washed over me: the soft murmur of my parents and brothers chatting in the kitchen below me; Tito barking at the back door; and the radio on – as always – tuned in, I calculated, for the 12 o'clock BBC news.

I recognised the sound of the Saracen armoured-cars well before I drew back the curtains and saw them cruising along Kennedy Way, rifle barrels projecting menacingly through narrow slits in their sides; the unmistakable drone, then the loud slow revving of their engines as they circled the roundabout to accelerate up the hill.

The previous night, on our way home from Great Victoria Street station, my parents began to update me on what had happened while I was away. They were also impatient to hear about France. As I started to regale them with tales of Marie-Joseph breaking the cat's shoulder, of eating frogs' legs and gathering armfuls of plums in scorching weather, my father took a shortcut across Barrack Street on to the Falls Road. The street lights were extinguished as usual but a flashing torchlight, cutting through the darkness, signalled that we were approaching an army checkpoint.

He switched off the headlights and eased the car forward gently. We knew the routine. My mother reminded us all to keep quiet as a soldier – with his face blackened – approached the driver's side. Royal Green Jackets. My father wound down his window. Not a word passed between the two as the soldier, with his SLR balanced on his hip, shone his torch on the five of us squeezed into the back of the Cortina.

'OK, mate,' he snapped. 'Drive on. Keep your lights off.' We relaxed and allowed ourselves to breathe out again. I knew I was home.

As we drove up the Falls Road, I learned that more than fifty people were killed across the North in August. I was shocked. More than forty of them lost their lives during the three and a half weeks I was away: Catholics and Protestants, Englishmen and Irishmen, IRA members, loyalists, security force members and civilians. With the exception of the few incidents that were mentioned in the letters sent from home, I was unaware of the scale of the ongoing carnage just, it seemed, like the rest of the world. Nothing, absolutely nothing, had changed.

I was pleased that for a couple of hours after I arrived home, my parents and their closest friends surrendered themselves to the delights of French country produce as they downed with gusto a bottle of *eau-de-vie*, distilled from plums grown on the magnificent de Marignan estate. The eye-watering potency of the attractively packaged and innocent-looking 'fruit juice' sent home by my hosts as a gift caught all of them by surprise.

I thought about Anne, freed from the burden of having to speak to me in slow, simple French every morning, flinging open the grey wooden shutters of our room and letting the first blast of early sunshine and heat flood in. She would watch the last traces of early morning mist disappearing over the hills, where her father's sheep were grazing contentedly, and would probably bemoan the fact, as she did most days, that she was no longer by the sea in Seignosse.

I suddenly understood what my father had long maintained: if you had a good imagination, you could easily dream up a holiday and convince yourself that you had really experienced it. However, the welcome glow of my suntan and the sun-bleached hairs on my arms, proved to me that I had been to another world.

Sun, Sept 3

We all got up and went to 11 Mass. Church area full of soldiers, obviously trying to catch somebody on way in to Mass.

Feel great now due to tan and I know I look well – sure it will soon all disappear. Weather had been beautiful before Mass but now it has become very dull and cool. We had a lovely dinner and I'm gradually getting into the ways of Irish life again! 2 explosions (done by Prods) this morning to make sure of that!

Army were here again diverting traffic away from a protest up the road about schools' occupations.

Got a few things ready for school tomorrow – not looking forward to it.

Mon, Sept 4

Dead beat and the thought of school nearly killed me. However, got up and went in looking very spruce! Met everyone again and compared sunburn! Got half day, thank goodness. It's queer to be Higher 6th now – as Sister Virgilius says, 'the elite of the school'.

Arrived home and nearly died when I saw a Saracen tank parked at our gate. Came round the back and found what I thought was half the British Army in the back garden. A .38 revolver had been found at the back and army spent from 10.30 till 2.30 p.m. investigating and taking it away. All sorts of captains and colonels in kitchen!

~~~

I levelled my eyes on our garage roof, determined not to make eye contact with any of the leering squaddies, not much older than me, hunkered down on the pathway to our back door. Quivering with embarrassment and self-consciousness, I endured their sullen, silent stares as I walked the length of the tarmacked path.

More of them were positioned in our backyard, framing their eyes with their hands and pressing them against the windows to peer into our living room; others were poking through my mother's well-tended shrubs with their rifle-butts and trampling through her flower beds. Without speaking, and with my heart thumping, I squeezed past a soldier standing on the steps and blocking the back-door, only to find another three inside questioning my mother about the revolver's discovery. Within the confines of our kitchen, the male English voices, the battle fatigues, the side arms and SLRs assumed terrifying proportions and dwarfed everything else in the room.

Later that day, I flicked through a copy of *The Sunday News* which my father kept for me and came across a half-page article bearing the triumphalist headline – in inch-and-a-half high letters – 'How the West Was Tamed'. It included a map of Andersonstown, with photographs of the eight army encampments which now encircled our area: Casement Park; Andersonstown Barracks; the three schools which the soldiers had taken over; and three purpose-built bases which they named Fort Monagh, Silver City and Fort Apache. I pasted it inside the back cover of my scrapbook and, in the days that followed, witnessed the full impact of the Army occupation.

It seemed as though the 4,000 extra troops who were flown in for Operation Motorman had all been sent to West Belfast. Silent, shadowy figures, with their faces blackened and rifles cocked, moved stealthily around Fruithill; lurking in gateways and crouching under our windows at night. They patrolled the streets round the clock, stopping and questioning pedestrians, spread-eagling young men against walls and interrogating drivers at vehicle checkpoints. My father showed me newspaper coverage of a dossier he helped to compile for the Citizens' Defence Committee, detailing cases of the 'inhuman and degrading treatment' being meted out by the army in Catholic areas.

Troops were installed in local schools – bunkered down behind mountains of sandbags and masses of barbed wire, camouflage webbing and high, wire fencing. Aidan's school, De La Salle, where Jim was due to start that very week, remained closed after the summer as a result. Soldiers occupied County Antrim's main Gaelic football stadium, Casement Park, preventing young local footballers and hurlers from playing their national games. And, in the meantime, the IRA stepped up its campaign of deadly gun and bomb attacks.

Within three days of coming home, I realised that West Belfast was tenser, more beleaguered and besieged than it had been when I left, a few days after Operation Motorman began. I certainly did not feel any safer.

Wed, Sept 6

I'm bored with school already and I'm only back 2 days. I don't know how I'll survive another year! Wasn't too bad a day, i.e. had plenty of free classes. Got out at 3.00 and came straight home.

Thurs, Sept 7

Army in the street since 7.30 a.m.! 3 people killed last night.

A freezing cold day and I envy Aidan not having to go to school due to army occupation of it. Was late, although I left early – hard to get buses.

Told Elizabeth I wouldn't sit beside her in Mechanics class this year – I couldn't keep up with her. However, she took offence and refused to speak to me. I was really annoyed – I got it all fixed up after school again. Mother Emmanuel says we have to read the Bible extracts for next 2 weeks at Assembly. My morning is Tuesday – I'm dreading it.

Great fun in watching and listening to the news today – 16 men found with piles of guns (Prods) and 26 arrested last night on Shankill. As Daddy says, his head is better!! He bought himself a new suit today.

There's big bombs going off here at the moment. My hands are shaking.

2 men shot dead in rioting on Shankill, UDA and Paras.

Thurs, Sept 14

Electricity is ON.

I was early (or just about) for school – really dreading it because I hadn't any homework done and I only had three free classes. Did my usual lunchtime duties – succeeded in getting someone out against the wall for talking! Nearly died when I saw how she obeyed me!

Came home at usual time but got caught in blast-bombing and shooting at Leeson Street. Thought I would never get a bus. Arrived home at half four, had an early dinner in case electricity went off again but it didn't.

Daddy went to CDC but had to come home early due to shooting at Cupar Street. We heard

it up here. Went on all night, with bombs as well.
Imperial Hotel bombed, a passer-by killed.

~~~

Plus ça change, plus c'est la même chose, or so my new friends in France might have observed. In the twelve days since I came home, that same number of people were killed; their lives taken in equal numbers by the army, the IRA and loyalists. Everyone was claiming a stake in the 'war'.

As the evening newsreaders recited details of the latest horrors or acts of carnage, I felt myself sinking back into the same grim, miserable cycle that had prevailed the previous winter: coming home from school with the light already fading; being soaked and battered by the rain and wind when we had to walk; being told about one death after another, and hearing – day in and day out – about the latest explosions and shootings.

'It's not safe to go there', 'What time will you be home at?', 'Do you really have to go?' I began to fear that my life would stay like that forever. As my spirits flagged, my New Year resolve to update my diary every day weakened. My entries became sporadic. With so much variety and excitement to recount during my stay in France, the August pages of my diary were often too small to contain my jottings. Back home in September, I was finding it increasingly difficult to motivate myself to write with any regularity.

Sat, Sept 16

Boys are all going to the baths today. Mammy
and Daddy have decided to bring Tito to the vet
because of his 'cough' – getting worried. I went too

to sit in the car. Left Tito with the NSPCA – has to stay there till at least Monday.

Came home and had dinner, then I went back down town to buy a pair of indoor sandals for school. Jimmy came too. However, had a terrifying experience – got caught in middle of a UDA parade – 1000s of masked men, scared stiff and came home as soon as possible.

Had to walk through rioting on Falls Road – no buses. Vowed _never_ to go down town again on a Saturday.

Fri, Sept 22

Had intended getting up early to be in time for Assembly but just made it at 5 to 9. I wasn't nervous until I was in front of the microphone and my knees began to shake – over in 30 seconds however.

Got plenty of work done for a change during my free classes. Had to do 'bus-stop duty' after school – a new idea to prevent St. Dominic's savages getting the buses put off the road altogether! Worked all right.

When Daddy came home, he told us Tito was 'being done in'. Mammy began to cry and cried all evening! I came up to study after being round at the shops. Micky O'Neill serving in Murray's Shop – I must admit, I fancy him!

Soldier killed in Crossmaglen.

~~~

It was as though I was living two parallel lives: in one, I was spreading the Word of God before an assembly of a couple of hundred schoolgirls, asserting my authority on a pupil who chatted too much and trying to impose discipline on unruly and disorderly bus queues; in the other, I was fleeing in terror from thousands of loyalists and dodging stones and petrol bombs during Saturday afternoon rioting.

Sometimes I wondered which of the two lives would win out. Part of me was thrilled to have reached Upper Sixth successfully, but another part wondered whether there was any point making plans for more than a week or two ahead. When I voiced my doubts, in moments of despondency and frustration, my father never deviated from his mantra: 'Don't mind what's happening outside. Concentrate on getting your education.'

Our beloved dog Tito, meanwhile, grew more and more unwell. Our tan, black and white mongrel – a cute, short-haired cross between what and what we had no idea – finally fell victim to the nasty, rasping cough that had afflicted him since he stayed in boarding-kennels while we holidayed in Sligo.

We were heartbroken at his going, not least for the entertainment he provided when the army was about. As soon as he spotted soldiers in the vicinity of the house, he leapt up at the nearest window sill, barking furiously like something possessed, until the uniformed intruders went on their way.

Tito's finest hour saw him arriving at the kitchen door, proudly carrying not a sparrow in his mouth – as was his occasional wont – but a cluster of red and white feathers. It was the hackle off a beret belonging to a soldier in the Royal Regiment of Fusiliers. We never found out how or where he claimed it. He spent his final days lying on a rug, listless and lethargic, choking out a deep, dry, throaty cough. Tito's war against the British Army was over.

Mon, Sept 25

At lunchtime, I felt terrible – head splitting and temperature. All set to go home but don't want to neglect my prefect duties at such an early stage!!! Came home on my own – don't know where Oonagh and Eleanor were today.

Sister Eusebius gave out UCCA handbooks today, UCCA forms next Monday. I'm dreading it, for I still haven't decided for definite on social work.

After tea, watched the news – the first day of the Darlington conference. Did homework, watched 'Panorama' – about guess where?!

Daddy came home from CDC at 11. Soldier shot dead, Falls Road.

Tues, Sept 26

Got up slightly earlier than usual, but it didn't help me to leave any earlier for school. Daddy took my watch to leave it in to be fixed – hope it can be. Nearly fell asleep during philosophy. Suzette's birthday – due to my lack of money I can't buy her anything <u>yet</u> ...

... I was almost in tears over dilemma of what

*university to go to. No one in the house can offer
me any assistance – pray for help, only answer.*

*Soldier shot in Derry on Saturday dies. Notes:
Another Catholic found shot dead, on Holywood
Road. Bomb exploded outside club at Unity Flats
– 27 in hospital, obviously UVF job.*

Wednesday, Sept 27

*No coffee for my lunch! Full morning, all morning,
in school today – spent Philosophy class discussing
university next year. Miss Hamilton has put me off
Queen's, although I was not really over-anxious to
go there anyway. But I haven't much choice.*

*Came straight home after school. Was supposed
to stay in to do prefect duty but I couldn't be
bothered. Mammy made a lovely tea – apple-pie
and all included.*

*Watched the news – it lasted till 7pm today due
to the end of the Darlington Talks. Worked till 10.
Am dying with the cold so I intend going to bed
early.*

*Man injured last night at Unity Flats died
today. SAS (i.e. Army plain clothes) shot 1 man
dead at Donegall Road – innocent passer-by.
Catholic teenager killed by UDA.*

Fri, Sept 29

*I went into school very reluctantly today – found
Sr. Karen in very bad mood, so I didn't want to
cross her path!*

After school we were told that there was 'a bit of trouble' down the Falls Road and to avoid it if possible. But when I was going home, Mrs McGlade called me in to ask me how many were dead!

(P.S. Later found out that 3 dead – 1 soldier, and 2 IRA – one Provo and 1 Official, woman).

～～

I was at my wits' end, trying to decide what to do. For the second time in a couple of months I was, as in Paris, a child standing on the brink of an adult world, with no idea where or what to study. 'Please God, tell me what to do', I prayed every night. 'Should I go away or stay in Belfast? Please God let me know the right thing to do.'

Being the first in my family to have the opportunity to go to university, I owed it to my parents to make them proud. My exam marks to date indicated that I would get the A-Level grades I needed and the generous grants system meant that it was financially possible. Beyond that, I was at a loss with no older siblings to advise me. I toyed with the idea of studying to be a social worker, but only because I could think of nothing else. I refused to contemplate becoming a teacher although many of my classmates opted for that profession, and my chosen A-Level subjects – English, French and Maths – closed off many other career paths.

The entrance requirements and the list of '-ology's' detailed in the UCCA (Universities Central Council on Admissions) handbook – psychology, sociology, archaeology, anthropology and so on – bamboozled me, as did the enticements offered by the multitude of UK universities vying for our applications. A college place in Britain would be my passport to a 'normal' life but so too, ironically, would a place at Queen's University, just a couple of miles away in safer, leafy South Belfast. When I was brutally honest with myself, I admitted that I was not brave enough to wrench myself away from my family again, on a long-term basis.

I cut a nine-line, single-column story out of *The Irish News* and pasted the two-inch square piece of paper into my scrapbook. It recorded – in a matter-of-fact, comment-free fashion – that 'The death toll, since trouble in the North began in 1969, reached 600 on Tuesday night. The total this year is 389 …'.

I had become inured to all but the most gruesome or heart-rending deaths, or to those of people I knew or felt I knew because they came from my neighbourhood. I tried to picture a gathering of 600 people. It would be similar, I estimated, to the number of people who would pack into our church for Mass on a Sunday morning; it would be more than the number of girls who crammed into our assembly hall at school.

I was shocked that the toll had crept so high without me noticing, but looking through the pages of my scrapbook, I saw how it had come about: '2 bodies in burned out car'; '3 civilians die in gun battle'; 'Short Strand toll confirmed to be eight'; 'Seven killed in carnage at Oxford Street'; 'Two shot in West Belfast', and so on.

Sat, Sept 30

Left for Cooley at 11.30. At Newry it was 12.30, so we decided to dine there rather than go on to

Dundalk. Called in to the Copper Grill and had a gorgeous lunch. Mammy and Daddy both in great moods.

Afterwards, went on to Dundalk, Dunnes Stores – got a new jumper, navy and white – it's very nice. Spent hours in Dundalk – Daddy bought Mammy a new dress-ring – it's lovely, so she's happy too! We went out to Granny's and had our tea there but left early to get home before dark.

More gun-battles on Falls Road, woman shot yesterday, died. Man shot accidentally by <u>drunk</u> soldiers died – another soldier shot dead in Ardoyne.

Body of Catholic student found too. A Catholic pub blown up, and 1 killed, 10 injured, 'no warning'.

Mon, Oct 2

Looking forward to today – going over to Queen's for Maths lectures. Left after first class. Sr. Karen in terrible mood these days – had her latest victim in tears today.

When we got to Queen's, met Micky O'Neill with the St Mary's party – I really have a 'tinge' for him. However, I never saw anyone more scruffy than he and the other fenians, compared to the Prods.

By the time the afternoon lectures came, I – like everyone else – couldn't keep my eyes open.

Lectures just too much. Glad when they were over, although I really enjoyed myself all day.

Daddy arrived home late – Mammy was worried, thought he was assassinated or something. Terrible thought – but a fact of life here now.

~~~

Watching my mother's pale, drawn face as she urged us to 'say a wee prayer that Daddy's alright' while she busied herself making dinner, I wondered how long we would have to go on living like that.

Women like my mother were living in a constant state of anxiety, seeing husbands out the door and praying they would come home safely. They kissed children goodbye and packed them off to school, imploring God to return them unharmed. They spent sleepless hours in bed, or paced the floor well into the small hours, listening for the turn of their sons' or daughters' keys in the door. They themselves set out to work and to shop, wondering where the next bomb or bullet might strike.

What a difference fifty miles made. As I whiled away a carefree Saturday across the border in Dundalk with my family, another five people – including a Queen's University medical student – were killed in Belfast. The 23-year-old Catholic was kidnapped by loyalists after leaving his home in the north of the city and was found shot dead a few hours later.

A few days earlier, I convinced myself that going to Queen's would guarantee me a normal life. When I saw the Queen's

University flag flying at half mast, as a mark of respect for the murdered student, confusion and uncertainty engulfed me again. I was forced to concede that no part of my immediate future would be spared the stranglehold of violence.

CHAPTER 14

'A pity ALL the Catholics hadn't been killed'

Fri, Oct 6

During Religious Knowledge class, we were addressed by Sister Virgilius about UCCA forms, we're getting them on Monday. I wish I knew what to do or had some guidance from somebody – but I haven't!

Being as efficient as usual at lunch-time, and returning from opening the cloakrooms, I met Sister Karen. She asked me to bring two groovy fellas to the labs. Very suspicious-looking characters – looking for a broken electric fire, which didn't exist. The only girl they knew at St Dominic's was now in Crumlin Road jail for armed robbery!!

Queen's 'Freshers' hop' is on tonight – wouldn't mind going but not with usual ones – would just be a boozing session.

~~~

I lifted the calendar down from the kitchen wall and counted off the weeks since my last 'proper' night out: thirty-one long weeks – seven and a half months – since I was bewitched and thrillingly intimidated by the dark, boozy atmosphere of my first university disco.

I was longing to experience again the excitement of my Students' Union debut: the reverberations pulsing through my body as we danced frenetically to the pounding, deafening beats of 'Brown Sugar' and 'All Right Now'; the swirling, ultraviolet strobe lighting that spanned the hot sweaty dance floor of McMordie Hall, endowing us with film-star smiles and showing up the white underwear beneath our tops and dresses; and the alcohol-fuelled advances of older male students, keen to try their luck with a group of overly excited schoolgirls.

Instead, I whiled away another night in the house, as I had done so many times before, regretting life passing me by. Watching and waiting. Always on the look-out, but for nothing in particular. I gazed out the bedroom window, lost in a trance instead of studying. I peeked around the sides of the curtains, following army foot-patrols through our garden or up and down the street. I peered into the far distance, trying to locate the origins of billows of smoke rising over the city – wondering whether it was a building or a vehicle that was burning.

Occasionally, my thoughts drifted back to the sunshine and freedom of France but as the days grew shorter, I increasingly lost myself in dark reflection about my city and my future. I found myself becoming too scared to walk to Suzette's house on my own after nightfall, even though it was only fifty yards away. I was nervous about putting the rubbish out at night, for fear of stumbling over a soldier lying on his belly outside the back door.

Camouflaged soldiers with blackened faces lay on their

stomachs on the unlit footpaths, their rifles trained on passers-by. A short, shrill whistle or a terse, barked command would signal the winding up of a vehicle checkpoint and precede the heavy thudding of military boots, as soldiers darted from behind walls and hedges to clamber into waiting Saracens. A narrow beam of light, cast from an invisible torch across a patch of grass, would give away the presence of a six- or eight-man army patrol making its way stealthily through our garden.

I wasn't alone in my social isolation. Going into the city centre at night, where cars remained banned, was rarely an option for most men and women. Few people wanted to walk through the dark, deserted streets from drop-off points beyond the steel security barriers which ringed the main commercial area. Once the shops and offices closed their doors for the night, the centre of Belfast became a ghost town.

The IRA was causing hundreds of thousands of pounds of devastation, blasting local hotels out of existence; Catholic-owned pubs were a favourite target for loyalist car bombers. Stout-hearted dance hall and bar owners, who were struggling to ward off closure by cutting staff and curtailing opening hours, pleaded with the government for assistance.

Most people, like my friends and me, opted to stay at home or very close to it. I consoled myself with the hope that having finally made up my mind to study English, French and Sociology at Queen's, I would be socialising there – in an oasis of near-normality – as a brand new undergraduate in exactly a year's time.

Sun, Oct 8

Mammy is staying in bed today, she has a cold. Went to 11 o'clock Mass. Deliberately avoided Eleanor – felt like a tramp, vow I'll go to bed early. Came home, Mammy still in bed. Made the dinner – took ages to get ready. I was determined not to do the dinner dishes – Aidan did them. I must admit he and John did their share of work today for a change. After dinner, did some studying – Maths test tomorrow for UCCA assessment.

Soldiers invaded park this evening over carhijackings, at least that's their excuse. Got smiles and waves from one but Mammy told me to leave the window. Fierce shooting tonight, followed by road-blocks. Just like old times. Mammy went to Gordons' and I went to bed.

Mon, Oct 9

The thought of another week of school half kills me. Got UCCA forms and all the do's and don'ts of filling them in. Getting a Maths test today for our UCCA assessments – the result? I'll be getting an assessment of 'F' – I couldn't even do one part of it!! ...

There was a funeral on today – funeral of Daniel McAreavey, IRA volunteer (17) shot dead on Friday. The funerals up and down this road, every day nearly, are terrifying.

When waiting for Mr. Magenis to give us a lift home, saw the soldiers 'lifting' 2 fellas – completely innocent, walking along the road. One escaped (great!), other got beaten around the head and thrown into Saracen. Pray for him in there.

Tues, Oct 10

Cold and tired and so began to devise a plan for not going to school (coupled with dread of Maths results!) Got up and fiddled about till 10 to 9, decided to go, went to get a bus and after 2 had passed by, I came home again, went down road in a taxi with Mammy.

Boring day in school. Miss Smith didn't have our Maths results – have to prolong agony till tomorrow.

Mammy had been at 'Stanley Rupert' College as the bus conductor called it (Rupert Stanley) and got into conversation with a wee Protestant woman from Newtownards Road. She told Mammy it was a pity all the Catholics hadn't been killed in 1969! Mammy fled.

Paddy Steele called, had a good wee chat – he said 'Cheerio, darlin', see you later' – however he didn't return with the eggs as promised. Hope nothing has happened to him.

Sat, Oct 14

Mammy feeling poorly – she stayed in bed. Said she didn't sleep a wink (I don't believe it!). As a very dutiful daughter, I cleaned up, baked, made dinner etc. Jim and I got ready to go into town – straight to Spinning Mill to look for material and home again. I wasn't going to risk previous Saturday experience again!

Fooled about in my room for a few hours trying to study but succeeded in getting nothing done. Went to bed after BIG supper at 1.

2 Catholics assassinated in pub in Tate's Avenue.

Sun, Oct 15

Catholics intimidated, shops burnt. Catholic church desecrated by Tartans in East Belfast.

~~~

I was petrified to think that another woman, probably with children of her own, could be so filled with hatred that she would, by implication, tell my beloved mother to her face that she wished she and the rest of us had been eliminated.

The 'clues' we all used to decipher one another's backgrounds immediately told anyone meeting my mother for the first time, or chatting to her for more than a few minutes, that she was a Catholic. Her name, the hint of a southern brogue which softened her accent, and the location of her playgroup were certain giveaways. I was convinced, after my mother's run-in with the woman at the East Belfast college, that the loyalists were 'on' to her – that she had been 'outed' as a Catholic venturing into a Protestant area and that they would deal with her accordingly.

I couldn't fathom such bitterness and venom, especially in

a woman. We lived in the same city but the similarities ended there. As a Protestant from the east of the city, the stranger inhabited a Belfast which was a world away from mine. It wasn't just the River Lagan that separated us; centuries of history and culture divided us as well.

I remembered being stunned at the start of the year when the loyalist leader John McKeague said he was sorry more people weren't killed on Bloody Sunday. I was even more shocked that after all the death and injury inflicted on our communities in the eight bloody months since then, an ordinary, working-class East Belfast woman hadn't had her fill of bloodshed. Gangs of gunmen, motivated by the same hatred, felt the same way.

My father suggested that my mother should give up her childcare classes, but if she was to secure the qualifications she needed for managing her playgroup she didn't have that option. Life had to go on and toddlers in West Belfast were in need of nurturing more than ever.

Mon, Oct 16

Mammy telephoned from the playgroup to say that it was being raided by the army – found a rifle – she came home at about 5.

Terrible rioting on Shankill, Sandy Row etc. Worst rioting for ages. 2 UDA men killed by army vehicles. Delighted. Catholics have suffered through army for long enough.

Went to bed after watching TV at about 12. Mammy went out and fell over a soldier in the drive! She came in to tell me before she went to bed.

~~~

The experiences of that summer and autumn left me battling with my Christian values. When the news reported that two people were run over by army vehicles during loyalist rioting in East Belfast, I barely gave the deaths a second thought. I already knew there was *no* chance that I – or anyone close to me – would have any connection with the dead men.

I knew instinctively that it was wrong to derive satisfaction from anyone's suffering but I could not help myself. If soldiers in Belfast were going to do what soldiers did around the world, I wanted them to do it to 'the other side' for a change. I wanted them to get 'stuck into' rioters in Protestant areas, with the same zeal they employed against Catholics. I thought of the woman in East Belfast who wished only death on my community and, although weighed down by guilt when admitting it, I felt no sympathy for her or her co-religionists, whatever they might be enduring.

Day after day, the army was encroaching more and more on our lives. Andersonstown was saturated with soldiers and I was incensed at the one-sidedness of it all, as loyalist paramilitaries also stepped up their pressure on the Catholic community. In less than a week at the start of October, we watched the funerals of three men who died in separate violent incidents, going along the Falls Road; one was killed by the IRA, another by the UDA and the third by the Army. A young mother, who died saving her baby daughter from a loyalist car bomb, was also buried that week.

Two of three men shot dead by the UDA in the middle of the month lived within walking distance of my home. Each time such a killing took place, I registered that the victim could just as easily have been my father, brother or a male relative of one of my friends.

Another one of *our* people had been killed; more of *our* children had been orphaned; more of *our* parents and women had been bereaved. It didn't matter a whit that I didn't know the victim personally. I simply absorbed my share of the hurt caused by yet another assault on my community.

Only occasionally, when a journalist unearthed some heart-rending detail about a victim's personal life – that he was the father of an unborn child, for example, or that he was engaged to be married, or was the second in his family to be killed – did I allow myself to acknowledge that both sides of the community were suffering.

Tues, Oct 17

Took Mammy up on her offer of staying off. Got up for my breakfast, then went back to bed. She has to go to Rupert Stanley College.

However every time I got into bed, somebody telephoned or knocked. In and out of bed like a yo-yo – at one stage, phone rang. I was in a deep sleep and woke to find two window-cleaners staring in the window at me. Nearly died!

Finally I gave in and got up at 12.00. Made my dinner and started to make a skirt. Gentle knock on the door, I nearly jumped out of my skin.

Peeped through keyhole and saw fellow (like Paddy Steele) with white van. Decided not to open door to him. He passed in a note – I opened it –

large letters 'U.D.A'! However, Paddy later denied having anything to do with it – really angry about being accused.

Notes: Fierce rioting – worst gun-battles ever, in Prods v. Army. 2 people killed. Shankill, Ballysillan, Donegall Road, Shaftsbury Sq etc.

Wed, Oct 18

Daddy came home early – very depressed over UDA and army.

Terrible rioting last night – however, all is forgiven between UDA and army despite 2 deaths. Mrs Gordon came up after tea for follow-up to my 'UDA note' story. Paddy Steele called this morning to tell Mammy that others in Glenhill and Fruithill had received similar notes. He had again been accused in the wrong.

He told us 2 men stopped him at McGlade's – both in combat jackets, 1 with patch on eye and hand inside his jacket – to check if they were in Fruithill! He was terrified, so are we all now – UDA note was not a joke. Mrs Gordon reported it to the army.

Did homework. All quiet with Prods tonight, I think. Notes: UDA and army friends again – all forgiven. However, more Catholics burnt out. In Stella Maris school, 100 out of 240 left.

~~~

The 'UDA note' caused consternation and bewilderment verging on fear. It was so surreal I didn't know whether to be scared senseless or to dismiss it outright as a very sick practical joke. I wanted to do the latter and laugh out loud at the very idea of UDA men calling at our front door, but a nagging, spine-chilling voice kept whispering in my head that maybe, just maybe, they had done.

The figure who appeared at our door looked similar in outline to Paddy, our vegetable delivery man, and was wearing – like nearly all young men in both republican and loyalist areas – a green parka jacket. I found it more incredible than frightening to imagine that UDA members would risk driving into Andersonstown in broad daylight to post 'notes' – perceived to be threats – through the letterboxes of selected houses. My parents were equally mystified. 'They wouldn't dare,' they insisted, but they were persuaded, on the surface at least, to accept Paddy's emphatic denial that he was in any way involved.

I studied my father's face to try to read his reaction but he gave nothing away. A tasteless prank? A calculated republican ploy to frighten middle-of-the-road Catholics into fully endorsing – and supporting – the IRA as their defenders? Or a genuine threat, brazenly delivered by loyalist extremists? I didn't know which option to believe but I certainly preferred the first.

Fear – and a vivid night-time imagination – can do strange things to the mind. Safely cocooned in the quiet darkness of my bedroom, I allowed myself to think the unthinkable. I reasoned that it wouldn't be impossible for a gang with murder in mind to drive the short two-mile journey from the loyalist heartland of The Village, along the M1 to Kennedy Way, and into the first street on the right after that – Fruithill. It was too terrifying to contemplate the consequences.

Thurs, Oct 19

Feel rotten and look like a ghost, even Mammy commented on how pale I looked. Out to get a bus, however waited with Oonagh till 9 before getting one – followed by a 'late' mark. A boring day – went to a meeting of VSB (Voluntary Service Bureau) after school.

I'm supposed to be going to Carrickfergus tomorrow evening for the weekend, not at all anxious to go. Anyway, Elizabeth C. isn't in so I'll ring her and try to get out of it for the meantime. After tea, washed dishes and did homework. Ready to scream – interrupted at least 15 times by John and Aidan!

Have decided to go to bed early, so now – at 9.45, Good Night!

Back again – army arrived at gate at midnight. All out of bed again!

Fri, Oct 20

Managed to arise slightly earlier than usual today, after my attempt at having an early night. Into school and Frankie told me that Elizabeth C. had rung her to ask us to postpone our visit for two weeks. I do so with pleasure!

Came out of school directly at 3.35 and waited till 4.15 for a bus – ridiculous bus service on Falls

Road. Gunmen opened up with a tommy gun beside us. I nearly died off (literally!).

Paddy Steele called late tonight – didn't arrive till 8.30, to tell us that the 'note posters' I had on Tuesday were really UDA men. Terrified! Mammy rang army. At 9pm, a Major Gamble and Lieut ? arrived at house. Armed escort of 7 men out in the drive. I had to give 'evidence'!

Sat, Oct 21

At half nine I got up when I heard someone at the door – only the paperboy. Came back to bed – never so glad to be able to lie in bed. Didn't regain consciousness again till 5 past 12!

Went round to the shops and had dinner-cum-breakfast when I came back. After dinner, did some baking. Mammy got a cough-bottle today but it seems to have affected her, had to go to bed at 4. Heard shouting in English accents after tea – army. About 50 soldiers had invaded the park – searching for gunmen (as usual!). One Negro came in and got his arm stuck to Daddy's newly-painted window-sill. Daddy nearly blew his top!

~~~

I wanted to burst out laughing at the soldier's slapstick clumsiness, but my father's outrage at what had happened to his flawless paintwork stifled my urge. A stickler for perfection, he had spent the entire day sandpapering, filling and undercoating – puffing contentedly on his pipe – while probably simultaneously mulling over a strategy for dealing with the UDA. Just before the light faded, he applied the final, gleaming white gloss coat and stood back to admire his handiwork. The look of bewilderment on the unfortunate squaddie's face, when my father unleashed his West Belfast fury on him less than ten minutes later, was a study to behold.

I felt sorry for the contrite soldier as he endured the tongue-lashing, although I suspect that my father's outburst was more a rage against the army's virtual round-the-clock presence than against that hapless individual. He didn't deliberately set out to mess up the freshly painted sill, as well as his uniform sleeve, when he crouched down nervously seeking somewhere to position his rifle. The likelihood of a house-proud resident, painting his windows in readiness for winter, was probably the least of the soldier's concerns as he patrolled West Belfast in constant fear for his life.

Mon, Oct 30

First day of the Hallowe'en holidays. All the boys are at school – I'm the only one off. Mammy brought me up my breakfast in bed and I stayed there for quite a while i.e. 11. She is going to the playgroup.

I was thinking of either going into town or over to see Agnes, however all my problems were solved when Mammy rang from the playgroup saying I could go up to help make hats for Hallowe'en. She came down to collect me. Exhausting afternoon but very enjoyable.

Spent whole night making 30 Hallowe'en witches' hats and decorating them. I got fed up doing them. Mammy gave off to me!

Tues, Oct 31

Two wee Catholic girls, aged 4 and 6, killed. UDA bomb outside a Catholic pub in North Belfast. 100lbs explosives. 10 people injured.

Thurs, Nov 2

Back to porridge and school today – unfortunately.

Fri, Nov 3

Well, today's the day I have to comply with Elizabeth C.'s kind intentions and go to Carrick with her, Loreto and Frankie.

All day long I had to suffer the insult of being called 'a queer', going to a 'hen-party' etc. from the 'elite' members of the class. After school, we stayed in and had a row with Dolores and a couple of others, over the new school hero, Mr McAleavey. At 5, headed for Carrick. Arrived there well after 6. No tea ready for us – went out to the shops for sweets etc. to satisfy our hunger.

Listened to records and then like a crowd of bitchy cats, discussed everyone in school till 3 in the morning. All into one bed because of the cold. Good laugh till 4 a.m. Fell asleep.

Sat, Nov 4

After our rather late night, we decided we just couldn't get out of bed before 12. At 1pm, we were still in the process of getting dressed. A bitterly cold day.

Before 'breakfast', we went out for a walk along the front and almost got blown away. Returned for dinner, washed dishes for Mrs C and then nearly all fell asleep in the living-room. Elizabeth dragged us out into the cold once again and then at 4, we got the bus home.

Scared stiff when we reached town. Pitch dark, 100s of soldiers and police about.

〜〜

Despite long being desperate for an evening out, an overnight stay – with three other girls – in a cold, unwelcoming town in the depths of winter, wasn't the sort of diversion I craved. Being verbally abused by catty teenage friends, who were excluded from the well-intentioned invitation, made the prospect of the trip to Carrickfergus even less appealing. The clocks had just been put forward an hour to winter time and, with the drawing in of the nights, I wanted instead to slide into self-indulgent winter hibernation.

Carrickfergus – or Carrick – on the northern shore of Belfast Lough and about 15 miles from the city, was as different to Andersonstown as it was possible to be. A predominantly unionist town, boasting a fine medieval castle, it held no attraction for me in a cold, grey November. Even the address where we were staying – Scotch Quarter – had hostile, Protestant resonances. Given what was happening in Belfast, I was uneasy about going into that alien territory, although my parents didn't try to dissuade me. I couldn't wait to get home.

Sat, Nov 11

As we were having our 'breakfast', a knock on the door. I answered it – 2 soldiers. Out to do a census (although it's illegal!). Daddy explained all this to them, gave them NO information and very amiably, they left.

At 2.30, Máire Magenis called for me and we went to Arizona Street on our first Voluntary Service Bureau call to Mr and Mrs Bingham – over 70, he is bedridden. Chatted to them for a few hours, came home at 5.30.

Did homework till 12. Mammy made Christmas cake (bit early!). Catholic man shot dead, Crumlin Road.

~~~

'The earlier it's made, the better the flavour', she always said. I watched fascinated as my mother measured out the vast array of ingredients for the Christmas cakes – raisins, sultanas, currants, cherries and mixed peel – before leaving them to soak overnight in brandy. When her arm grew tired from beating the butter and sugar in the big brown stoneware basin, I took over. As we blended and mixed, my father – with mathematical precision – set about his annual task of lining the baking tins with layers of greaseproof paper on the inside and brown wrapping paper on the outside. Within hours the house was filled with the warm, rich aroma of spices and fruit, redolent of all our Christmases past. At last I had something to look forward to.

There was no evidence of Christmas when I called at the Binghams' home on my first uncomfortable visit as a member of the Voluntary Service Bureau. When my new friend, Máire, and I signed up to 'look after the socially isolated' for a few hours a week, I basked in a sense of smug self-righteousness (although I only undertook this 'good work' at the urging of the St Dominic's nuns). Frailty, decrepitude and dependency both repelled and frightened me.

A smiling, white-haired old lady opened the door of her old-fashioned terraced house and ushered us into a dimly lit Aladdin's cave, cluttered with furniture and ornaments. It reeked of old age; the stale smell of cooking, dead air and medication.

Dozens of Christmases had come and gone, leaving the old woman and her invalid husband alone with their memories and galleries of photographs. Black-and-white pictures were arranged along the length of the mantelpiece and hung on the heavily patterned wallpaper, telling of much-loved children who had grown up, married and moved on.

Mrs Bingham had been expecting us and had a tray set with china cups and matching milk jug and sugar bowl. She quizzed us about ourselves, school, our families and what we were going to do at university. All the while I grew increasingly apprehensive about meeting the old man whom I occasionally heard whimpering upstairs and whom she referred to lovingly as 'Daddy'.

The curtains were closed tight in the airless bedroom. On a bed in the corner of the dimly-lit room, I made out the shape of a bald, unshaven man, supported half upright against a pile of pillows, under a mountain of blankets and eiderdowns.

Mrs Bingham wiped her husband's drooling mouth and

told him brightly that two girls from St Dominic's had come to see him. He reached out a trembling hand and mumbled incoherently. The tightness of his grasp and the delight in his rheumy eyes expressed all the gratitude that he was unable to put into words. For a moment I was happy that I had allowed myself to be persuaded to visit them.

We prolonged the chat with the old lady as best we could, although her husband's habit of intermittently gasping 'Ah' was painfully disconcerting. I made up my mind, there and then, to eliminate another possible career option. I decided that I could never be a social worker.

When it was time to leave, Mrs Bingham seemed genuinely pleased to have had our company but like ourselves relieved that we were going. A difference of 60 years in our life experiences left us flailing for things to talk about. Unusually, in a home in West Belfast, no one talked about the Troubles.

It was unimaginable that the strife which dominated all our lives didn't impinge on theirs, and yet the bond they shared seemed to insulate them from it. All that mattered to that old woman, after a lifetime of mutual devotion, was her bedridden husband – not politics, armies, religion or power.

CHAPTER 15

'We'll all be butchered'

Sun, Nov 12

It was so cold that, in spite of the radiator, I had to sit with the eiderdown wrapped around me. At 3, I called for Máire Magenis and we headed, very reluctantly, to see Sister Karen in Turf Lodge. We had a wee cup of tea, said the Rosary in the oratory, saw around their playgroup and at 5.30 decided to go home. Thank goodness, Mr. Magenis called for us.

The wind is blowing the house down here, so I'm off to bed (9.30!)

Mon, Nov 13

The worst day I have felt all winter – temperature must be about minus 10 degrees!! Froze all day long in school.

Have to go to dentist after school. Came home soaking wet and nearly frozen to death. Took off uniform – put on vest (!), woolly socks, blouse, jumper, trousers etc. until I was well wrapped up. Plucked up courage enough to go to the dentist. Got a filling, he nearly killed me with the drill –

and I let him know!

Daddy is engaged on a CDC project on the UDA, i.e. anti-UDA. Making collection of UDA crimes etc. I spent one hour after tea cutting tiny letters out of the newspaper for him, in order to make words. He went to a meeting,

Notes: Another Catholic shot dead – Joseph McCrystal, Newtownabbey. Army shot dead IRA man. Soldier shot dead.

～～～

Belfast was in the grip of a foul, wet, November chill that penetrated through to my bones. I braved the journeys to school with my shoulders hunched against the driving rain, head tucked deep inside my maroon, black and white woollen scarf and my sodden overcoat pulled tight across my chest. At Mass, for the second Sunday in succession, we marked the Month of the Dead: thirty days when we were urged to pray for loved ones who had passed away.

We wrote the names of our deceased relatives and friends on slips of paper, placed them in white envelopes bordered with black, and deposited them in a large wooden box which rested at the foot of the altar throughout the month. The priest reminded us of our obligation to pray for 'the relief of the suffering of the souls in Purgatory' and for a hastening of the end to their sojourn there. I couldn't help thinking that those of us who were *alive* in our grey, wretched city were probably in greater need of prayer.

My heart ached for my father as, demoralised and disheartened, he applied himself to the thankless and seemingly futile task of drafting press statements for the CDC and updating his macabre archive of sectarian assassinations. Meticulously, he recorded the names and ages of the victims; where they were killed; whether they were abducted before being shot, or mown down randomly from a passing car; whether or not they were tortured and, if so, where their bodies were dumped.

At the height of the summer, when it was clear to all Belfast nationalists that the UDA and UVF were engaged in a murderous campaign against them, I was proud to be at his side, helping him compile evidence from old copies of *The Irish News*. Yet there he was a month before Christmas, *still* trying to get the Northern Ireland Office and the population at large to acknowledge what was happening.

As RUC spokesmen stated on the evening news that they didn't know why a particular Catholic was singled out, and when distraught relatives begged to know 'Why?', he shook his head in silent exasperation.

Among the records he kept was a street-map of Belfast on which he marked – in red and green biro pen – the locations of sectarian murders, cross-referencing them precisely to the victims' personal details. His archiving of the clusters of deaths, mostly in North Belfast and along the interfaces in the west of the city, was laborious, depressing, time-consuming work which went unobserved by all but those closest to him.

He enlisted my help to assemble a collage of newspaper headlines and photographs in the hope that an eye-catching visual presentation would grab the attention of the Secretary of State, William Whitelaw, when a CDC delegation was eventually granted a meeting with him. He may as well not have bothered.

The Secretary of State closed his deep-set, bloodhound eyes and drifted off into a doze as the group – including my father – delivered their presentation. My father felt almost as much pity as contempt for the British viscount, thrown into such an alien and bewildering mess.

The Prime Minister, Edward Heath, flew into Belfast to get what the BBC called 'a feel of public opinion'. On the same day, the news reported that 634 people had been killed in the three years since the Troubles began, nearly 450 of them in the previous ten months.

My friend Agnes, who by then was the Head Girl at St Dominic's, was among a group of Upper Sixth students from across the city who were invited to meet him during his 36-hour visit. When she related to me how Mr Heath paid no attention to her views on the conduct of the British Army, it reinforced the message emanating from my father's meeting with a drowsy Secretary of State: no one was listening.

Wed, Nov 15

Kept waking every half hour from about 6.30 onwards. Got to school to find out that there was absolutely no heating on in either St Thomas' or St Margaret's wing. Hands were blue with the cold.

A concert was run for the Voluntary Service Bureau at lunchtime – a great success, made £25.79½ p – but Sr. Virgilius was in one of her 'moods' – shouted at everybody, even staff, complained that the concert was very badly organised etc. and not worth the bother. She was then called all the current names of the day!

In French class, I was completely tongue-tied. Mme was really ignorant and sarcastic to me – I felt like packing school in! Came home and drowned my sorrow in drinking-chocolate. Did my homework – nothing except soldiers on the road.

Notes: Another Catholic shot dead by UDA – George Doherty, Sintonville Avenue (73rd assassination since July), by UDA.

Sat, Nov 18

Got up late again, I had no intention anyway of getting up early! When I came down, Mammy said she wanted to get John, Aidan and Jim new shoes, so they all went over to Crawford's and got all they needed – while I had my last year's boots sent down to the shoemaker's!!

After lunch, Mammy, Daddy, Paul, Aidan and I went down town to get Mammy a coat. Wandered and wandered around town till 5.30 and I suffered the degradation of being frisked by a horrible Military Policewoman – never again!

Met Agnes in town – told me about her meeting yesterday with Heath and his mates. She was the only one who had the guts to condemn the British army – Heath immediately brushed over it.

Sun, Nov 19

Had a late dinner and then I called up for Máire Magenis, so as to do our 'visit' to the Binghams.

Mrs Bingham was going over to her son's house so we had to mind 'Daddy'. He gave us photo albums to look through, very interesting pictures of him in the army in France etc. I succeeded in smashing a saucer out of her lovely china tea set. I nearly died but apparently she didn't mind.

Mon, Nov 20

Faced with a very important problem. Should or shouldn't I go to school? After all, it's Queen Elizabeth's 25th wedding anniversary and we have been granted an official holiday.

In the Catholic schools, it is optional due to, (1) School cannot close in respect to the Queen because of threat of IRA violence, (2) cannot remain open, because of danger to us from UDA.

I was very, very good! Came to school unlike the majority of others, e.g. in English class there were only 4, so at dinner-time I went home. Spent afternoon doing baking and watching the army over in Martins' farm.

~~~

All year I looked for excuses not to go to school, never more so than on those bleak winter mornings when the shrill 'brrng' of the alarm clock wakened me to the sound of sleet and hail rattling against the window. Yet, when I was presented with a perfect opportunity to stay at home and snuggle beneath the blankets, some perverse gene in my make-up persuaded me otherwise.

A gut instinct dictated that I *would* go to school – come rain, hail or snow – rather than allow any news reporter or political commentator to count me among the people celebrating the Queen's Silver Wedding Anniversary, thereby showing their allegiance to the monarchy.

I was lucky to be living in a nationalist area where the overwhelming majority of people were either openly hostile to everything pertaining to the monarchy or, at best, indifferent to the Queen's personal milestones. If I had been living instead in the north of the city or along one of the sectarian interfaces – obliged to conceal my Catholic school uniform under a plain overcoat every day – I wouldn't have had the luxury of taking such a 'principled' stand. I would have stayed at home, as many of my classmates did, knowing it was the safest thing to do.

Tues, Nov 21

Winter is definitely here to stay.

Forced myself into school, everybody is in again after yesterday's 'holiday'. Not too bad a day at school. Paddy Steele called with vegetables – Mammy over at Rupert Stanley. I chatted to him for a while and then he went away.

Mammy returned from RS and a big row ensued over the boys fighting. At 7, she was getting ready to go to a course in St Mary's. I was at the front door – a desperate burst of gunfire, loudest I have ever heard! I almost collapsed. Paddy Steele who had called back, rushed off to investigate!!

Did homework – spent 20 minutes on floor in the dark. Shooting at army in Kennedy Way. Soldiers running about everywhere. Another Catholic shot dead.

Wed, Nov 22

Siobhan had to get photos for her Trinity application form so I went down town with her at lunchtime. Like two mad women, racing around to get back in time. Came home at 3 o'clock (slipped out early with Anne Mulvenna and Máire Magenis).

Did homework as soon as I got in. Acted the idiot – I've been at it all day and I don't know why. Did homework till about 10.30. Mammy and Daddy went down to see Granny – she was disappointed her grandchildren weren't visiting her.

Bed at 1, after watching the army over in Martins. UDR man killed, Co. Derry.

Thurs, Nov 23

I got up very red-eyed after my 'watching' last night. I was late but not as late as Eleanor and Oonagh, whom I met at the bus-stop. Another cold day, can't wait for the weekend to come.

Another Catholic man was shot last night – just feel in despair. What hope is there for peace when UDA and UVF thugs can murder innocent Catholics every night? Came straight home from school. Watched news and did homework.

Daddy got phone-call to go to an emergency CDC meeting tonight – we left him down Falls Road (scared stiff).

Did homework till 10 – now going to watch Monty Python's Flying Circus.

Fri, Nov 24

At long last, Friday has come. Another desperate day – fits in with my mood.

Máire Magenis asked me to go to 'Macbeth' in QFT with her and Anne Mulvenna tonight. I have worked out that this will be my first night out since the wild March weekend in Dublin.

Máire and her daddy collected me at 6.15 and we headed for QFT, a little theatre up an alleyway off Botanic Avenue. Slogans all over the alley-walls – 'UDA OK', 'Paras for Derry' etc. Terrified – the type of place the UDA could murder somebody.

Mr. Magenis went home. After waiting about ten minutes we discovered that we couldn't get in – booked out.

My fertile teenage imagination went into overdrive, convincing me that my friends and I could become the UDA's latest victims on our first night out in Belfast for more than eight months. Maybe it was our choice of a controversial, X-rated film, coupled with the location of the small, 'private' cinema, I don't know. But I ended the short evening relieved to be safely home again.

The graphic violence, nudity and lurid portrayals of murder in Roman Polanski's much-hyped *Macbeth* held an inexplicable appeal for a section of Belfast's cinema-going public, including my friends and me. The film wasn't available on general release but was selling out at QFT – Queen's Film Theatre – an intimate, independent cinema behind a terrace of red-brick Victorian houses, comprising part of the university campus.

Access to the cinema was through a dark, narrow, high-walled alley, at right-angles to the busy Botanic Avenue, and was illuminated only by the light escaping through the open cinema doors. There was hardly a wall in Belfast which wasn't defaced with some sort of offensive slogan or graffiti, republican or loyalist, but I was in unfamiliar territory. My imagination was fuelled by reading so many of my father's accounts of recent UDA killings and abductions.

I was starting to get a sense that terror was stalking me. No matter where I went, even so close to the 'sanctuary' that was Queen's University, I couldn't escape its grip. The darkness of winter intensified my apprehension and I lost any desire to go out. Once I was home from school there was no question but that I was in for the night.

Sat, Nov 25

Feel terrible, obviously I'm loaded with the 'flu.

Intended staying in bed, however, at 11, heard Mammy yelling that the army were at the gate and on their way in. Couldn't think of any good reason for them to do so, therefore presumed we were going to be searched. Jumped out of bed and made myself respectable in spite of headache etc. etc. Soldiers only there to introduce themselves as KOSBs (King's Own Scottish Borderers) – I was furious!

Mammy and others went into town, she arrived home with lovely material for me for a suit – I was all chuffed! Suzette is back in hospital (as a patient), so did good deed and visited her. I took a lift in a car with 4 men – I didn't care – they looked honest!!

Went into town for more material. Out quickly – Tartans on rampage through Donegall Place chanting 'Taigs Out!' – so I got out!

Sun, Nov 26

Very cold, wet morning. Mammy told me to stay in bed and I complied, I can't say reluctantly, with her orders. Tried to do a bit of revision, unsuccessfully. Got up at dinner-time.

Seán MacStíofáin is on the 7th day of his 'hunger and thirst' strike – lawyer says he will be dead in 2 or 3 days. All we can do is pray for him.

Everyone is feeling intensely bitter. He is lying in hospital, starving himself to death obviously for his beliefs, while Craig, Herron etc. run about completely free!

In afternoon, I made more of my suit. I couldn't face doing any studying – too depressed to bother *about exams. Mrs G came up at about 11. I went to bed at 12 and kept vigil till 1!!!*

Mon, Nov 27

Heard Mammy's footsteps approaching my room when I woke – prayed she would tell me to stay in bed. No such luck! Got up but discovered I had no tights! Had to wash a pair – a good excuse to stay off. Jim is in bed sick, Mammy went around to the shops.

Mrs Gordon rang to say that Dr Peter Gormley and his 2 sons had been shot – 1 dead – on their way over to St Malachy's School, via Shankill. I cried and cried – thought it was Peter (19), however it was his younger brother (14).

I hate Belfast, I'm sick of the troubles. All I feel is despair that we've been sold out and that soon we'll all be butchered by the UDA/UVF.

Went to school at lunch time and came straight home after it. Watched TV and news – Seán MacStíofáin is dying. In despair, do homework and go to bed.

~~~

My brain reeled in shock and disbelief. I couldn't take in what my parents' best friend told me: that the kind and highly respected surgeon (who had removed my tonsils when I was six years old) had been shot along with two of his sons. I initially feared the son who was killed might be Peter, whom I had long admired from afar as one of the nicest and best-looking fellows in his school year.

My head was spinning as a torrent of images exploded inside it, leaving me distraught and bewildered. I couldn't stop visualising the ambush. I shuddered to think of a loyalist gang lying in wait, at breakfast time, for a happy and defenceless Catholic family making their daily journey from their home in leafy, 'safe' South Belfast to school in the north of the city.

The brutality of the attack shocked me, like Bloody Sunday all over again. My mother was shopping, my father was at work and I was on my own – unable to make sense of how anyone could attack a man who cared for the ill, regardless of class or creed, and his schoolboy sons.

Rory, who was killed, was only 14, a year younger than my brother John. The school uniforms which he and his brothers were wearing identified them as Catholics. I suddenly understood – with brutal clarity – why my school-friends who lived in North Belfast were exempt from having to wear our drab St Dominic's overcoats.

When I dried my tears, I didn't even feel angry; just empty and numb. I did what I did so many times before and tried to visualise what it would be like if my father and my brothers were attacked in the same way. I couldn't bear to think of it.

I held no brief for the cold, uncharismatic, IRA Chief of Staff, Seán Mac Stíofáin, but as I followed with morbid fascination the progress of his hunger strike, on that same day, I found myself thinking once again in terms of 'them and us'. The image of an Irish republican, languishing in prison and threatening to starve himself to death, appalled the impressionable 17-year-old in me, despite his reputed involvement in the IRA's vicious campaign.

I thought about the people I knew who were killed by loyalists that year. In May, it was our former neighbour Andrew; in July, it was Frank Corr; now, just four weeks before Christmas, it was young Rory. I wondered who would be next.

Wed, Nov 29 (night)

Another Catholic shot dead in a taxi by UDA/UFF gang – Mr Gearon. Since August, there have been 26 sectarian killings – 20 of them were Catholics i.e. almost 80%.

CHAPTER 16

'No longer is anyone unlikely to be shot.'

Fri, Dec 1

Friday has come at long last. Only one and a half weeks to go before the tests.

Long boring day. I'm getting to the stage where I detest school and everything to do with it. Same routine day in and day out. Came home for my lunch again – breaks the monotony – and got soaked in the rain. Came straight home after school i.e. after waiting 35 minutes for a bus.

Daddy didn't get home till 6.15. We were all scared stiff – with all the assassinations of Catholics, one never knows the next victim.

Watched Miss World, won by Miss Australia.

Then came the desperate news that 2 bombs had exploded in centre of Dublin. _2 dead_ and more than _70 hurt_. Definitely not an IRA job – probably UVF. Well arranged to get anti-IRA Bill passed in Dáil. Succeeded!

A Catholic shot last week died tonight – Antrim.

Sat, Dec 2

Woke early, felt unimaginable pleasure to know I didn't have to get up! Mammy, Jim and I went into town to get me a coat. In town at 12 – looked and looked, not even a coat I could have tried on.

While in Anderson & McAuley's, a bomb went off in Anne Street – 22 injured. Followed immediately by a series of bomb-scares. All big shops were closed due to them – thousands of people on the streets.

Panic. Streets being closed off while still full of shoppers. About 20 'Tartans' ran through the town yelling that there were bombs everywhere. Everyone terrified, we got home immediately.

Washed my hair. Tried to study, looked out window – two 'visitors' in the garden, at the bank at the bottom. Not army – no further comment.

Watched Midnight Movie and went to bed at 2.30am.

Catholic shot dead in East Belfast. Brutally tortured and burnt. Patrick Bensted. Woman shot dead in East Belfast – a Protestant but married to a Catholic.

~~~

The sound of my heartbeat pulsating inside my head almost drowned out the pounding feet and the clamour of voices raised in panic and confusion. A denim-clad loyalist mob, flaunting Ulster flags and tartan scarves, stormed through Royal Avenue whipping hordes of Christmas shoppers –

already terrified by the spate of bomb alerts – into a terror-stricken frenzy; probably the same louts, I realised, who forced me to flee a week earlier with their vicious 'Taigs out! Taigs out!' chants.

Hundreds of festive shoppers like my mother, 11-year-old brother and me – husbands, wives, elderly couples and old people on their own – surged backwards and forwards in the pandemonium, not knowing where to turn for safety. Rounding one corner, we ran into a sea of frantic people rushing to escape from another bomb scare in the opposite direction.

With my young brother between us, each of us clasping one of his hands, we fled from the mayhem towards Castle Street, in the direction of home. I prayed to God that we weren't running straight into the path of another IRA bomb, like the shoppers who had been caught in the Donegall Street, Bloody Friday and other explosions earlier in the year. Behind us, the lights on the giant Christmas tree in front of the City Hall glowed weakly. Seasonal shop window displays seemed grotesquely out of place as terrified customers rushed past and one store after another slammed its doors on another lost Saturday's trading. For the second Saturday in a row I was driven out of my own city centre, although Belfast no longer felt like *my* city. It was a hostile and terrifying place, filled with threat and dread.

A few hours later, the sight of two, shadowy male figures, moving stealthily between the bushes at the bottom of our garden, set my heart racing. I turned off the bedroom light, held my breath and watched out the side of the curtains – not knowing or wanting to know what they were doing.

Their sinister presence was unexpected and unexplained, and I began to shake. 'Serves you right,' I thought, acknowledging that if I had had my head down studying, instead of staring into the darkness as usual, I wouldn't be feeling so anxious.

Sun, Dec 3

Exhausted after my late night. I was last up. Aidan, Jim and Paul went down the garden on my advice after our nocturnal visitors and hey presto, found a Kennedy's carrier bag with 2 guns.

Daddy got up like a shot (pun, pun!). He expertly examined them – turned out to be two toys – very realistic looking, could scare you enough to hand over money or a car! However, we left them back – whoever finds them can keep them.

Watched Catholic Ex-Servicemen's Association (CESA) march from home – about 2,000 of them. Horrible feeling – think they'll be slaughtered. UDA and Vanguard say they will stop them!

Went up to Mr and Mrs Bingham with Máire, going to Xmas party with them on 17th.

CESA march stopped by army at King Street. Catholics will never march through their city (i.e. Prods' city). Daddy used my full 12 photos on them, now out of film.

Did my English, just finished now at 11.

*Watching to see if our 'visitors' return to claim
their property.*

Man shot dead in E. Belfast – a Protestant.

Tues, Dec 5

*Definitely the coldest morning of this year.
Endured a hard struggle before I managed to get
out of bed.*

*Mammy is going over to Rupert Stanley College
today – Daddy in house on his own, so I'd better
come home for my lunch to make sure he's alright!
Raced home and, God love him, he had dinner
beautifully ready – soup and all, ready to put out.*

*Got no revision at all done, too tired. Came
downstairs at 11 (Elizabeth C. on the phone for
30 mins) – and had an argument with Mammy
and Daddy about young people in pubs.*

Wed, Dec 6

*I decided yesterday to take half day. I have no
choice now because I've no French conversation
homework done. Not a bad morning in school, I
was late as usual!*

*Bad night last night – 4 dead in past 24 hours.
(There's a bomb after going off! One earlier at
bottom of Dunmisk.)*

*Came home at lunchtime, took taxi again –
couldn't be bothered waiting for a bus. Daddy off
all this week. Tried to study after tea and managed
to get homework done. Hardly any studying for*

exams – start this day week.

Suzette came up – didn't stay any longer than 40 minutes. She left at 9.45. Her mother rang at 10.45 looking for her. Don't know where she is – probably in somebody's house, hope so. John in bed early – he's worried sick about his exams.

Whitelaw sets up 'investigation squad' for assassinations.

Fri, Dec 8 (Holy Day)

Great knowing I didn't have to face school. Bitterly cold day, the frost didn't clear at all. Feel absolutely fed up with everything!

We went to 11.30 Mass, I had intended going down town but owing 'to circumstances beyond my control', we had to stay at home. Mammy made a Christmas pudding.

I came up to study and revise at 8.00 p.m. on the dot – by 9.45 I hadn't even opened my bag – looking out the window and chewing my nails. At 11, came down.

After another Catholic being shot dead, we are really getting scared.

No longer is anyone unlikely to be shot. 71 Catholics, 37 Protestants (sectarian assassinations).

~~~

Try as I might to study, there were too many interruptions on an average night in West Belfast and too many violent incidents drawing me to the evening news, for me to be able to concentrate properly.

I doubt if I was ever so badly prepared for my exams but my ability to dedicate myself exclusively to my books for hours on end had evaporated. In the past, I prided myself and even enjoyed drawing up colour-coded revision plans and sticking to them rigidly: making meticulous notes, ticking off each subject area as I finished it and marking off the days I allocated to each topic.

My father's words of advice rang in my ears: that education was more important than anything if we wanted to get good jobs; that as Catholics in Unionist–controlled Northern Ireland, we needed not only to do as well in exams as our Protestant counterparts, but better than them; and finally, that my brothers and I were getting opportunities that he, having left school at 14, never had. That final reminder, more than anything else, made me feel guilty for slacking.

With the Christmas tests fast approaching though, I was struggling to keep on top of my normal homework, let alone make any progress with revision. The steadily mounting death toll distracted me from worrying unnecessarily about my academic future.

Sat, Dec 16

Going to Dundalk today. Panic stations – usual pre-outing fuss.

Had lunch in Newry. Met Granny and Auntie Jo in Dundalk. Never regretted anything so much in my life – every time we wanted to go anywhere, a whole procession – 11 of us. Not a very good idea! Didn't get my coat after it all.

*Granny almost persuaded us to stay overnight
– finally decided to come home.*

*Hate coming home. Pouring rain – wettest
night I ever experienced. Stopped by army – they
were nearly drowned. Gave Jim and Paul sweets. I
could have cried for them – being away from their
families to protect a pack of savages on both sides
here.*

~~~

Whether it was a result of the weather, exam pressure, the frustration of yet another failed day's Christmas shopping or teenage hormones, I don't know – but I was moody and emotional, knowing neither what I wanted nor where I wanted to be. Nothing was making me happy.

After our recent Saturday afternoon experiences, I had been forced to accept that Christmas shopping in Belfast city centre was a bad idea. Dundalk, however, was buzzing, as shoppers from both sides of the border threw themselves into the annual spending frenzy, dashing between shops to escape the downpours and calling out the season's greetings above the blaring of Christmas music. I was in anything but a festive mood.

I sighed petulantly and refused to stand correctly in front of the mirror as I was forced to try on a stout, moss-green wool coat in Deary's department store, one of Dundalk's oldest 'outfitters'. An assurance from my grandmother that, 'It'll last you a lifetime,' was the last thing I wanted to hear.

The family-run store was cluttered and dark, with long polished wooden counters and an antiquated system of vacuum-chutes and pulleys for transferring money to the cash office upstairs. How I longed for the bigger, brighter shops in Belfast and I cursed the IRA and the Tartan gangs who had ruled them out of bounds to me. 'What do I want a coat for anyway?' I thought disconsolately. We would probably all soon be dead.

I didn't want to go back to 'stink-bombs Belfast', as 8-year-old Paul still called it, but I didn't want to stay on in Cooley either. The enforced shopping expedition had been a well-intentioned attempt by my southern relatives to engender in us some festive cheer but it turned out to be a nightmare. Even leaving the Troubles aside, I doubt if anyone could have devised a Christmas outing to accommodate the wishes of such a disparate group: two grandparents, parents, an aunt, an uncle, three recalcitrant teenagers and two pre-teens.

I wondered wistfully whether my mother and I would ever again experience the leisurely, women-only shopping trips which were such an enjoyable part of our weekends before Belfast descended into chaos.

On our drive back to the North, my heart went out to the young soldiers who stopped us at the border crossing. I detested the sight of British soldiers on the streets of Belfast but when I saw, up close, the rain-lashed faces of the two young squaddies who stepped out in the darkness to stop our car, I felt only pity for them. They looked no more than 18 or 19 years old, dripping wet and cold, but were courteous to my father. He dismissed their seasonal act of 'generosity' – passing sweets through the car window to my youngest brothers – as part of the army's so-called 'hearts and minds campaign', but acknowledged it would have been churlish to refuse them on such an awful night. They should have been in England, I thought, at home with their families for Christmas.

The following day, Máire and I were true to our word and brought the Binghams to the St Vincent de Paul pensioners' Christmas dinner in the local parish hall. 'Daddy' was strapped into a wheelchair, with a tartan rug wrapped around him and a yellow paper hat on his head. The smell of overcooked Brussels sprouts was sickening and my festive cheer was forced.

When the holidays eventually arrived, however, and I was freed from the drudgery of nightly homework and revision, my younger brothers' excitement began to infect me. I relished the task of dispelling the December gloom: helping my father to steady the Christmas tree in the corner of the front room, jagging my fingers on its needles and inhaling the deep scent of fresh damp pine; draping the tree with tinsel, then switching on the fairy lights to see them work their twinkling magic in the dark; stoking blazing coal fires; wrapping presents for friends and family in the secrecy of my bedroom, and helping my mother as she toiled lovingly to fill the house with the warmth of fresh baking.

The savagery continued outside but, cosseted and insulated within my West Belfast home, I was swept up by the Christmas momentum. After almost a year of recounting in my diary the details of so many grim days, my resolution finally waned.

Notes

Tues (night) – Catholic boy (16) assassinated; Wed – Catholic girl killed in bomb at father's pub, Killeter; Friday – policeman shot dead, Lurgan. UDR man shot dead in Armagh. 6 attempted assassinations, 3 Prods – 3 Caths; Saturday – Catholic shot dead near Enniskillen. St Brigid's Catholic Church bombed. Man shot dead (Catholic), York Road.

~~~

The inside back cover of my Collins diary was laid out as a '1973 Year Planner'. As 1972 drew to a close, I glumly filled in the only high points of my coming year: a concert by the Celtic rock band, Horslips, at Queen's University on February 5; two visits, a fortnight apart, to the Binghams in the same month; the first part of my A-Levels on April 2 and, on June 14, the end of my time at St Dominic's.

I accepted that my relationship with my beloved red journal had run its course. My friend throughout the year – the confidante with whom I shared my innermost hopes and fears and to whom I bared my soul – offered me no escape from the all-pervasive sense of hopelessness. I was weary of the one-sided conversation – the virtually unbroken monologue of gloom and desperation – which echoed back at me as I turned each page. I searched for some solace but was met by a stony silence in return. I closed my diary and that year of my life.

Sun, Dec 31

Worst New Year's Eve I have ever experienced in my life.

We had no one here with whom to 'celebrate' it – anyway, not much to celebrate!

At about 10, I went upstairs to have a bath, intending then to go to bed. However I felt that as everyone else was staying up to welcome in New Year, I ought to do the same.

IRA truce (or at least temporary ceasefire) ends today. Waited for midnight – went outside to hear if any horns were blowing, as was the tradition. Not a cat stirring – absolute silence.

I couldn't bear it – started to cry. Everyone too afraid to go out now. I hate Belfast!

Went to bed and cried myself to sleep.

The thought of another year, like the one which has just gone out, is too unbearable to contemplate. Heard Mr McGlade coming up to 'first foot' and fell asleep.

All I can do is dread 1973. White Paper due out in Spring. This, plus assassinations plus freedom of UDA, doesn't carry much hope of a happy New Year.

Just hope that I and the rest of the family are still here this time next year!!

EPILOGUE

'Thankful to be alive.'

There is something strangely soothing about city centres especially on a summer Sunday morning. They assume a gentler rhythm, making the world feel calmer, almost serene. Traffic hums lightly along virtually deserted roads and buildings seem to grow in stature, towering in sharp relief against a clear blue sky. Workers, drivers and shoppers – drained by the stresses of the week – sleep away their anxieties, while the buildings reclaim the territory as their own.

On such a tranquil Sunday morning in July 2012, I walked with my 83-year-old mother across Belfast's Oxford Street, to mingle with the locals and tourists drifting contentedly through the nineteenth-century St George's Market. We browsed among stalls of curiosities, crafts and vintage clothes, tantalised by the aroma of sizzling pork, and lulled by the soothing airs of the jazz quartet playing in the pool of sunlight seeping through the market's ancient glass ceiling. Belfast had changed so much, we reflected. We could have been in any modern European city.

Our easy Sunday fell within a ten-day period which marked – in stark contrast – the fortieth anniversaries of the deaths of almost forty people, killed in Northern Ireland in

July 1972. Six of them died on Bloody Friday, in the explosion at Oxford Street bus station – just yards from the market through which we now wandered, totally at ease.

Belfast – evolving today as a thriving, vibrant, metropolis – has been transformed. The grim, deserted, fear-filled streets of my teens now teem with young people, seeking out fun and excitement. Tourists in St George's market buy Ulster linen tea towels commemorating the ill-starred 'Titanic' – the Belfast-built liner whose fate is now spawning a multi-million pound tourism industry. The shopping areas, from which my mother and I often fled in terror – for fear of bombs or riots – now host glitzy retail centres, clamouring for business seven days a week and attracting shoppers from near and far. Brand new hotels and restaurants sit side by side with old pubs which weathered the storm of violence, and all bustle now with visitors and young professionals. Belfast is unrecognisable as the city of my youth.

On a similarly sunny day, in June 2010, my career as a journalist brought me by a circuitous route to Guildhall Square in Derry. With my newly rediscovered teenage diary in a bag at my feet, I joined in the rapturous applause which greeted the pronouncement by the Prime Minister, David Cameron, that the army killings on Bloody Sunday were 'unjustified and unjustifiable'. I felt a sense of completeness – that life had turned full circle – as he brought the curtain down on the event I had recorded with shock, sadness and anger in the opening pages of my journal in 1972.

In the days following the British government's unprecedented apology, I read for the first time in nearly 40 years my own account of my life during the worst year of the Troubles. The innocent 16-year-old, who pasted paper butterflies on the cover of her brand new diary, could not have foreseen that by the end of December that year she would be consumed by dark thoughts of death. Nor could she have imagined that subsequent decades would claim another 3,000 lives and bring so much fear and grief.

By the time I worked my way through page after page of my new-found journal, the desolation I felt on the last day of 1972 was as fresh in my memory as if it was yesterday: the black, silent streets; the miasma of despair; the sense that it could have been our last Christmas together as a family. I had set my diary down after reading it, emotionally spent, crushed and submerged by the bleakness of its final entries and the weight of violence and hopelessness in the preceding pages.

Suddenly, though, a wave of gratitude engulfed me, displacing the sadness which had threatened to overwhelm me. Like a blind woman newly blessed with sight, I understood – for the first time – how incredibly lucky I was. Instead of being felled by the recollections of that awful year, I realised that I should have been down on my knees, giving thanks to God that all my immediate family had been spared, not only through the year after I completed my diary, but for decades afterwards.

'... *Just hope that I and the rest of the family are still here this time next year.*' However improbable it had seemed to me on the last day of 1972, our family made it through the Troubles unscathed. My beloved father died peacefully in 1994, just four months before the Provisional IRA announced the 'complete cessation of military operations' which signalled the end of its twenty-five-year armed campaign. Thankfully my mother, four brothers and I were all 'still here' when I – a married woman with three grown-up children – finally unearthed my schoolgirl account.

I clutched the diary tightly and appreciated for the first time what a treasure I had in my hands. The journal with which I had become so disenchanted towards the end of 1972, and which had become such a bind to complete, threw new light on my teenage self, on life in my divided city during the most violent year of its history, and on the obligation bearing down on all of us to open ourselves to one another's stories.

Unlike the relatives of the 3,500 victims of the Troubles, I never experienced the harrowing anguish of walking behind the coffin of a loved one whose life was brutally cut short. I never had to make a lonely prison visit. I haven't been maimed or scarred by physical injury, or had to seek relief from mental or emotional damage through alcohol or drug dependency. I *did* know terror, fear and despair, yet I am one of the lucky ones.

It is pointless to speculate on what might have become of me if I had been born in Dublin, London, Edinburgh or Cardiff, instead of Belfast. My experiences bore little in common with those of girls the same age in other such cities. I can't help wondering, though, how my story might have differed if fate had dealt me a less benign hand.

I do not doubt that if loyalist gunmen had killed my father, if an IRA bomb had blown my mother to pieces while she was out shopping, or if soldiers had shot dead an innocent, unarmed, teenage brother of mine, the course of my life could have been radically changed. If I had been born a Protestant instead of a Catholic, or if my father had worked for the security forces rather than the Post Office, my perspective on what happened in 1972 would have been very different.

In the painful throes of writing this book, I often worried whether I had a story to tell at all. I am not a 'personality'. I neither killed anyone, nor was anyone directly related to me killed. I was neither a victim nor a protagonist, in the commonly accepted meaning of the terms.

I am nobody of any consequence to anyone beyond my small circle of family and friends. I have no stories of earth-shattering loss or momentous achievement. My hard-working parents were not wealthy but neither did we experience the deprivation and hardship so widespread in the Belfast of my youth. Indeed, I was privileged to escape to France, for almost a month, at the height of the mayhem. At times when I was writing this book, I even wondered whether I should feel guilty that I hadn't suffered *enough*. Doubtless there are far more dramatic stories to tell, but this is my story, simple and unremarkable as it is.

In writing it, I did not set out to produce the definitive history of 1972 (I was too protected from the worst of the Troubles to be able to do so). I have not tried to tell the story of the people of West Belfast or of the nationalist community during that year, because I was only a minuscule part of it. I certainly have not attempted to describe the experience of the unionist community because – for reasons of age, circumstance, history and culture – I remained closed to it. I do not have the resources to produce an academic analysis of the causes and factors which precipitated the most violent year in Northern Ireland's history.

My story, of one year in the life of an unexceptional Catholic schoolgirl, shows what conflict does to a community. It tells what happened to decent, God-fearing people when they lost faith in – or respect for – the authorities which governed them. It offers an insight into how circumstances and events brutalised ordinary men and women, while the fear of retribution cowed others into silence and inaction. It records how – in many instances – the instinct for self-preservation overrode traditional Christian values. It is also, I hope, a witness to the resilience of tens of thousands of ordinary families who became victims of a conflict not of their making.

I was shocked to discover how the passage of time dimmed my memory of the base savagery and ghastliness of 1972. More than forty years had elapsed during which a peace process was engineered, culminating in April 2014 in the first ever state visit to Britain by an Irish president. Irish tricolours and Union flags flew side by side along the route to Windsor Castle, where Queen Elizabeth II hosted a ceremonial banquet in honour of President Michael D. Higgins. Among her guests was Northern Ireland's deputy First Minister Martin McGuinness.

In a scene inconceivable when I wrote my diary, the former IRA commander stood for the UK national anthem and toasted the Queen, the head of Britain's armed forces.

In the four decades preceding that momentous occasion, the details of a multitude of violent deaths were reduced to an amorphous blur for all but those left mourning lost loved ones. In many cases the bereaved continue to search for elusive answers to questions such as 'Why?' and 'For what?'

The years softened, and in some cases obliterated, my memory of much of the obscenity that enveloped our lives. The mind plays tricks. Perhaps, while the conflict was raging or still fresh, ordinary people *needed* to 'forget' so that we could move on with living; maybe now, though, when it appears Northern Ireland has moved to 'a better place', we should take time to remember the horror.

By the time I rediscovered my journal in 2010, violence – or the threat of it – had overshadowed half of my life. Nevertheless, I was still horrified by the experiences my 40-year-old diary had evoked and by the way it breathed life into my long-forgotten memories.

As, page after page, I delved deeper into my journal, I resolved never to trust my memory again; so many of the incidents I recorded had vanished or been erased from my consciousness. Were it not for the real-time accounts of certain events and my reactions to them – captured in my own teenage scrawl – I would have struggled to believe that I was ever part of them.

I discovered that I had forgotten the chilling feel and horrible taste of fear. It was hard to accept that I used to waken in the mornings in dread of hearing the death toll from the gun battle which had kept me awake the night before. I had forgotten what it was like to go to bed with my head swimming with sickening images of the aftermath of a no-warning bomb attack or a gruesome loyalist killing. I marvelled at how parents like mine wove the necessary business of rearing families, going to work and getting children out to school, into the fabric of life in a city that seemed hell-bent on self-destruction.

I grew angry when my diary reminded me how the simplest details of our lives were affected by the permanent threat of violence and the oppressive military presence on our streets. I became upset when I was confronted with the memory of the desperation that drove me down on my knees to pray, in May 1972, because my family had no means of defending ourselves should the need have arisen.

There were times, as I was waded through the pages of my diary, reliving those awful months, when I felt I could read no more. The interminable catalogue of death and destruction came close to overwhelming me. 'How in under God,' I wondered, 'did ordinary men and women - people like my parents - rear families and stay sane under such appalling circumstances?' God help those who were less fortunate than I.

So many innocent people – Catholic *and* Protestant – died because they were in the clichéd, 'wrong place at the wrong time'. So many young men and women died needlessly, fighting for Ireland, Ulster or the Crown. So many lives were sacrificed on the altars of sectarianism, patriotism and service.

I couldn't help but shed tears when I became absorbed in the humbling task of checking out the personal details and dreadful final circumstances of the many victims to whom I had made only passing reference, recording them merely as nameless, faceless, statistics. They included men and women doing their jobs, pensioners and children, people with learning disabilities, men rendered vulnerable by alcohol, teenagers and young men accused in the wrong of being gunmen or bombers.

I winced with horror when I read the details which emerged at the inquest into the death of a Catholic man whom I recorded matter-of-factly in my diary as having been 'brutally tortured and burnt'. The inquest was told that a cross, and the letters 'IRA', had been branded on his back, probably with a hot iron. A dispassionate 'Soldier shot dead', recorded on a different page, became the heart-breaking, tragic story of a family torn apart – a young woman widowed and her three-month-old twin daughters orphaned. I read of another widow who didn't even know her husband was in the IRA until he was blown to pieces by his own bomb; she recognised her stitching on a scrap of material from the trousers she had shortened for him.

The records in my diary were sparse and cursory; the language detached and dispassionate, utterly inadequate for conveying the depth of the suffering which had been inflicted. But, at 16 or 17 years of age, I was recording events that no one so young should have to contemplate. I console myself that I wasn't old or mature enough to adequately convey the scale of the horror, but that doesn't ease my sense of having done scant justice to many of the victims.

I felt uncomfortable at being confronted with dozens of killings I omitted to record. I never did so out of malice or ill will towards those victims, but because the deaths didn't impact directly on me or my community. It was also due to the enormity of the carnage. My sole preoccupation, in the face of such terror, was with the welfare of Belfast's nationalist population and those nearest and dearest to me.

I felt dismayed when I came across details of a woman and her husband – a farmer and off-duty member of the Ulster Defence Regiment – who were gunned down as they watched television in their isolated Fermanagh farmhouse. I don't recall ever hearing about the killings and I didn't mention them in my diary.

I looked with incredulity at the entry for 31 July where I recorded – only as a 'note' – a line about one of the worst atrocities of the Troubles. I was on holiday in my aunt's home in Sligo, rejoicing in being free from the murder and mayhem which was shackling my life in Belfast, when the Claudy bombers claimed nine innocent lives. Operation Motorman, which preceded it, is recorded merely as a postscript.

In December, I made no reference to the loyalist gun attack which killed five men in a bar in Derry. After almost 500 violent deaths in just twelve months, I had reached the point where I was too war-weary and too hopeless to record it.

Loyalism and its murderous manifestations terrified me. Fear, distrust and the belief that the security forces were aggressors rather than protectors – that my community was on its own – blinded me to much of the suffering the IRA was inflicting on the unionist community. My feeling of vulnerability at the time also shut my eyes and closed my ears to the enormous pain the same organisation was inflicting on the Catholic population, who looked to it for protection. Innocent Catholic men, women and children were among those killed in crossfire and explosions; IRA members were blown to bits by their own bombs; civilians were abducted, tried and executed by 'kangaroo courts', among them Jean McConville.

The widowed, West Belfast mother of ten was among the disparate group of unfortunates who were abducted and killed by the IRA, before being dumped in unmarked graves. Her grisly fate, in December 1972, earned the nondescript 37-year-old an unenviable place in Northern Ireland's tortured history. Her 'disappearance' went unreported until the New Year, so it wasn't mentioned in my diary either.

Gripped by fear of the loyalist threat, I didn't allow myself to dwell on the stark realities of the IRA campaign. The IRA came from the same community as I did and, in desperation, I had to believe that they were on my side. If *they* weren't there to protect my family and me, who else could we rely on?

With the evidence of my diary in front of me, I was forced to acknowledge that I had been preoccupied with loyalist assaults on my community, to the exclusion of nearly everything else. Given the terror that was unfolding around us, I understand why. What I was unable to see back then, and what I have come to understand since, is that the same was true in reverse within the unionist community. The words of St Matthew's Gospel, which were read by the First Minister, Peter Robinson, during Queen Elizabeth's visit to Enniskillen in June 2012, are relevant to both sides of our community, as we slowly emerge from conflict:

> Why do you see the speck in your neighbour's eye, but do not notice the log in your own eye? Or how can you say to your neighbour, 'Let me take the speck out of your eye', while the log is in your own eye? You hypocrite, first take the

log out of your own eye, and then you will see
clearly to take the speck out of your neighbour's
eye.

(Matthew, 7: 3-5)

We all lived the nightmare. In a population of only one
and a half million people, many separate battles were being
fought. The Catholic or Protestant family living at a sectarian
interface had a different enemy to the part-time UDR man
on an isolated farm along the border; the threat facing a man
or woman trying to run a business in Belfast city centre was
very different to that confronting a young Republican in the
heart of Derry's Bogside.

Many a night, as I wrestled with the uncomfortable and
unpalatable truths which my diary revealed about me and the
society I lived in, I shut down my computer and despaired of
ever working my way through to the end of my reflections.
I was uneasy with the shockingly candid, but unchristian,
sentiments I expressed when my community was most under
siege. I was appalled at how ordinary people like me became
inured to violence, and at how cheap life had become. I
despaired at what human beings in the 'civilised' Christian
world were capable of doing and becoming. Ultimately,
though, the revelations made me persevere with my writing,
in the hope that a reminder of the depths to which we had
plummeted might prevent other generations from following
the same path.

Time and again I asked myself how families came through
not just 1972, but the two and a half decades afterwards as
well. Sometimes I wonder what became of Carol, the little

'refugee' burned out of her home in North Belfast and cast like flotsam on the surging tide of terror, upheaval and uncertainty. No child should have to endure such horrors, or be kept awake by violence, death, or fear for his or her tomorrow. Having latterly experienced the relatively simple challenge of guiding my own three children into young adulthood, I am in awe of what my parents did.

Like the overwhelming majority of people, in much-maligned West Belfast, my parents forged ahead in the face of appalling difficulties with their duty of care: loving, providing, nurturing and, above all, protecting. They strove to instil discipline and Christian values in the midst of chaos and disorder; somehow they held the ties of family life together. They steered me and my four brothers through a nightmare that began when the youngest was only 5 years old and which lasted until after he, himself, became a husband and father. I am eternally in my parents' debt.

No one can ever measure what role, if any, prayer played in preventing an awful situation becoming worse. If hope is the message of Christianity, perhaps that was the guiding hand that brought us through to the other side and stopped us, as a society, from being dragged into all-out hell.

Prayer, faith, friendships and mutual support held communities together when violence and fear were testing human resilience to its limits. It is a tribute to the strength and bravery of ordinary men and women – parents, teachers, members of the clergy, people who cared enough to give of their time and energy – that the wheels of 'normal' society kept turning in the midst of such adversity.

In the early 1980s, while the conflict was still raging, I

had an opportunity due to my career as a BBC journalist to record a radio interview with Dr John Robb – a retired consultant surgeon and liberal Northern Irish Protestant – who believed that Ireland should ultimately be united. In the course of a long conversation afterwards, he wanted to know at what point I, as a member of the nationalist minority, would feel I had achieved equality and was no longer 'a second-class citizen'. I was stumped for a moment but the answer suddenly came to me:

'When I can say my name out loud in strangers' company and not be uncomfortable that people know I'm a Catholic.'

Decades later, on a hot summer day, I stood on the shore at Portstewart – the North Derry seaside town where my husband, Paul, and I have spent our married lives. Through remarkable coincidence and the vagaries of my husband's friendships, the best man at our wedding in 1981 was Peter Gormley – the student whom I had feared dead, and whose young brother was killed in an attack recorded as a November entry in my diary.

As I shielded my eyes against the early August sun, I reflected yet again on how Portstewart, with its quaint promenade, stunning cliff walks and magnificent, blue-flagged strand, was a world away from the strife-torn Belfast where I grew up. I watched the scores of day trippers, lured to the coast by the heat, and thought about my own fun-filled, childhood outings to the seaside during those cherished family visits to the Republic.

I recalled too how I struggled to come to terms with the violation of some of those repositories of happy childhood memories. In 1979, a member of the British royal family,

Lord Louis Mountbatten, was killed with three other people when an IRA bomb ripped through his boat, in the sea where we used to swim at Mullaghmore. In 2003, a man walking his dog accidentally uncovered the remains of Jean McConville – the best known of 'the Disappeared' – on 'our beach' at Shelling Hill, where they had lain buried and undetected for three decades since 1972.

I felt happy that the families around me on the beach in Portstewart would go home from *their* day at the seaside free from the ghosts of my childhood – the fear of a shooting, a bombing or the discovery of a body.

I reflected, too, on my recent carefree visit to St George's Sunday market, and delighted in having had the good fortune – after all those aborted shopping trips of the past – to experience with my mother, the emerging 'new' Belfast.

Finally, I thought about my own three grown-up children, Maura, Paul and Orla, and rejoiced that the barriers which constricted my world in Belfast have been toppled in theirs.

They number Catholics, non-Catholics, people of no religion and of different skin colour among their best friends and loved ones.

My children have no fear of saying their names out loud.